D1765877

THE UNIVERSITY OF
WINCHESTER

Martial Rose Library
Tel: 01962 827306

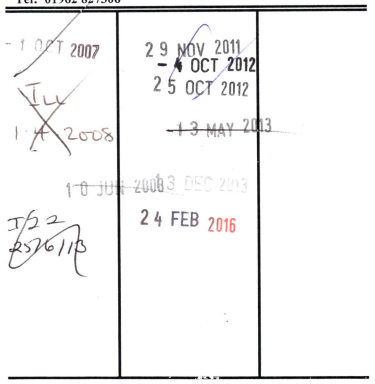
To be returned on or before the day marked above, subject to recall.

Jack Cade's
Rebellion of 1450

JACK CADE'S REBELLION OF 1450

I. M. W. HARVEY

CLARENDON PRESS · OXFORD
1991

Oxford University Press, Walton Street, Oxford OX2 6DP
Oxford New York Toronto
Delhi Bombay Calcutta Madras Karachi
Petaling Jaya Singapore Hong Kong Tokyo
Nairobi Dar es Salaam Cape Town
Melbourne Auckland
and associated companies in
Berlin Ibadan

Oxford is a trade mark of Oxford University Press

Published in the United States
by Oxford University Press, New York

British Library Cataloguing in Publication Data

Data available
ISBN 0–19–820160–5

Library of Congress Cataloging in Publication Data
Harvey, I. M. W.
Jack Cade's rebellion of 1450/I. M. W. Harvey.
Includes bibliographical references and index.
1. Cade's Rebellion, 1450. 2. Great Britain—History—Henry VI
1422–1461. 3. Social conflict—England—History. I. Title.
DA257.H37   1991
942.04'3—dc20   91–10160
ISBN 0–19–820160–5

Typeset by Cambrian Typesetters
High Street, Frimley, Surrey
Printed and bound in
Great Britain by Bookcraft Ltd,
Midsomer Norton, Bath

To J. R. R.
and to the memory of
B. A. W.

PREFACE

THERE has never been any doubt that Cade's rebellion stands among the major political events to take place in England during the fifteenth century. It is one of the period's great popular uprisings. Although it achieved scarcely any of its political aims its repercussions were significant. The rebellion itself encouraged the return to England of the duke of York to attempt a reform of the government, whilst its unmet demands and harsh suppression alienated a whole region of England from its Lancastrian ruler. It is a story which helps to make more intelligible the way in which Henry VI's reign ultimately dissolved into the Wars of the Roses. This book has sought to illuminate not only the course of the rebellion and its associated troubles during the early 1450s, but also the nature of the society from which it sprang, for Cade's rebellion acts as mirror in which is caught a reflection of the disastrous failure of kingship of Henry VI.

Until fairly recently the subject of Cade's rebellion has been treated somewhat inadequately by historians. At the end of the last century G. Kriehn brought out his pioneer *The English Rising in 1450* (Strasburg, 1892) which was, however, based largely on the evidence of chronicles alone; and in 1950 Helen Lyle produced a short pamphlet for the Historical Association, *The Rebellion of Jack Cade, 1450*. In 1970 Dr Barron in her so far unpublished University of London doctoral thesis contributed a masterly chapter on Cade's rebellion in London. But it was not until 1981 that a thorough study of the subject as a whole came out as a chapter in R. A. Griffiths, *The Reign of King Henry VI: The Exercise of Royal Authority, 1422–1461*, an invaluable work which has greatly facilitated the writing of this book. In that same year another helpful but less detailed account came out in B. P. Wolffe's *Henry VI*. Another most useful work in dealing with the subject of Cade's rebellion has been R. Virgoe (ed.), 'Some Ancient Indictments in the King's Bench referring to Kent, 1450–1452', in *Documents Illustrative of Medieval Kentish Society*, ed. F. R. H. Du Boulay (Kent Record Society, 1964).

For the events of 1450 our major sources are some ten or more chronicles of near contemporary date, or at least based on contemporary narratives, which give a fairly detailed account of events in and around London. By and large they do not contradict one another on essentials. What is largely, although not entirely, lacking for 1450 is evidence from king's bench indictments. The rebels from Kent, Surrey, and Sussex were pardoned in large numbers and it is for this reason that indictments do not survive to suggest to us how they rose, from which villages, or who their ringleaders might have been. Fortunately this is not true of Wiltshire, where insurgents were comprehensively indicted, or of Essex and Suffolk, where subsequent indictments would be presented in 1453 concerning the 1450 rebels there. A few further suggestions as to what was going on in the affected counties during 1450 can be gleaned from records of proceedings in chancery. In contrast to the 1450 rising, those troubles which came after it during the early 1450s go unmentioned by the chroniclers, but are well documented in the records of the king's bench.

Throughout the book place-names are spelt in their modern form while county boundaries remain those of the fifteenth century. The expressions 'men of Kent' and 'Kentishmen' are employed loosely, meaning no more than simply the inhabitants of the county, without any suggestion that those referred to come from one particular side of the river Medway.

It is a pleasure to thank those who have assisted so generously in the completion of this book. I only regret that it is not possible to thank everyone by name. One of my most long-standing debts of gratitude is that which I owe to those who taught me as an undergraduate at Aberystwyth, particularly to Professor R. R. Davies who has been of kind support ever since, and above all to Professor E. B. Fryde who supervised the thesis upon which this book is based. Neither the thesis nor the book does justice to his scholarly standards or to his patience and generosity over the years. I also owe a major debt of thanks to the President, Fellows, and staff of Corpus Christi College, Oxford, who provided me with ideal conditions in which to complete this work during four delightful years spent with them. Dr T. M. Charles-Edwards, Dr G. L. Harriss, Dr J. D. Howard-Johnston, and Dr C. F. Richmond were all kind enough to read the text of the thesis: their suggestions contributed very greatly towards its revision into its present form. Naturally, they bear no responsibility for the book's omissions, inaccuracies, and infelicities. I am grateful to the staff of the several archives and libraries I have had cause to use, most especially to the staff of the Public Record Office at Chancery Lane. Thanks are due also to Dr C. C. Dyer for his helpful criticism of certain passages in the book and to all the members of the Department of Medieval History at the University of Birmingham for the great good grace with which they bore with a distracted colleague during 1989–90.

Over the years of my preoccupation with south-eastern insurgents I have been sustained by much helpful discussion, hospitality, and kindness. Particular thanks go to George and Dorothy Bourne; Thomas and Gifford Charles-Edwards; Edmund and Gwenno Fryde; John and Jennie Harvey; Nicholas and Catharine Stansfeld; and my brothers. The most enduring support of all has come from my parents.

CONTENTS

LIST OF MAPS

ABBREVIATIONS

Arch. Cant.	*Archaeologia Cantiana* (Kent Archaeological Society)
Bale's Chron.	*Six Town Chronicles*, ed. R. Flenley (Oxford, 1911)
Benet's Chron.	'John Benet's Chronicle for the Years 1400 to 1462', ed. G. L. Harriss and M. A. Harriss, *Camden Miscellany*, 24 (Camden Society, 4th ser., 9, 1972)
BIHR	*Bulletin of the Institute of Historical Research*
BJRL	*Bulletin of the John Rylands Library*
BL	British Library
Brut	*The Brut, or the Chronicles of England*, ed. F. W. D. Brie, ii. (Early English Text Society, 136, 1908)
CCR	*Calendar of the Charter Rolls*
CCLR	*Calendar of the Close Rolls*
CFR	*Calendar of the Fine Rolls*
Chron. of London	*A Chronicle of London, 1189–1483*, ed. N. H. Nicolas and E. Tyrell (1827)
CPR	*Calendar of the Patent Rolls*
Davies Chron.	*An English Chronicle of the Reigns of Richard II, Henry IV, Henry V, and Henry VI*, ed. J. S. Davies (Camden Society, OS 64, 1856)
Econ. HR	*Economic History Review*
EHL	C. L. Kingsford, *English Historical Literature in the Fifteenth Century* (Oxford, 1913)
EHR	*English Historical Review*
Fabyan's Chron.	Robert Fabyan, *The New Chronicles of England and France*, ed. H. Ellis (1811)
Gough	MS Gough London 10, printed in R. Flenley (ed.), *Six Town Chronicles* (Oxford, 1911)
Great Chron.	*The Great Chronicle of London*, ed. A. H. Thomas and I. D. Thornley (1938)
Gregory's Chron.	J. Gairdner (ed.), *The Historical Collections of a Citizen of London in the Fifteenth Century* (Camden Society, NS 17, 1876)
HMC	Historical Manuscripts Commission

KR	King's Remembrancer
London Chrons.	*The Chronicles of London*, ed. C. L. Kingsford (Oxford, 1905)
LTR	Lord Treasurer's Remembrancer
PBA	*Proceedings of the British Academy*
PL	J. Gairdner (ed.), *The Paston Letters* (6 vols., 1904)
Political Poems	*A Collection of Political Poems and Songs relating to English History, from the Accession of Edward III to the Reign of Henry VIII*, ed. T. Wright (2 vols., Rolls Series, 1859–61)
PCC	*Proceedings and Ordinances of the Privy Council of England*, ed. N. H. Nicolas (7 vols., Record Commission, 1834–7)
PRO	Public Record Office, London
RC	Record Commission
RP	*Rotuli Parliamentorum*
RS	Rolls Series
Short English Chron.	*Three Fifteenth-Century Chronicles*, ed. J. Gairdner (Camden Society, NS 28, 1880)
Stevenson	*Letters and Papers Illustrative of the Wars of the English in France during the Reign of Henry the Sixth, etc.*, ed. J. Stevenson (2 vols. in 3, Rolls Series, 1861–4)
TRHS	*Transactions of the Royal Historical Society*
VCH	*Victoria History of the Counties of England*
Virgoe, 'Ancient Indictments'	R. Virgoe (ed.), 'Some Ancient Indictments in the King's Bench referring to Kent, 1450–1452', in *Documents Illustrative of Medieval Kentish Society*, ed. F. R. H. Du Boulay (Kent Record Society, 1964)
Wedgwood, *Biographies*	J. C. Wedgwood (ed.), *History of Parliament: Biographies of the Members of the Commons House, 1439–1509* (HMSO, 1936)
Wedgwood, *Register*	J. C. Wedgwood (ed.), *History of Parliament: Register of the Ministers and of the Members of both Houses, 1439–1509* (HMSO, 1938)

1

THE SOUTH-EAST OF ENGLAND

IN 1450 such was the strength of popular discontent throughout southern England that in many places it broke out into violence and rebellion: nowhere were the outbreaks as sustained or organized as those in the South-East. It is a circumstance which requires some explanation. Certainly this regional particularity had a lot to do with the sequence of political and military events of that year, but the full explanation lay in the landscape and society of the South-East itself.

The 'South-East', for these present purposes at least, comprises the five counties of Kent, Middlesex, Surrey, Sussex, and Essex. The term is more than just a convenient tag used to tie together five adjacent counties, since the area has a certain regional unity of its own. The chalk escarpment of the North Downs runs west–east through Surrey and Kent to end just on the Essex bank of the Thames; the large, roughly circular, wooded prominence of the Weald extends from eastern Sussex and the corner of south-eastern Surrey into central Kent; whilst the Thames ebbs and flows in its wide estuary bounded to the north by Essex and to the south by Kent. But that which above all binds these counties together into a geographical and, what is more, a political coherence is a common proximity both to London and to the Continent. This circumstance is one of the most important factors in explaining why the major popular uprising of Henry VI's reign occurred here in the South-East.

A crow flying at a good height over Kent from Canterbury to Sevenoaks at any time during the first half of the fifteenth century would look below to its right and see flocks of sheep grazing the treeless, level stretches of the Isle of Sheppey and the marshes north of Cliffe, Cooling, and St Mary's Hoo, just as far away in the distance to the left there would be sheep grazing Romney Marsh. But a more striking feature of its bird's-eye view would be the hedged and wooded nature of the landscape. Woodland was to be seen both on the chalk Downland west of Canterbury and on the Chartland, the hill country

The English Counties Known to Have Seen Popular Disturbances in 1450

with its numerous quarries at the foot of the Downland escarpment.[1] There in the Downland at Sevenoaks it would see expanses of wooded slopes on the Weald stretching away to the south into Sussex. Likewise, areas of woodland were to be found in Surrey, Essex, and northern and eastern Sussex.[2] As always, timber was a cash crop worth farming. Large-scale landlords who leased out most of their other property often chose to continue exploiting their woods directly. They were encouraged to do so by a tendency for timber to increase in price throughout the century.[3] In the twelve months from Michaelmas to Michaelmas 1427–8 the archbishop of Canterbury's woodward at his important wood at Bexley in north-western Kent sold 5,000 talwodes (a largish variety of firewood) and 5,500 tosards (a smaller variety); but during a similar period 1447–8 he sold 9,000 talwodes and 11,000 tosards, along with twenty-seven oaks sold to a shipman.[4] Nor was it always just the large-scale landlords who were in this business. Lumbering could well take up a substantial proportion of an average Kentish farmer's acreage alongside his arable and pastoral interests. In the 1430s John and Margaret Brenchesle had property on the edge of the Kentish Weald in Benenden and Rolvenden comprising 150 acres of arable, 140 acres of marsh, meadow, and pasture, and 150 acres of woodland.[5] And in Sussex in the second half of the century, when derelict lands belonging to Battle Abbey were being brought into use again, the new tenants sometimes chose to turn the land to timbering or to cattle pasture rather than to resume their use as arable land.[6] Not all woodland, however, was put entirely to commercial use. Some landowners had enclosed part of their woodlands and turned them into deer parks. Such parks could be of considerable size; large enough, for

---

[1] A. M. Everitt, 'The Making of the Agrarian Landscape of Kent', *Arch. Cant.*, 92 (1976), 1–31, now also printed in id., *Landscape and Community in England* (London, 1985), 61–91. For a detailed description of the physical characteristics of the different regions of Kent, see ch. 3, 'Regions and Pays', in id., *Continuity and Colonization: The Evolution of Kentish Settlement* (Leicester, 1986), 43–68.

[2] O. Rackham, 'The Medieval Landscape of Essex', in D. G. Buckley (ed.), *Archaeology in Essex to A.D. 1500* (Council for British Archaeology, Report no. 34, London, 1980).

[3] F. R. H. Du Boulay, *The Lordship of Canterbury: An Essay on Medieval Society* (London, 1966), 215–18. It is some gauge of the high demand for timber that in 1446 a clerk of the king's works could make an illegal sale of a parcel of woodland belonging to the royal manor of Eltham in Kent at an astonishingly over-priced £1 an acre. E143/25/13.   [4] Lambeth Palace Library, ED 246, 254.

[5] KB9/251, m. 145.

[6] E. Searle, *Lordship and Community: Battle Abbey and its Banlieu, 1066–1538* (Toronto, 1974), 369–70.

example, in the case of the duke of Buckingham's park at Penshurst in Kent, for a big gang of poachers allegedly to carry off no fewer than eighty-two deer in one raid in the middle of the century.[7] Poaching was a particularly exciting and popular sport pursued with enthusiasm throughout the country.

In the absence of the acid uplands which characterize the northern and western extremities of Britain, arable crops could be grown through most of these five south-eastern counties. Wheat and barley predominated on the most fertile soils, as, for example, on the rich soil of the foothills of north and east Kent. Fringed to the seaward side by coastal marshes and inland by the not so fertile Downland, these gently undulating foothills were the main grain-growing districts of Kent, the county's most populous and affluent portion, and one of the factors contributing towards making the South-East one of the richest areas of the country. An example of the kind of farm found here is the manor of Ackholt, on the edge of this belt a few miles south of Wingham in east Kent, which in 1445 had all of its 274 acres down to arable crops but for ten acres of woodland.[8] This was an important area of supply for the London market; wheat was sent by boat up the Thames estuary from harbours of the north coast such as Faversham and Margate. Another prominent cereal-growing belt, likewise enjoying ideal soils and gradients, was the south coastal belt of Sussex which had a farming economy specializing in the growing of grains in combination with the raising of sheep which supplied the necessary manure, although the latter were increasingly being supplemented by cattle. Here too the most popular crops were wheat and barley. Such was the concentration of arable farming on this coastal plain of Sussex that it created a demand for teams of reapers during the harvest period and drew a seasonal labour force down from the Weald.[9] This relative wealth of eastern Kent and maritime Sussex within the South-East was of long standing and was reflected in the figures of the 1334 subsidy a century earlier.[10]

Throughout the South-East oats, peas, beans, and a certain amount of rye were grown alongside the more commercially valuable wheat

[7] Virgoe, 'Ancient Indictments', 254–5.
[8] KB9/251, m. 12.
[9] P. F. Brandon, 'Demesne Arable Farming in Coastal Sussex during the Later Middle Ages', *Agricultural History Review*, 19 (1971), 118–19.
[10] This was reflected in the assessments for the 1334 subsidy. See R. E. Glasscock, *The Lay Subsidy of 1334* (Oxford, 1975), p. xxviii.

and barley. Fields of peas and beans, scenting the surrounding roads and lanes during their summer flowering, were grown primarily for human consumption. Other leguminous crops, vetch and 'horse-meat', had been grown as animal fodder and as improvers of the soil in an important way since the late thirteenth century in the cereal belts of Kent and Sussex, an innovation that had shown these regions to be at the forefront of farming methods in England.[11]

Yet the emphasis should not be laid too heavily on arable crops alone. Speaking generally, the five counties would best be described as having a notably balanced mixed farming economy. Indeed, there was an observable trend in the later Middle Ages away from cereal farming towards more pastoral farming.[12] Even in the grain-growing belt of Kent itself a farmer would prefer to combine intensive livestock husbandry with raising arable crops. The manor of Ackholt, mentioned above as an illustration of the importance of arable farming in this area, is somewhat misleading in its suggestion of an area of exclusively arable cultivation. William Aldelond, who grew wheat and barley in the parish of Minster on the Isle of Thanet in the north-eastern corner of the Kent grain belt, left behind him as his winter minimum of livestock five (presumably draught) horses, twenty pigs, eight bullocks, and a flock of a hundred sheep, when at the end of January 1445—a month of short days and cold east winds—he drowned himself.[13]

The large orchards which until very recently were one of the most characteristic features of the Kentish countryside were possibly a much less conspicuous aspect of the landscape during the fifteenth century, although the presence of apple mills suggests large-scale apple growing.[14] The imaginary landscape described in a poem probably of Henry IV's reign, *Mum and the Sothsegger*, may have

[11] Brandon, 'Demesne Arable Farming', 123; B. M. S. Campbell, 'The Diffusion of Vetches in Medieval England', *Econ. HR*, 2nd ser., 41 (1988), 193–208.

[12] M. Mate, 'Pastoral Farming in South-East England in the Fifteenth Century', *Econ. HR*, 2nd ser., 40 (1987), 523–36. This trend in the South-East towards more pastoral farming was not, however, an even one throughout the century. It was greatly set back during the 1430s and 1440s by bad weather and disease, and, in the case of sheep farmers, by declining markets.

[13] E357/38 Kent and Middlesex: Lands, tenements, goods, and chattels of traitors, outlaws, felons, and fugitives.

[14] It is thought that refugee Flemings in the sixteenth and seventeenth centuries were the first to introduce market gardening to Kent and that they probably also did much to encourage fruit growing. S. G. McRae and C. P. Burnham, *The Rural Landscape of Kent* (Wye, 1973), 106. References to apple mills are to be found in inventories of goods of rebels in 1381.

conformed closely to the actual appearance of some rich rolling
portion of Sussex or Kent in high summer: here is a landscape of green
woods and hedges, homesteads set among mown meadows, and
harvested corn fields where blackberries and honeysuckle grow along
the waysides. Beans, broom, and wild meadow flowers blossom, there
are plums and pears in the orchards, grapes in the garden, deer out on
the dale; sturdy horses and cattle graze the pasturelands, and, hidden
in the available shade, sheep lie in the cool as their lambs sport along
the hedges.[15]

Sheep, the most numerous of the different livestock present in the
South-East, were kept rather less for their mutton than as dairy
animals and wool producers, and for their use in manuring arable land.
John Leventhorp, who in the early 1420s leased out to farm his dairy at
Wennington in Essex a few miles south-east of Romford on the edge
of Thames-side marshland, included in his lease fifty-six cows and
168 sheep for milking.[16] Likewise, at Easter 1450 at another Essex
grange a John Bewham took on the dairying of seventeen cows and 300
ewes.[17] The flat open marshlands of southern Essex, where the salt
breeze carried a clinking of sheep bells along with the cries of the
waders, were widely renowed for their fine cheeses.[18]

Wool from the south-eastern counties was none of it of the highest
quality grade required by the medieval wool trade. In a list of 1454,
grading fifty-one different kinds of English wool, the wools of
Middlesex, Kent, and Sussex were placed almost at the bottom of the
list, worth, in the case of Kentish wool, four marks per sack. This
compared with fourteen marks per sack for the finest English wools
from the March of Shropshire and Leominster. None the less, these
'slight' wools of Kent and Sussex were not without their export market
and they also had the local cloth industry to supply.[19] The evidence

---

[15] J. Burrow, *English Verse 1300–1500* (London, 1977), 260–1. I am grateful to Dr
P. A. Robinson for bringing the judgement of another mind to this passage.

[16] Essex Record Office, D/DL M33. I am grateful to Mr S. P. Potter of Purleigh for
bringing this document to my attention.

[17] SC6/848/16. For further illustration of the importance of flocks of sheep for milk
production on the Essex coastal marshlands during this period, see J. R. Smith, *Foulness:
A History of an Essex Island Parish* (Essex Record Office Publications, Chelmsford, 1970),
10–13.

[18] *VCH* Essex, ii. 369–70. For an instance of a merchant selling 164 Essex cheeses in
Calais in 1448–50, see E101/194, m. 26ᵛ.

[19] E. Power and M. M. Postan (eds.), *Studies in English Trade in the Fifteenth Century*
(London, 1933), 49–50.

points to large flocks of sheep particularly on the South Downs and throughout Kent.[20]

In a region where the influence of great magnate houses was conspicuously absent, the agricultural and mercantile wealth of the South-East found its reflection in a numerous gentry class, particularly in Kent. It has been estimated that the total number of gentry families resident in Kent between 1422 and 1509 was two hundred and fifty-six.[21] This Kentish gentry was both abundant and of quite modest means. A very high proportion of them—almost half according to taxation returns of 1450—were lesser gentry: gentlemen, rather than esquires or knights.

Below the ranks of the gentry, and nudging up close to them, was a class of prosperous peasantry, men described as either yeomen or husbandmen, some of whom were landholders and cultivators on such a scale that to call them peasants is perhaps misleading. The terms were not employed rigidly but in a general fashion a yeoman held a greater acreage than a husbandman.[22] They were in large part a product of that widespread depopulation, resulting from the Black Death of 1348 and its subsequent outbreaks, which had changed landlord–tenant relations so dramatically in favour of the tenant. Land became more abundant and the cost of labour rose. Their financial difficulties led large-scale landholders to abandon the direct exploitation of their estates. The demesne manors of the archbishop of Canterbury, for instance, like those of many of the large estates, were wholly farmed out by 1450, and many of the lessees came from the growing ranks of well-to-do peasantry.[23] The century after 1348 became a time of rising expectations and increasing self-confidence among tenants for whom the traditional encumbrances of feudal tenure were slipping away. Since the late fourteenth century in Kent, Surrey, Sussex, and elsewhere such men had been prospering from farming the archbishop's land together with his livestock, buildings, and, where these were important, rights to customary services. And if a

---

[20] For a well-documented account of the organization of sheep farming by a Kentish landowner as important as Christ Church Priory, Canterbury, especially during the boom of the first quarter of the fourteenth century, see R. A. L. Smith, *Canterbury Cathedral Priory* (Cambridge, 1969), 146–56.

[21] For the remarks of this paragraph, see P. W. Fleming, 'The Character and Private Concerns of the Gentry of Kent 1422–1509', Ph.D. thesis (Swansea, 1985), 61–3.

[22] C. C. Dyer, *Standards of Living in the Later Middle Ages: Social Change in England c.1200–1520* (Cambridge, 1989), 15, 22–3.

[23] Du Boulay, *The Lordship of Canterbury*, 221.

man held some of his land from the archbishop, he was quite likely by
the mid-fifteenth century also to be leasing from a couple of other
large landowners and from several of his own neighbours too.
Competent managers with valuable local knowledge (sometimes
themselves former estate officials for landlords), these men rationalized
and increased their holdings assiduously, often in jigsaws of small
plots.[24] The grant by Simon Sage, of Litlington in the Cuckmere
valley not many miles from the Sussex coast, who in 1458 alienated all
his lands in neighbouring Exceat and Westdean, is a catalogue of tiny
plots. He had one fifty-acre piece of arable, a ten-acre piece of
meadow, and seventeen acres of saltmarsh, but the remaining thirty
and more acres of his property came in four-, three-, one-, and half-
acre portions, no doubt patiently accumulated with aspect and soil in
mind.[25] Some of the more prosperous families of this group can be
seen abandoning the traditional Kentish custom of partible inheritance
in favour of primogeniture in order to ensure that their carefully
garnered family estates might be passed on intact.[26]

It is worth looking at this group in some detail in order to convey
how different south-eastern society of 1450 was from what it had been
in 1381 when it participated in the Great Revolt, since at first glance
the two risings would seem to be strikingly similar. On both occasions
men within riding distance of London took themselves to the capital to
petition the king. Both risings were precipitated by the war against the
French. Both were protests against misgovernment and the failure of
the judicial system and produced murderous violence against some of
the central and local ministers and officials regarded as the source of
these evils. But the Great Revolt had important features largely, or
even wholly, lacking in 1450. The intolerable fiscal demands of the
Crown during the decade before the rebellion of 1381 had no parallel
in 1450. Above all, as we have seen, in the seventy years dividing the
two revolts there had been changes in the organization of agrarian

---

[24] The leasing to *firmarii* who were usually prosperous peasants and small
landowners by Christ Church Priory, Canterbury, is discussed in Smith, *Canterbury
Cathedral Priory*, 193–4; Du Boulay, 'Who were Farming the English Demesnes at the
End of the Middle Ages?', *Econ. HR*, 2nd ser., 17 (1964), 443–55; B. Harvey, 'The
Leasing of the Abbot of Westminster's Demesnes in the Later Middle Ages', *Econ. HR*,
2nd ser., 22 (1969), 17–27; R. H. Hilton, *The English Peasantry in the Later Middle Ages*
(Oxford, 1975), 18.
[25] *Abstracts of Sussex Deeds and Documents*, Sussex Record Society, 29 (1924), 25–6.
[26] A. F. Brown, 'The Lands and Tenants of the Bishopric and Cathedral Priory of St
Andrew, Rochester, 600–1540', Ph.D. thesis (London, 1974), 297.

society so fundamental as to alter radically the nature of economic and social grievances of which the population of the region might complain: serfdom and the pressures of the seigneurial system had ceased to be an important issue. There is no impression in 1450 that the insurgents of the South-East were seeking to reform the social order of their day. The great legacy of 1381 for this region was not so much its grievances as the common tradition of insurgency which it furnished. There is evidence that memory of 1381 acted as a spur to action in the risings of the 1450s.[27]

Their increasing literacy and material prosperity have made the yeomen and husbandmen a group about which it is possible to be quite precise. They were not wealthy on any scale but the better off among them knew a solid domestic comfort by the standards of the time. Their homes, better constructed than in many parts of the country, had bacon hanging in the roof, silver spoons on the table, a chimney over the hearth, and feather beds to sleep on. They indulged a taste for vivid colours in clothing and hangings; gave affectionate pet names to their cows (here an Almond, there a Nightingale); remembered the local poor in their wills; owned a book or maybe two; and wanted their sons sent to school.[28] The more wealthy among them were not easily discernible from the lower ranks of the gentry. John Cotyng from Sittingbourne in Milton hundred may or may not have been a rebel in 1450 but he certainly had his name placed among those granted a pardon after it was over.[29] Howsoever, as a landlord and entrepreneur he represents the most prosperous kind of Kentish yeoman, one who had everything to lose if the terrible rumour of 1450 were true that Kent was to be made a wild forest in revenge for the death of the duke of Suffolk. To be more precise he had, give or take a few acres (since this was his total in 1459), more than three messuages, twelve virgates, and an additional twenty-seven acres. That is, a total of some 387 acres. In addition to this he owned a house, the Swan in Sittingbourne, furnished with a good display of silver and plate, two barns, and also

[27] KB9/955/2, m. 2; this evidence is discussed in Ch. 6, below.

[28] On the advanced nature of Kentish domestic architecture in the fifteenth century, see E. Melling (ed.), *Kentish Sources*, v. *Some Kentish Houses* (Maidstone, 1965), 4–7. Evidence for the remaining statements in this paragraph comes from the reading of wills, Kent Record Office (Maidstone) PRC 32/2, PRC 17/5. An example of how fruitful a source of information wills can be for examining late medieval Kentish society is the essay by P. W. Fleming: 'Charity, Faith, and the Gentry of Kent 1422–1529', in A. Pollard (ed.), *Property and Politics: Essays in Later Medieval English History* (Gloucester, 1984), 23–54.   [29] *CPR*, 1446–52, 362.

stalls in the market-place at Milton and Sittingbourne.[30] Living within the smell of the sea and only half a dozen miles or so from the castle of Queenborough on the Isle of Sheppey, which the French had attacked in April 1450, the threat of enemy occupation or looting must have been an acute anxiety for him and a great many men of coastal Kent that summer.

Property consciousness was the hallmark of this group. To take an example of a more modest yeoman, Henry atte Bregge, the younger, farmed in the village of Laughton set in the low-lying countryside east of Lewes in Sussex. He apparently enjoyed a little illegal sport and may have taken an interest in national affairs, but more than anything else his overriding concern was with his own farming affairs. In April 1449 he is to be found being fined for keeping a greyhound bitch, a franchise granted only to those with property valued at over 40*s.* a year. Since his father was fined at the same time for keeping a greyhound dog this looks suspiciously like a family poaching enterprise.[31] He may perhaps have been involved in the rising of July 1450, yet in the first week of August of that year, which would have been almost immediately upon his return from the turbulence of the capital, he was busy protesting in the local manor court over a long-standing grievance, that a neighbouring landholder had not scoured out his ditch properly for years and that as a consequence Henry's own meadow had been under water and useless, causing him a farthing less than 40*s.* in damage; in response to which his neighbour was equivocating, acknowledging some damage but disputing the amount.[32]

At the lowest end of the yeoman–husbandman group were men such as Thomas Jerveys, a husbandman farming during the 1440s at Thundersley, just north of Canvey Island on the Essex bank of the Thames. In the summer of 1443 he had twenty acres under wheat, twenty-seven acres under barley and dredge, and twenty-four under peas and oats. He was recorded as owning three horses (one of them no longer fit to work), two cows, and seven piglets, but with seventy-one acres under crops almost certainly had many more than this.[33] Such a holding would have lent him status in the local community, for there were those whose holdings were too small to support them and

---

[30] 'Sittingbourne Wills', *Arch. Cant.*, 41 (1929), 49–50.
[31] BL Add. Roll 32471.
[32] His name is on the pardon roll but this is inconclusive evidence. *CPR*, 1446–52, 345; BL Add. Roll 32004.
[33] E357/37 Essex and Herts.: Lands, tenements, goods, and chattels of traitors, outlaws, felons, and fugitives.

who were habitually obliged to hire out their labour. The livestock of such a labourer in the parish of Otford just north of Sevenoaks in Kent in the summer of 1445 consisted of no more than three young bullocks and a pig; in addition he had a mere three roods of land sown with wheat and two acres sown with peas and oats.[34]

There is no sure way of estimating how large a fraction of society the yeomen were, but after Cade's rebellion in 1450 a long pardon roll was drawn up of some 3,000 and more names from the south-eastern counties. A few of the county hundreds present on it enumerate sufficiently large numbers of their inhabitants to be statistically interesting. There is Milton hundred with an unparalleled 314 names from fourteen villages; Shamull hundred with 123 individuals from ten different towns and villages, and an additional twelve men from whereabouts unknown in the hundred; Eyhorne hundred with 211 men from seventeen localities; and Maidstone hundred with ninety-four individuals from six towns and villages. All these were hundreds from around or near the Medway valley in northern and central Kent. Looking at these lists of names the yeomen and husbandmen are very conspicuous. Not every name is accompanied by occupation or status, but among the greater number who are, a substantial 30 per cent in the hundred of Maidstone are designated as either yeomen or husband-men, a proportion which rises to a rough 50 per cent in the hundreds of Eyhorne, Milton, and Shamull. Even in Sussex where the greatest number of names in any given hundred is a mere sixty-seven from Netherfield hundred, forty-five from Steyning hundred, thirty-three from Swambergh hundred, and thirty-two from Longbridge hundred, the proportion is 35 per cent, 55 per cent, 51 per cent, and 84 per cent respectively. And in the Surrey hundred of Wallington and Brixton with its plentiful 243 names 37 per cent of persons are designated as either yeomen or husbandmen.[35]

Whilst the yeoman class may have come to rule the fields by the second quarter of the fifteenth century, the status of the artisan was little changed. Of course the distinction between the two groups was very far from absolute; much of the manufacture of textiles had moved from the towns into rural areas where cloth workers were commonly also smallholders. But the concentration of artisans—cobblers, glovers, fletchers, tallow-chandlers, carpenters, and cordwainers—continued to be in the towns and large villages. Some of these retailed their own

---

[34] KB9/254, m. 62.   [35] *CPR*, 1446–52, 338–74.

goods in shops or stalls at the weekly markets and at their towns' fair days. Often they formed a vocal, mobile, and independent-minded element in the community, prominent in the religious and political dissent of the period.

In some instances one particular craft or trade predominated in a town. This was the case, for example, at Thaxted in northern Essex where since the later fourteenth century approximately 40 per cent of the working male population may have been employed in tool manufacture as cutlers or sheathers.[36] In some coastal towns of the South-East it was shipping and fishing which gave the greatest employment, although, it must be added, this was not the case as often as might be expected. It was true of Hythe where a majority of the working population were fishermen,[37] and where the work of craftsmen, for example that of the net knitters,[38] was often allied to the fishing trade. The boats of Sussex and Kentish ports such as Brighton, Rye, Romney, Hythe, and Folkestone fished the local inshore waters for plaice and mackerel, and from June onwards their larger boats went up to the North Sea fisheries of Scarborough and Yarmouth to catch herring.[39] Oyster fisheries were a local speciality of the estuaries of the north Kent and south Essex coasts.

Apart from fishing, another important source of revenue for the boat owners and shipmen of the region was the carrying and supplying trade over the Channel to the English troops operating in France and to the permanent garrison in Calais. Here was a network of trade, indeed, which extended all over the south-east of England and beyond. Calais formed a more or less captive market. Set on flat and marshy ground, the castle and town could not even supply its own building materials of freestone or timber: in 1440 the woods of three Essex monasteries supplied 1,400 great oaks, and woods at Langley Park near Leeds Castle in Kent supplied a further 1,760, all for the harbour and waterworks at Calais.[40] The garrison could buy some wheat in the

---

[36] KB9/26/1, mm. 24, 30, which supplies a list of men from Thaxted who rose in support of the duke of York at Chelmsford on 22 and 23 Feb. 1452. It appears to name a large proportion of the able-bodied male population of the town: of the 268 named, 106 were described as either 'shether' or 'coteler'.

[37] A. J. F. Dulley, 'Four Kent Towns at the End of the Middle Ages', *Arch. Cant.*, 81 (1966), 103.   [38] Mentioned, for example, KB9/253, m. 34.

[39] Dulley, 'Four Kent Towns', 105–7.

[40] R. Allen Brown, H. M. Colvin, and A. J. Taylor (eds.), *The History of the King's Works*, i. *The Middle Ages* (London, 1963), 426, 439. Even lime had had to be brought over regularly from Kent until a kiln was built at Calais 1438–9 to burn local chalk. Bricks, however, had been made over there since the fourteenth century (ibid. 426–7).

March of Calais and wheat and wine were on occasion acquired from Norman and Breton traders, but its main traffic in live cattle and sheep, bacon, stockfish, saltpetre, arrows, and the like came through the ports of London and Sandwich.[41] As regards cross-Channel passengers, Dover enjoyed a monopoly of the Calais traffic; mariners were not allowed to take merchants and pilgrims from Calais to any other Kentish port.[42]

The whole enterprise created all kinds of incidental benefits for the area, such as a demand for pasturage near Sandwich for hundreds of cattle and sheep whilst they awaited embarkation[43] and a demand in the quarries of the Maidstone area for stone missiles for siege machines.[44] An outgoing stream of troops, pressed labour,[45] food-stuffs, and military equipment, together with incoming merchants, merchandise, and visitors, made the main roads of the region among the busiest in the country; the hostelry business could not but benefit as it inflated its prices to suit demand. At Rochester, a stopping-place for travellers *en route* from Dover to London, an innkeeper in the July of 1445 thought some French ambassadors in the peace negotiations between England and France suitable customers to buy fish from him at three times its true value. It was, of course, the same story with the wine they bought too.[46]

Porchester and Southampton on the south coast were both used as disembarkation points by visiting embassies which then took their road to London through Hampshire, Sussex, and Surrey, as an alternative to the Dover–Canterbury–Rochester–Dartford route. This meant that a large portion of the population of the South-East were exposed at

---

[41] E101/194/6, mm. 1, 1ᵛ, 13, 13ᵛ, 25–9ᵛ, and elsewhere. For the business of maintaining Calais and its March during its early years as an English possession, see S. J. Burley, 'Victualling of Calais 1347–65', *BIHR* 31 (1958), 49–57.

[42] *CPR*, 1446–52, 427–8.

[43] E101/194/6, mm. 3, 30ᵛ.

[44] L. F. Salzman, *English Industries of the Middle Ages* (Oxford, 1923), 88. In 1418, for example, 7,000 stones for guns of divers sorts were ordered from the quarries of Maidstone and elsewhere. *CPR*, 1416–22, 134.

[45] Royal purveyors were given powers of impressment to gather masons and carpenters for the work at Calais and bring them to ports of the south coast for embarkation. Unlike Normandy, Calais had a strict policy of employing none but English workmen. This created one more nuisance for the roads and villages of the South-East and Hampshire. *The History of the King's Works*, i. 427, 463.

[46] KB9/252/1, m. 82. The embassy had an altogether unfortunate experience of Rochester. Their journal reports that Rochester had an epidemic that July, that the water was unclean, and that accommodation for themselves and their horses was so unsatisfactory that they went out to nearby villages. Stevenson, i. 95.

various times, and most particularly at the time of the bringing over of Henry VI's new French queen in 1445, to very colourful and vivid manifestations along their own parish roads of the ever-important French connection.[47]

There was another side, however, to the South-East's cross-Channel dealings. Soldiers and camp followers were quartered in the countryside on their way to and from France and were apt to commit every sort of outrage. Ships were commandeered to transport troops. A zone was created, twelve miles wide and extending in length right round from Sandwich to Appledore, from which purveyors might take (regardless of the inconvenience and without any sure guarantee of repayment) livestock or grain exclusively for the supply of Calais, its marches, and Kent's own Dover castle. The rich arable lands of the Isle of Thanet and the central hundreds of Maidstone, Eythorne, and Twyford also came under this special preserve of royal purveyors that made a parasitic neighbour of Calais in times of stress.[48] When in the late 1440s commerce was badly disrupted by an increase in piracy and England through military defeat lost a friendly French coast in Normandy the whole business of proximity to France was to turn very sour. Sandwich in particular declined through this disruption: its exports of wool and cloth dropped dramatically in 1449, whilst its wine imports fell to a quarter of what they had recently been. As a key Kentish port, Sandwich's decline had repercussions upon the health of the whole county's trade. In neighbouring Sussex in 1448 the French had burnt Rye and Winchelsea.[49] All along the Thames estuary, at Gravesend, Cliffe, Hoo, and on the Isle of Sheppey on the Kentish bank, and at Horndon, Tilbury, Fobbing, and Shoebury on the Essex bank, beacons stood in readiness for firing. They formed part of a network which extended from the coast inland throughout the South-East, manned by local tithingmen, watching day and night for signal of enemy attack.[50] Additionally there were solitary religious who lived on

---

[47] The new queen, Margaret of Anjou, landed at Porchester from where she went to nearby Southampton and thence to London. B. P. Wolffe, *Henry VI* (London, 1981), 182.

[48] These special arrangements were reaffirmed on 15 May 1449 in the light of the worsening military situation of that spring. *CPR*, 1446–52, 244.

[49] R. A. Griffiths, *The Reign of King Henry VI: The Exercise of Royal Authority, 1422–1461* (London, 1981), 631–2.

[50] H. T. White, 'The Beacon System in Kent', *Arch. Cant.*, 46 (1934), 80–1. A contemporary drawing of Kentish beacons may be seen in an early fifteenth-century map of the Isle of Thanet which illustrates a chronicle of St Augustine's Abbey, Canterbury (Trinity Hall, MS 1, fo. 42ᵛ). R. A. Skelton and P. D. A. Harvey (eds.), *Local Maps and*

the coasts acting as self-appointed keepers of lights and as coastguards, men such as the hermit who sat in the cliff at Dover gazing upon the sea.[51]

There was a busy domestic carrying trade along the roads of the region with the movement of passengers, pilgrims, and local materials: chalk from Lewes perhaps, or from Northfleet, pot clay from Wrotham, or timber from Sevenoaks to name a few.[52] Certainly the Thames was as much a thoroughfare as a barrier with ferries plying across from Kent to Essex and back at points such as Gravesend, Greenwich, Greenhithe, and Higham.[53] The condition of the roads varied from season to season, but it was possible to move about the countryside at a fair speed. An estate official of the archbishop of Canterbury could ride in May from Pinner Park in Middlesex via Hayes to Otford in Kent and down to Wadhurst, Frankham Park, and Mayfield in Sussex attending to business at each of these manors as he came to them in a matter of four days.[54] Moreover, the trade in a commodity as perishable as fresh fish, carried by rippiers from Folkestone, Hythe, and Rye to London, confirms the suggestion of serviceable roads.[55] Indeed, Kent was notorious for the speed with which news could travel from one end of the county to the other. The London to Dover road had become all the swifter since the replacement early in the century of the ford over the Darent at Dartford by a bridge, and since the construction of a new stone bridge over the Medway between Rochester and Strood.[56] However, there was a constant problem of upkeep. At Dartford the occupant of the hermitage at the foot of the bridge solicited alms for the repair of the bridge, whilst the repair of the highways was regularly remembered by

Plans from Medieval England (Oxford, 1986), pl. 8, discussed pp. 119–26. Fear of the French notwithstanding, the system of watch-keeping by tithing men sometimes failed: Walter atte Gate of Waldron, Sussex, for example, was fined 6*d.* at his local hundred court in Apr. 1450 for defaulting on his vigil at 'le Bekene'. BL Add. Roll 32472.

[51] R. M. Clay, *The Hermits and Anchorites of England* (London, 1914), 51, 53, 222–5.

[52] Mention is made of these local commodities, for example, in the parker's account for Mayfield (Sussex), Lambeth Palace Library, ED 714; in the reeve's account for Northfleet (Kent), SC6/1129, m. 12; in the parker's account at Wrotham (Kent), ibid. m. 11; and the manorial accounts for Otford (Kent), ibid. m. 2, during the 1440s and 1450s.

[53] *VCH* Essex, viii. (1983), 58. The Higham–Tilbury ferry is mentioned, for example, in connection with the transporting of Kentish wool to Colchester in 1441. *CCLR*, 1435–41, 418.   [54] Lambeth Palace Library, ED 715.

[55] Dulley, 'Four Kent Towns', 102.

[56] J. Dunkin, *The History and Antiquities of Dartford* (London, 1844), 191; C143/448/19.

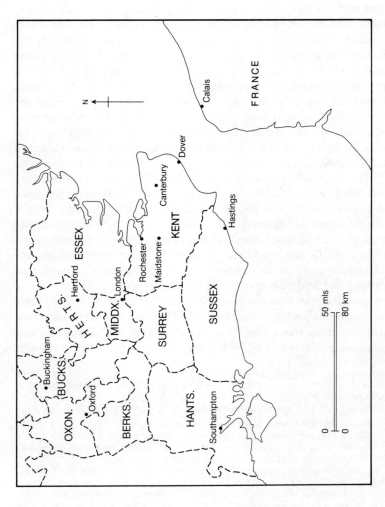

The South-East of England

men in their wills. Bequests were frequently made for the upkeep of local roads, sometimes for attention to be given to specified stretches.[57]

There is one industry which merits special attention: the manufacture of cloth. By the 1430s woollen cloth enjoyed a position of major importance among the exports of Henry VI's England, rivalling that of wool. When in the middle of the century the trade went into marked temporary decline the workers of this labour-intensive industry naturally suffered badly from insecurity of employment.[58] The commercial and industrial depression is an essential element in any explanation of the popular unrest of this period. In the chapters which follow it will be seen again and again that the cloth workers were the most persistent insurgents of mid-fifteenth-century England: in the Midlands, in Wiltshire, in East Anglia, and in Kent—men such as the weaver from Faversham, William Horne, who at Canterbury on 14 June 1451 was adjudged to be hanged for high treason and whose goods were forfeit, his most valuable possessions being his two looms.[59]

The volume of the export trade in woollens from England was normally subject to cyclical fluctuations of two or three years, but the period 1448–50 saw—at least as revealed by official customs' records—an abnormal downswing in quantity by some 35 per cent from the 1446–8 figure. This change marked the beginning of a depression in the trade which would continue throughout the two following decades. Not until the mid-1470s did a long-term recovery begin.[60] The export of wool, dealt in largely by English merchants and mainly channelled through Calais, as a monopoly of the English staplers, was less likely to be seriously crippled than the trade in cloth which was dealt in as much by alien merchants as by Englishmen. It

[57] For example, the will of John Bunting of Milton dated 1464–5 gives 40s. 'to repair the bad road between Middleton church and Colshale'. 'Milton Wills', *Arch. Cant.*, 44 (1932), 91–2.

[58] M. Mate, 'Pastoral Farming in South-East England in the Fifteenth Century', *Econ. HR*, 2nd ser., 40 (1987), 527.

[59] E357/42 Kent and Middlesex: Lands, tenements, goods, and chattels of traitors, outlaws, felons, and fugitives.

[60] For details of English exports of woollen cloth at this period, see Power and Postan, *Studies in English Trade in the Fifteenth Century*, 23 ff.; G. V. Scammell, 'English Merchant Shipping at the End of the Middle Ages: Some East Coast Evidence', *Econ. HR*, 2nd ser., 13 (1961); E. M. Carus-Wilson and O. Coleman, *England's Export Trade, 1275–1547* (Oxford, 1963), 122–3; J. L. Bolton, *The Medieval English Economy 1150–1500* (London, 1980), chs. 8 and 9.

was marketed as widely as the Baltic, the Low Countries, and
throughout the Mediterranean—they knew in Byzantium that the
British Isles produced the best wool in the world and had a flourishing
cloth industry.[61] At the end of the 1440s, however, the English cloth
export trade fell victim to a combination of failed diplomacy, warfare,
and commercial rivalry. In 1435 England had lost its alliance with
Burgundy and this led to repeated disruptions in its dealings with the
all important market of the Low Countries (so far as legal trade was
concerned). In 1448 active fighting recommenced in France just as
English–Hanseatic rivalry entered upon a further phase of mutual
damage with the suspension in 1447 of Hanseatic privileges in
England.

Some of the finest broadcloths in England were made in the area
around the southern Cotswolds, and just to the south in southern
Wiltshire and Berkshire there was an important industry producing
smaller and less heavily fulled types of cloth marketed variously as
kerseys, dozens, and straits. Another equally important cloth-producing
area concentrating on the production of smaller cloths existed along
the Suffolk–Essex border.[62] In this area around the river Stour and its
tributaries where the grinding and pounding of water-mills, some for
fulling cloth and some for corn, accompanied the normal sounds of the
river,[63] kerseys and straits were manufactured in large quantities at
towns such as Dedham, Sudbury, Clare, Hadleigh, and Lavenham.
Cloth production was also important in certain other towns of Essex
and Suffolk such as Coggeshall, Braintree, Bury St Edmunds, and
Halstead. A woollen district, although not of the importance of either
the Wiltshire–Gloucestershire or Suffolk–Essex groups, extended
through the southern counties of England from Hampshire through
Surrey (Guildford was an important centre), to the villages of the
Kentish Weald and beyond.

The Weald had the advantages of access to the fuller's earth, found
plentifully to the west around Nutfield and Reigate in Surrey, which
was needed in the finishing of more valuable varieties of cloth, of fast-
flowing streams to power fulling mills, and above all a surplus

---

[61] A. Ducellier, 'La France et les Îles Britanniques vues par un byzantin du XVᵉ
siècle: Laonikos Chalkokondylis', in *Économies et sociétés au Moyen Âge: mélanges offerts à
Edouard Perroy* (Paris, 1973), 439–45; R. H. Britnell, *Growth and Decline in Colchester,
1300–1525* (Cambridge, 1986), 169.

[62] Carus-Wilson, 'The Woollen Industry', in *Cambridge Economic History*, ii, ed.
M. Postan and E. E. Rich (Cambridge, 1952), 355–428.

[63] DL29/40/747 (Dedham ministers' accounts).

population lacking sufficient employment. For example, during the 1440s in the villages of Smarden and Pluckley, just on the edge of the Low Weald or Vale of Kent, a few miles west of Ashford, it is likely that almost a quarter of the male population was engaged in the cloth industry.[64] Serving the cloth villages of the Weald was the important town of Maidstone to its north in the lower Medway valley. Here were the drapers and chapmen who acted as middlemen between the workers of the Weald and the London merchants: commerce and connections with the capital were continuous.[65] It was a familiarity which could breed contempt, as in September 1442 when two Londoners set upon a Bearsted draper and a Maidstone servant carrying goods for his master as they rode along the roads of Kent. The robbers made off with thirty yards of woollen cloth worth 35s. and eight pieces of woollen cloth worth 7 marks.[66] But it is precisely this dubious side of the connection between Maidstone and the capital which, by entering the criminal records, allows us a closer look at the chapmen's wares. Another robbery by the same pair of Londoners that September, this time from two Maidstone chapmen, permits us to discover that in this district of Kent there was not only a market for cloth dyes but also for cloves, ginger, cinnamon, dates, sugar cane, and silk.[67]

The Wealden cloth villages nurtured a tradition of religious dissent so strong as to constitute one of the more distinctive features of this singular district—a tradition encouraged by large parishes, scattered settlements, and the weakness of the local manorial structure.[68] This was a Lollard district, which would, moreover, take its full share in the political unrest in Kent during the early 1450s. Indeed, with its wooded, incised valleys, its comparative absence of large, nucleated

[64] This figure is taken from lists of names of those men from Smarden and Pluckley who were pardoned on 7 July 1450 for having risen with Cade. *CPR*, 1446–52, 363–4, 365–6. The lists for these two villages are exceptionally full, appearing to name a large proportion of the working male population and giving their occupations. At Smarden, of the 101 names, 22 are employed in the cloth industry; at Pluckley, the figure is 10 out of 51.

[65] For examples of Maidstone men (a draper, spicer, chapman, husbandman, and tailor) in debt to London citizens, see *CPR*, 1416–22, 284; *CPR*, 1429–36, 98, 157; *CPR*, 1436–41, 208; *CPR*, 1452–61, 619.

[66] KB9/248, m. 19.

[67] Ibid.

[68] A. Everitt, 'Nonconformity in Country Parishes', in J. Thirsk (ed.), *Land, Church and People: Essays Presented to Prof. H. P. R. Finberg*, Agricultural History Review, 18, suppl. (Reading, 1970), 189–91.

settlements, and its sense of remoteness and secrecy, it was a natural refuge for fugitives.[69]

Besides the manufacture of cloth the economy of the area was based on small pastoral holdings, local crafts, iron smelting, and its allied charcoal burning. It was a peculiarity of the land holdings here that Kentish manors all over the county, some of them many miles distant, owned discrete portions of woodland or clearing—denes. In the fifteenth century the manor of Wye, for example, away to the north-east of Ashford on the river Ouse, owned eight denes there.[70] There is no doubt that the Weald's distinctive nature was recognized at the time. It is likely that a Wealden man could be identified by his speech. Caxton, who was born and learnt his native tongue in the Weald during the 1420s, wrote in a preface to one of his English translations, that there was spoken 'as brode and rude englissh as is in ony place of england'.[71]

But to return to the textile industry, signs of the industry were present throughout the South-East. It had made a spinster of many women and had dotted the river valleys with its tenter grounds, fulling mills, and plots of dye plants and teasels. In 1452 at Braintree in Essex the bailiffs declared that the art or mystery of weaving was practised in their town more than any other and had been so from time beyond memory.[72] Just to their north was the greatest of the Essex cloth towns, Colchester. A wide variety of cloths were made there from a low-quality russet, regarded by some as fit only for hermits or the corpses of the humble, to high-quality varieties exported by Italians.[73] A man possessing one of the skills of the industry was not likely to be left unemployed long provided relations with foreign customers were good. Many of the immigrants who were resident in England at this time came from the Low Countries and were employed in the manufacture of cloth, bringing to it their expertise. Among the 128 aliens in Kent who failed to evade the oath of allegiance in 1436 the

---

[69] For example, John Wilkyns, who led an uprising in Kent in May 1452, sought hiding in the Weald, E404/68, m. 133.

[70] Five in Biddenden, one in Halden, one in Tenterden, one in Woodchurch. Cf. R. Furley, *A History of the Weald of Kent*, ii. pt. i. (London, 1874), 413.

[71] *The Prologues and Epilogues of William Caxton*, ed. W. J. B. Crotch, EETS, OS 176 (London, 1928), 4.   [72] *VCH* Essex, ii. 330.

[73] Ibid. 384; E. B. Fryde, *Studies in Medieval Trade and Finance* (London, 1983), 351. (ch. 15: 'The English Cloth Industry and the Trade with the Mediterranean c.1370–c.1480'). Lollard knights specified in their wills the use of russet for their grave-clothes as a sign of their humility. K. B. McFarlane, *Lancastrian Kings and Lollard Knights* (Oxford, 1972), 211.

occupation is known of only eleven, but of these four were weavers and one a mercer. Similarly, of the twelve aliens whose occupations are known in Essex that year, three were weavers and five were tailors, two of whom lived in Colchester.[74]

London was the chief centre for bargaining in English cloth. Wherever the finished cloth of the South-East ended up it was likely either to have travelled through London or to have been bargained for there and delivered directly to harbours of shipment elsewhere. In the middle of the fifteenth century London was the market for those great exporters of English cloth, the Italian merchants. The business was transacted in Blackwell Hall which had been specially constructed for the purpose in the last years of the previous century. At the beginning of the century wool destined for the Mediterranean had left England from London, Southampton, and Sandwich, but by the middle of the century the Venetian galleys had almost ceased to go up the estuary to London, and Southampton with its excellent harbour and Sandwich as an outport to London were the main ports dealing in this trade.

To discuss any aspect of the South-East at this time, whether it be political or economic, makes little sense unless the counties are seen in their proper regional context as a hinterland, closely connected to this expanding capital city. For all its orchards, straying pigs, and countryside of grazing cattle close by its walls, London was a truly urban community by the standards of its day.[75] The fifteenth century saw it outpace more decisively such cities as York, Norwich, Chester, and Bristol. It is estimated that in the mid-fifteenth century 30,000 to 40,000 people lived in the city and its close suburbs.[76] London was the great market for the wares of this adjacent region, its grains, fish, fruit, cloth, iron, timber, stone, and manpower. When in 1439 there was a general shortage of corn the mayor of London was ordered to send purveyors into the city's normal regions of supply—Sussex, Kent, and East Anglia—to buy grain to feed the inhabitants of the city.[77]

The South-East was a region inhabited by a gentry class who had

[74] M. R. Thielemans, *Bourgogne et Angleterre: relations politiques et économiques entre les Pays-Bas Bourguignons et l'Angleterre, 1435–1467* (Brussels, 1966), 556–9.
[75] For example, in 1447 a London butcher could allegedly take a dozen cattle from fields at Tyburn, KB9/996, m. 17.
[76] C. M. Barron, 'London and the Crown 1451–61', in J. R. L. Highfield and R. Jeffs (eds.), *The Crown and Local Communities in England and France in the Fifteenth Century* (Gloucester, 1981), 88.
[77] *CPR*, 1436–41, 253; A. F. Butcher, 'The Origins of Romney Freemen, 1433–1523', *Econ. HR*, 2nd ser., 27 (1974), 19.

been up to London and quite possibly looked at the king. Conversely, every well-to-do merchant or craftsman who made a prosperous living in London looked to Middlesex and the counties of the South-East for property in which to invest. Landed property not only set a seal upon a man's affluence and gentry status but also provided him with a solid asset.[78] And so a citizen and saddler of London might hold a manor in Surrey;[79] a London dyer look to south-western Essex for land in which to invest;[80] and a London alderman such as John Gedney enjoy a desirable warren out in the Middlesex countryside at Tottenham (so desirable, that is, that men from the parish of St Clement Danes would trouble to visit it by night and unannounced).[81] During the mid-1430s Kent and Middlesex were the counties which attracted the greatest number of such Londoners with money to invest in land. The 1436 lay subsidy roll for London revealed that there were 358 men there with assessments of over £5, of these fifteen were detailed as holding land in Hertfordshire, seventeen in Surrey, thirty-three in Essex, thirty-five in Middlesex, and thirty-seven in Kent.[82]

In short, London, the political, financial, and commercial capital of England, with the royal court just outside its walls at Westminster, was the hub of the south-eastern counties and part of what made them a region. It was a singularity of the South-East, and a very significant one, that its regional capital should also happen to be the country's capital.

[78] A. Brown, 'London and North-West Kent in the Later Middle Ages: The Development of a Land Market', *Arch. Cant.*, 92 (1976), 145.

[79] *CPR*, 1446–52, 184–5.

[80] *Feet of Fines for Essex*, iv. *1423–1547*, Essex Archaeological Society (1964), 42, 45.

[81] KB9/997, m. 4; S. L. Thrupp, *The Merchant Class of Medieval London* (Chicago, 1948), 345. For other examples of aldermen who held property in the South-East during the reign of Henry VI, see ibid. 334–5, 352, 373.

[82] Brown, 'London and North-West Kent', 145.

2

THE GROWTH OF DISCONTENT
DURING THE 1430s AND 1440s

POPULAR unrest and rebellion were to be a major feature of the crisis of Henry VI's reign which occurred during 1449–50. Up until that time—at least in Henry's English possessions—they were rare events.[1] The only exceptional year in this regard was 1431, during Henry VI's minority, when a rising with Lollard associations was attempted in southern England. It is worth noting in some of its details because whilst Cade's rebellion would be very different in purpose and organization many of the satellite risings associated with it both in 1450 and during the years immediately after occurred in places of strong Lollard tradition.

The Lollards were scarcely a sect at all in a formal sense and differed widely in their religious attitudes and practices. They had in common a desire to return to a simpler Christianity purged of the trappings of worldly institutions and they emphasized the primal authority of Scripture made accessible by translation into English: hence their nickname, the 'Bible-men'.[2] Other characteristically Lollard attitudes were the denial of priestly sacramental powers (anyone could baptize or hear confession), the refusal to venerate images, the denial of the efficacy of pilgrimages to the relics of saints, and the denial of the carnal presence of Christ's body in the Sacrament.[3] Lollard teachings had first been inspired by the writings of John Wyclif (died 1384) but very early on had left behind their beginnings in Oxford among scholars working in Latin. By the 1430s they were sustained and propagated largely in industrial villages and

---

[1] There were uprisings in Henry's French possessions, such as that which occurred in 1435 in the Caux region north of Rouen shortly after the death of the duke of Bedford. C. T. Allmand, *Lancastrian Normandy 1415–1450: The History of a Medieval Occupation* (Oxford, 1983), 40, 63, 234.

[2] C. Babington (ed.), *The Repressor of Over Much Blaming of the Clergy* (2 vols., RS, 1860), i. p. xxii.

[3] M. H. Keen, 'Wyclif, the Bible, and Transubstantiation', in A. Kenny (ed.), *Wyclif in his Times* (Oxford, 1986), 1–16.

towns by artisans and craftsmen literate in English.[4] Adherence to
these teachings appears to have been particularly prevalent in textile-
producing centres populated as they were by literate, indoor craftsmen
who had established links with outside towns and ports. In these
communities books and ideas might journey with the middlemen
amongst the workers.[5] Bristol through which much cloth was marketed
was an important Lollard centre in the West; in the South-East the
weaving villages of Essex and south-west Kent appear to have given an
early home to Lollard beliefs.

Lollards would seem to have existed in pockets of concentration.
Within the country as a whole they were never anything but a minority,
and, despite their sometimes revolutionary aspirations, they achieved
nothing in the public, political sphere during the fifteenth century.
Their calls for disendowment and for the use of the Church's
temporalities to relieve taxpayers and to pay for the army in France all
came to nothing. The short-lived and small-scale uprising of 1414 led
by the Lollard knight Sir John Oldcastle, which had planned to destroy
Henry V and his brothers, had been harshly repressed. After that date
the support given to Lollardy by influential laymen had faded away.[6]
However, Lollardy as a persistent, covert tradition of radical thinking
acted significantly upon the political sphere. Signally, the districts to
join most actively in political protest in the mid-fifteenth century
would be those of known Lollard sympathies. Lollardy can be likened
to embers, glowing before the conflagration of 1450, and still
smouldering on after that outburst had been doused.

The authorities, then, despite the decisive defeat of the 1414 rising,
were warranted during the decades which followed in their permanent
mistrust of any views or behaviour smacking of Lollardy, for these
threatened the secular as well as the ecclesiastical hierarchy. Those
found guilty were made public examples: the gallows at Tyburn
became known as the 'Lollers galewes';[7] throughout the 1420s clerical

[4] For an enquiry into how 'with the passage of time the intellectual content of Lollardy
dwindled, and the movement became essentially a working-class tradition of dissent',
see J. A. F. Thomson, 'Orthodox Religion and the Origins of Lollardy', *History*, 74
(1989), 39–55; also Keen, 'The Influence of Wyclif', in Kenny, *Wyclif in his Times*, 127–
45, and R. N. Swanson, *Church and Society in Late Medieval England* (Oxford, 1989),
329–47.

[5] J. F. Davis, *Heresy and Reformation in the South East of England 1520–1559* (London,
1983), 2; K. B. McFarlane, *John Wycliffe and the Beginnings of English Nonconformity*
(London, 1952), 161.

[6] Ibid. ch. 6; McFarlane, *Lancastrian Kings and Lollard Knights* (Oxford, 1972), 143.

[7] KB9/1057, m. 12.

versifiers inveighed against these *ingrati, maledicti, daemone nati*;[8] convocations and synods for their part kept issuing statutes and ordinances against Lollards, false preachers, and the possession of sacred books in English. Norfolk, Essex, and London were among some of the places which saw men burnt as heretics at this time.

In addition to what might be termed this doctrinal Lollardy there existed a long tradition of anti-clericalism which it suited prosecuting authorities to conflate and confuse with Lollardy. Anti-clericalism, which as we shall see could manifest itself in acts of horrible violence, was one of the most common forms of seditious behaviour: an effective way to deal with it at law was to call it Lollardy. The word 'Lollard' had long been employed in a derogatory fashion, meaning an idler or a vagabond; by the mid-fifteenth century the term was used very loosely by royal officials and justices' clerks to mean no more than priest-hater or even just general trouble-maker. A word, indeed, which was ideal for making the authorities prick up their ears if one wished to get one's enemies or relatives into trouble. These were tactics, however, which were effective only if employed judiciously. In 1434, for instance, Thomas Tournour, a Middlesex labourer, misjudged the matter and ended up getting himself taken to court for accusations made on insufficient grounds.[9]

The Lollard rising of 1431 was in many respects a political affair. The rebels of 1431 were apparently almost all laymen (this had not been the case in 1414), and when some of them came to be indicted no charges were made of doctrinal unorthodoxy. Their offences lay scarcely in their beliefs at all but rather in their attitude towards the Church, in particular its clergy and its wealth. To this extent the rising of 1431 may not have been a thoroughgoing Lollard revolt in the strictest sense.[10]

The troubles began in the spring of 1431, after the king had been absent from the realm for a year. They started in the form of pamphleteering and the flagrant advertising of heretical and subversive opinions. During March and April in the parish of St Giles without Cripplegate in the northern suburbs of London, between the open

---

[8] *Political Poems*, ii. 128.

[9] KB9/958, m. 30. I am grateful to Dr C. R. Burgess for a helpful discussion on the subject of this paragraph.

[10] Thomson, *The Later Lollards, 1414–1520* (Oxford, 1965), 61. It is his view that 'Lollardy may have helped to prepare the ground for the rising, but it is unlikely that it did anything more'.

spaces of Finsbury fields and the clutter of the city proper, Lollards fomented discontent against the existing order of Church and government.[11] At secret meetings they composed letters and bills expounding their views on church doctrines and, more especially, on their plans to disendow the Church. These bills were distributed to towns of the Midlands and the West such as Salisbury, Oxford, Northampton, and Coventry, to be placed on doors and windows as public notices.[12] Their productions continued into May when they allegedly drew up a detailed list for the replacement of the great prelates and peers of the realm with Londoners from their own ranks. For example, a London weaver, John Cok, was to become the duke of Gloucester and lord of Westminster, whilst a fellow citizen, Ralph Bukberd, was to become head of the Carmelite friars of London.[13]

Yet it was in the West and Midlands, especially in Wiltshire and Berkshire at Salisbury and Abingdon, that most of the outbreaks of trouble took place. As in London, support came in significant proportion from workers in the cloth industry. At Abingdon a group had done its active share in the billing campaign of April, distributing bills on the same network to London, Salisbury, Coventry, and Marlborough.[14] The leader and probably the instigator of much of this religious disaffection was a weaver from Abingdon in Berkshire, William Mandeville, who had assumed the name of 'Jack Sharp of Wigmoreland'. In May some men from Salisbury joined the campaign. On 9 May a group there, including a weaver of the city, a clerk, and a weaver from Westbury some twenty miles and more away to the north-east, and a fuller all the way from Abingdon, distributed and put up in the city and in other towns bills and posters containing heretical statements.[15] Their alleged plan of action was to make an energetic assault on Salisbury cathedral in order to raze its buildings to the ground and to carry off its goods and relics. It was intended that this should set the pattern for a country-wide purge of the possessions of abbeys and priories. On 15 May a gathering of Lollards marched in upon Abingdon from the neighbouring village of East Hendred to

[11] KB9/225, mm. 2–4, 21, 22. For a more comprehensive look at Lollard troubles in the late fourteenth century and early fifteenth century, see M. E. Aston, 'Lollardy and Sedition, 1381–1431', *Past and Present*, 17 (1960), 1–44.

[12] *Annales monasterii S. Albani*, ed. H. T. Riley (2 vols., RS, 1870–1), i. 63–4; KB9/225, m. 21.

[13] KB9/225, mm. 2–4, 22; a passing allusion is made to this in reference to Russell. *Gregory's Chron.*, 172.   [14] BL Add. MS 14848, fo. 89–[r–v].

[15] KB9/227/2, mm. 1B, 2, 23.

attack the abbey.[16] Two days later, on 17 May, Sharp's followers made
their presence known in Frome in eastern Somerset close to the
Wiltshire border.[17] There a dyer from the town and other Lollards
distributed subversive religious literature, again exciting others to rise
up and attack religious houses.[18] In indictments later presented at
Salisbury and Frome the juries outlined the activities just mentioned
(certainly a biased first source for our information) and added, no
doubt for good measure, that the Lollards were also out to kill the
dukes of Bedford and Gloucester and other magnates who opposed
their opinions, be they archbishops, bishops, dukes, earls, barons, or
knights. According to one chronicler, the rebels at Abingdon said that
they would have three priests' heads for a penny.[19] Religious dissent
was here tantamount to anarchy and it is not surprising to find either
chroniclers or commissions dealing with them ready to believe these
Lollards capable of any atrocity.

Since Oldcastle's rising in 1414 the secular government had taken
on a more active role in seeking out and dealing with aberrant religious
views in conjunction with the ecclesiastical authorities. In 1431 a
special commission under the duke of Gloucester, who was then acting
as regent for the absent king, undertook the task of dealing with these
offenders who were regarded as much as traitors as heretics. And it
was before Duke Humphrey that Sharp, who had been put to flight
and who was finally apprehended at Oxford, appeared that May.[20]
Indeed, indictments made before special commissions and justices of
the king's bench form a great bulk of our evidence about Lollard
activity (or alleged activity) at this time. Tilting the balance of the
evidence slightly, there remains a copy of one of the handbills
distributed by Jack Sharp and his followers at the time of his trial in
which we hear the Lollards put their own case, rather than listen to the
allegations and hearsay of juries and chroniclers.[21] This longish
document in English addressed to Henry and 'to alle the Lordys of the
reme of this present Parlement' is a version of the Lollard disendowment bill which had been presented to parliament probably in 1410,

---

[16] Thomson, *The Later Lollards*, 58–9.

[17] KB9/227/2, mm. 1A, 36.

[18] This dyer appeared before the king's justices the following year and was actually
acquitted. Thomson, *Later Lollards*, 30.

[19] *London Chrons.*, 97.

[20] *PCC*, iv. 107–8; *Gregory's Chron.*, 172; *Annales monasterii S. Albani*, i. 63–4.

[21] BL MS Harleian 3775 fo. 120ª, printed as App. F, *Annales monasterii S. Albani*, i.
453–6.

and so by this date its ideas had long been in circulation.[22] The petition argues that the wealth of the temporalities of bishops, abbots, and priors was being wasted and should be utilized far better and to the general good of the realm if it were redistributed in favour of the king and used for the creation of a specified number of earls, knights, esquires, and houses of alms. This point is underlined by an impressive list of all the major English and Welsh bishoprics and abbeys and the value of their temporalities which such a scheme would release. The theme is amendment and reform, 'that alle the temporaltes of chyrches thus apropred azens Crystes lore be turned to Godde, and to the prosperyte of the reme'.

However reasonable and sound this may have seemed to the Lollards it was of course heretical and treasonable rubbish as far as Duke Humphrey or any other law enforcer was concerned. The duke acted with speed and dispatch in taking justices around the country. Jack Sharp, along with a group of his fellow Lollards, was hanged, drawn, and quartered on charges of treason.[23] His head was set on London Bridge as a sober warning to that Lollard contingent which the authorities well knew existed in London, whilst his quarters went to two other main centres of trouble, Oxford and Abingdon.[24] John Russell, the main London ringleader beside Sharp, charged also as a thief, was likewise hanged and drawn. The authorities made examples of other followers wherever there had been disturbances, for example in Coventry and in Salisbury where that June at least two of the Lollards involved in the activities of the previous month there were found guilty of treason and felony and sentenced to be hanged, drawn, and quartered. Severe penalties for conspirators against the peace seemed all the more in order at a time when the young king was absent from the country in France.

II

Throughout the 1430s Lollard doctrines continued to be taught and discussed, albeit in a less overtly proselytizing fashion, probably all

---

[22] The Lollard Disendowment Bill, of which several copies remain, is printed and discussed in A. Hudson (ed.), *Selections from English Wycliffite Writings* (Cambridge, 1978), 135–7, 203–7.

[23] *Gregory's Chron.*, 172; *Davies Chron.*, 54; *Brut*, 457; *Annales monasterii S. Albani*, i. 63–4.   [24] *London Chrons.*, 97; *Brut*, 457.

over the country and most certainly in southern England where little gatherings continued to meet 'to jangle of Job or Jeremye'.[25] Whilst up at Tendring in north-eastern Essex a franklin and his wife were teaching heretical propositions such as that the sacrament of Christ's body was not his actual body and translating the Gospels into English for their teaching,[26] another layman down at East Woodhay in Hampshire was preaching the Gospels in English in his home.[27] Eccentric views were also aired concerning marriage, baptism, confession, and religious images in east Hampshire and west Surrey where a commission of 1440 uncovered what appears to all accounts to have been a well-established local Lollard tradition centred in the vicinity of Odiham, Crondal, and Farnham.[28] Meanwhile, at Selhurst in Sussex, it was the parish priest himself who owned the four Gospels in English and allegedly taught the 'pestiferous opinions of John Wycliff'.[29]

In Kent, where on the flat coastal marshes north of Rochester Sir John Oldcastle's fortified manor house, Cooling Castle, stood as a landmark to a seditious Lollard past, an active Lollard tradition persisted. It was particularly strong in the Weald. This was a county where the images of saints were liable on occasion to have their heads lopped off.[30] Although there is no evidence for Kent's direct involvement in the 1431 risings there was some kind of rising here in 1438 which may locally have been quite serious.[31] It would appear that the preaching of a certain William White, a chaplain who abjured his heresies before the archbishop in Convocation in 1422, sowed the seed for what was to be a persistent heretical tradition at Tenterden in the Weald.[32] By 1428 the matter had been serious enough to warrant a (partially frustrated) round-up of suspects in the district by Archbishop

---

[25] *Political Poems*, ii. 243.   [26] KB9/996, m. 63.   [27] KB9/1059, m. 30.

[28] KB9/234, mm. 77, 78. The parishioners of Odiham had been receptive to Lollard ideas from the time of Lollardy's first beginnings in the early 1380s when their own vicar had invited followers of Wyclif to come and preach there. McFarlane, *John Wycliffe and the Beginnings of English Nonconformity*, 91.

[29] W. R. W. Stephens, *Memorials of the South Saxon See and Cathedral Church of Chichester* (London, 1876), 140–2.

[30] *Political Poems*, ii. 246. This poem is undated although thought to belong to some date about the reign of Henry VI. It is just possible that the iconoclasticism belonged to a particular few years and so I could be antedating it by my suggestion here that it was prevalent during the 1430s.

[31] For this subject in greater detail, see Thomson, *The Later Lollards*, 173–81; also id., 'A Lollard Rising in Kent: 1431 or 1438?', *BIHR* 37 (1964).

[32] M. E. Aston, 'William White's Lollard Followers', in *Lollards and Reformers: Images and Literacy in Late Medieval Religion* (London, 1984), 71–99.

from the villages of Tenterden, Romney, Cranbrook, ?n, Rolvenden, Woodchurch, High Halden, and Staplehurst. ar 1431 saw public abjurations wrung from two Wittersham men and from a Hadlow and a Brenchley man; these two latter men doing penance at Tonbridge and Malling as well as in their own parishes and in Rochester cathedral, suggesting that either their preaching or some Lollard influence had reached these villages. When in 1438, as a royal letter described it, 'aswel lollardes as other robbers & pillers of oure peple, were, in grete noumbre, & in ryotous wyse, gaderyng in the said Shire of Kent',[33] five men from Tenterden were executed for heresy at Maidstone. Other offenders in the rising were carted off to be imprisoned in London. Again, two years later, in 1440, Tenterden's notoriety as a centre of disaffection was signalled for all to see when a man executed for treason had his head set on a pike in the village, whilst two of his quarters were sent for public display at Cranbrook and Appledore. Tenterden and other Lollard villages of the Weald may have subsequently played some kind of part in the risings of 1450. John Glover, one of the Wittersham men to have made a public abjuration in 1431 on the charge of having associated with other heretics and having been present at the reading of reprobate books, may have been the man who took advantage of the opportunity of a royal pardon in 1450 following Cade's revolt. The same may be true of Thomas Harry of Halden, one of those men from the Weald imprisoned in Newgate in 1438 on suspicion of heresy, who had his name included on that same pardon roll of 1450.[34]

III

Lollards apart, there was little in the way of overt popular insurrection during the years of Henry's reign before 1450. Some kind of uprising may have threatened in March 1443 when Edward Hammys, a London tallow-chandler alias soldier, and John Oddeshole of Lewes, soldier, allegedly associated at Isleworth in Middlesex with a couple of hundred other men from Middlesex, London, Hertfordshire, Essex,

---

[33] BL Add. MS 14848, a letter from Henry VI to the abbot of Bury St Edmunds, printed in *Archaeologia*, 23 (1831), 339–41. For the dating of this letter to 1438, see Thomson, 'A Lollard Rising in Kent'.
[34] Thomson, *The Later Lollards*, 176, 178; *CCLR*, 1435–41, 197–8; *CPR*, 1446–52, 361.

Surrey, and Kent ~~with the intention of~~ *intended to* attack~~ing~~ Henry and various magnates of the realm.[35] On the day this happened Henry was several miles downstream at Eltham in northern Kent and nothing came of it—although the allegations here of regional support coming from several counties are interesting and suggestive.

More significant for the 1440s than any such single incident, however, is what would appear to be a new degree of restlessness among Henry's subjects. This is to be measured less in planned uprisings against the king than in criticisms levelled against him by his people which, in the criminal records at least, reach a peak at this time. The infant Henry had begun to acquire his first critics and would-be assassins early in life, as he acquired his first set of teeth, but it was the late 1440s and early 1450s which saw the nadir of his popularity in the country as reflected in contemporary charges of seditious speech.[36] Before the second half of the 1440s recorded criticisms of Henry are few, but during the thirteen years between 1444 and 1457 some twenty-six charges of seditious speech came before justices of the king's bench. The accuracy of such charges may be doubted, of course, but their significance remains: even false accusers in the interest of their own plausibility would reflect something of the kinds of accusations or abuse which were being cast against the king in the common talk of the time. What strikes one about these charges is that the same kind of thing was being said (or being said that it was said) all over the country. The constant underlying theme of such speech was that men simply did not regard Henry as fit to be a king. At best he was regarded as a hapless idiot, and at worst as a predatory menace to his country's domestic finances and its foreign affairs. He was a fool, a simpleton;[37] he looked like a child;[38] he had murdered his uncle, the duke of Gloucester, in 1447;[39] he was losing all the wealth of the crown;[40] he was grasping;[41] he was no soldier;[42] it was the earl of Suffolk and the bishop of Salisbury who really had power;[43] indeed, it was because of their influence that Henry was still

---

[35] KB9/245, m. 13.   [36] For example, KB9/203, mm. 2, 5.

[37] 1449, Norfolk, KB9/262, m. 78. The subject of seditious speech against the king is treated at rather greater length in B. P. Wolffe, *Henry VI* (London, 1981), 16–18.

[38] 1446, Suffolk, KB9/260, m. 85; 1449, Cambridgeshire, KB9/262, mm. 2, 5.

[39] 1447, Gloucestershire, KB9/256, m. 13.

[40] 1446, Suffolk, KB9/260, mm. 9, 85.

[41] 1446, Suffolk, KB9/260, m. 85; 1448, Lincolnshire, KB9/260, m. 1.

[42] 1448, Middlesex, KB9/260, m. 87.

[43] 1446, London, KB9/996, m. 55.

childless;[44] Henry were better dead;[45] if 'the comy[n]s were well
avysyd they schuld aryse and destruye hym and all hys consell that is a
bowte hym'.[46] These sentiments were expressed during the 1440s.
From 1450 onwards, once the commons of the South-East had
actually risen, such sentiments were if anything to increase in rancour.
Would God (it was to be said) that the captain of Kent—that is to say,
Cade—was reigning instead of Henry;[47] how much better it would be
if the head stuck on London Bridge was not Cade's but his.[48]

Some regions of the country may have felt more strongly about
Henry than others. As early as 1438 a gang of thieves, predominantly
Londoners, could go down to Rainham in Kent and be sure of drawing
a big crowd (some seventy are said to have turned up) by making plans
and suggestions for Henry's destruction. Having lured together and
excited the locals in this way the thieves then went about what may
perhaps have been their true business of the night: stealing the
valuables from Rainham church. The following night on the road back
to London they ransacked Meopham church.[49] Northern Kent, then,
even in the late 1430s would appear to have been an excellent place for
such decoy techniques and quite possibly had a reputation in the
London area as a place where feeling was running high against the
king.

IV

This vehement and persistent criticism of Henry VI requires some
explanation. Half hidden by his portrayal as a royal saint, he remains to
the historian an elusive, inept, and colourless figure.[50] Certainly, as we
have seen his detractors suggest, he did lack those attributes expected
of a medieval monarch: prowess on the battlefield; an even-handed
distribution of royal justice and favours; qualities of firm leadership
and financial independence. It was his misfortune to have inherited his
father's military commitments and large debts without Henry V's own
military enthusiasm and administrative flair. Henry VI surrendered to

[44] 1446, Suffolk, KB9/260, m. 85.
[45] 1447, Gloucestershire, KB9/256, m. 13; 1449, Suffolk, KB27/760 *rex* side, m. 3.
[46] 1446, Suffolk, KB9/260, m. 85.
[47] 1453, Southwark, Surrey, KB9/273, m. 103.
[48] 1451, Southwark, Surrey, KB9/265, m. 92.
[49] KB9/230A, mm. 24, 28, 29.　　　　　　[50] See Wolffe, *Henry VI*, ch. 1.

the will and influence of stronger-minded and more active men. He blighted his court with favouritism, offered pardons and grants with thoughtless liberality, and affronted his subjects with the concessions offered to France in his search for a permanent peace.

By the late 1440s this lack of royal leadership had put the country into the hands of an unscrupulous court party headed by the duke (as he became in 1448) of Suffolk, William de la Pole, and a few others, notably the bishop of Salisbury and the bishop of Chichester. They, it was reckoned, were the ones with the real power. Cardinal Beaufort, the king's great-uncle, had earlier worked to develop a clique of his supporters around the king, so ousting the influence of Gloucester, the king's uncle and heir. By the 1440s, however, Beaufort was ageing.[51] From 1441 onwards Suffolk, then steward of the royal household, had begun to attend the king's council regularly, forming part of the marked trend towards adding figures from the royal household to Beaufort's satellites in the council.[52] By the end of 1446 Beaufort was no longer involved in active politics and when he died in 1447 control of the royal household was securely in the hold of a small grouping of men—largely Suffolk's dependants and often household men—whose influence extended equally through household, council, and departments of state. Heading this privileged group were Suffolk himself, by 1449 grand chamberlain of England, Adam Moleyns, keeper of the privy seal and bishop of Chichester, William Aiscough, bishop of Salisbury, and James Fiennes, Lord Saye and Sele. Indeed, Suffolk had 'made his influence about the young king unassailable—except by violence',[53] and violence was what was shortly to come.

Among the members of the Suffolk 'court party', Adam Moleyns, doctor of laws and dean of Salisbury, had acted since 1438 as both clerk of the council and of the privy seal but was made keeper of the privy seal in 1444. He was closely involved with the embassies negotiating with France during the 1440s, being sent across the Channel in the later part of the decade as the king's plenipotentiary, and was there to ride out of Le Mans at its surrender in 1448. Much of the hostility felt towards him then and later stemmed from one complaint: he delivered Maine to the French. Reginald Boulers, abbot

[51] G. L. Harriss, *Cardinal Beaufort: A Study of Lancastrian Ascendancy and Decline* (Oxford, 1988), 359–62.

[52] For greater detail concerning the growing influence of the household in the king's council, see R. A. Griffiths, *The Reign of Henry VI: The Exercise of Royal Authority, 1422–1461* (London, 1981), ch. 12.   [53] Ibid. 285.

of Gloucester, was another councillor closely involved in the Anglo-French *rapprochement* of the 1440s. He was appointed in January 1448 alongside Adam Moleyns as the king's plenipotentiaries to treat with Charles VII's negotiators. The reaction of the people of Gloucester, who denounced him as a traitor who had sold France for a sum of money and who in their fury ransacked his abbey's property, anticipated Moleyns's own crueller fate of January 1450.[54]

William Aiscough, who came to be regarded by the mid-1440s as having, alongside Suffolk, such power as to set the king's rule at nothing, had held the office of bishop of Salisbury since 1438, although his diocese scarcely ever saw him.[55] He had acted first as the king's chaplain then as his confessor during Henry's youth and was close in his confidence. He officiated at Henry's wedding ceremony in 1445. During the 1440s he became one of the most regular attenders at the meetings of the council. Walter Lyhert, bishop of Norwich, was another absentee prelate much more involved with his role at court as a royal councillor than with his pastoral duties in his own diocese. He, like Moleyns, took an active part in the negotiations with the French, leading an embassy in 1447 which met Charles VII and amongst other things agreed to yet another extension of the existing truce. Like Moleyns he was seen as one of the leading implementers of Henry's peace policy.

There was a lower echelon in Suffolk's circle, below the prelates, drawn from amongst the esquires of the body and yeomen of the chamber. Three individuals in particular from this group were hated beyond any others: Thomas Daniel, John Trevilian, and John Say. Their greed and the success with which they engrossed the king's favours explains much of the hatred they incurred. In an assessment of Henry VI's reign made after Edward IV's accession one of the major grievances which remained in the mind was that under Henry's rule 'the Duke of Suffolk, the Lords Say, Daniel, Trevelian, and other mischevious people around the king were so covetuous towards themselves'.[56] Daniel, originally from Cheshire, had his main connections in Norfolk, marrying a sister of John Howard, the future duke of

[54] Wolffe, *Henry VI*, 197; *EHL*, 355–6.

[55] Thomas Gascoigne gives absenteeism as the major cause of resentment amongst Aiscough's murderers in 1450. Thomas Gascoigne, *Loci e libro veritatum*, ed. J. E. T. Rogers (Oxford, 1881), 158–9.

[56] *A Chronicle of the First Thirteen Years of the Reign of King Edward the Fourth by John Warkworth*, ed. J. O. Halliwell (Camden Society, OS 10, 1839), 11.

Norfolk. Daniel acted as sheriff of Norfolk and Suffolk 1446–7, as JP for Norfolk December 1447–October 1450, and was appointed constable of Castle Rising in western Norfolk in 1449.[57] Besides this he acted as MP for Cornwall 1445–6, and for Buckinghamshire in 1447 and 1449, as well as holding various offices in the royal grant, including that of king's remembrancer in the exchequer. His influence in Norfolk by the second half of the 1440s was such that men speculated as to whose rule would be the greater, his or Suffolk's. But by 1449 their rivalry was transformed into an alliance through which Daniel became an acknowledged adherent of Suffolk: Daniel played a prominent part in the story of the events in Kent in 1450.

John Trevilian was from Cornwall and through the king's favour obtained grants of lands, wardships, stewardships, and keeperships there as elsewhere.[58] During the 1440s he represented the borough of Huntingdon in parliament at least twice and in 1446 was made keeper of the armoury in the Tower, the same year in which he was made joint constable of Hadleigh castle in Essex.

Sir John Say of Broxbourne (five miles south-east of Hertford) like Daniel held offices largely in East Anglia but also in Hertfordshire. He was escheator for Cambridgeshire and Huntingdonshire 1445–6 and for Norfolk and Suffolk 1446–7. In February 1447 he was first elected to parliament as member for the city of Cambridge in the notorious parliament which met not far away at Bury St Edmunds, and that same year he obtained as a gentleman usher of the chamber the manor of Lawford up in northern Essex not far from the Suffolk border. In 1448 he began acting as JP for Cambridgeshire. He had been a member of the embassy of 1444 which Suffolk led to negotiate the royal marriage, and it may have been as one of Suffolk's clients that he found his way to many of his household and local East Anglian offices. During 1449–50 he held the office of sheriff of Norfolk and Suffolk.[59] The degree to which he was seen as Suffolk's creature can be heard in a popular poem composed after Suffolk's death which had Say intoning at the duke's funeral offices, *Manus tue fecerunt me.*[60]

There were other popular compositions in which Daniel, Trevilian,

[57] Wedgwood, *Biographies*, 253–5.
[58] Ibid. 873–4; *Trevilian Papers*, pt. 1, ed. J. P. Collier (Camden Society, OS 67, 1857), 27–37.
[59] Wedgwood, *Biographies*, 744–6.
[60] J. S. Roskell, *Parliament and Politics in Late Medieval England* (3 vols., London, 1981), ii. 155.

and Say figured. The influence and prominence in the king's council of this trio in particular was never seen as anything but malign:

> The Cornysshe Chowgh [Trevilian] offt with his trayne
> Hath made oure Egulle [Henry] blynde

went one of these works.[61] Whilst elsewhere:

> Tome of Say and Danielle bothe,
> To begyn be not to lothe.[62]

With men holding positions in the royal household and in the counties, Suffolk's affinity extended tentacle-wise through southern and eastern England. Suffolk's own hereditary estates were above all in East Anglia—his Wingfield inheritance.[63] His adherents were most prominent in Norfolk, Suffolk, Kent, Surrey, and Sussex. They took over these areas both socially and politically, impinging upon some of the older established gentry. The courtiers went about the buying up of estates and the securing of property in a rapacious and often violent manner.[64] In 1447, for instance, John Trevilian, the esquire of the body just mentioned, together with another household squire, Thomas Bodulgate, forcibly expelled three esquires, William Wangford, William Ludlowe, and Stephen Wymbyssh, from the manor and castle of Stone in Kent, two miles east of Dartford and not far down river from London (although on this occasion Trevilian and Bodulgate were not acting against older established gentry but against men of their own standing). They were to hold the manor for at least the following three years.[65] Kent made rich pickings for such opportunists. It was a wealthy county, the advanced level of whose economy had created an unusually large gentry class divided by numerous feuds. The same wealth also appears to have encouraged there 'a peculiarly sophisticated body of abuses and corruption in local government and justice'.[66]

The Fiennes family offers one of the best examples of adherents of

---

[61] *Political Poems*, ii. 223.   [62] Ibid. 229.

[63] Roskell, *The Impeachment of Michael de la Pole Earl of Suffolk in 1386 in the Context of the Reign of Richard II* (Manchester, 1984), 205–8.

[64] Griffiths, *Henry VI*, 630–1.

[65] Virgoe, 'Ancient Indictments', 221–2. William Wangford was a JP and serjeant-at-law; William Ludlowe may be the individual of that name who was yeoman of the cellar 1440–61 and who was exempt from the Act of Resumption of 1450. Wedgwood, *Biographies*, 561–2.

[66] E. B. Fryde, from his chapter in the forthcoming *Cambridge Agrarian History of England and Wales*, iii. (Cambridge, 1991). I am most grateful to Professor Fryde for giving me access to this manuscript.

Suffolk who through royal service and patronage came to be one of the most influential families in the South-East. Their family home was at Herstmonceux in Sussex, a fashionable brick castle erected by Sir Roger Fiennes on a grand scale during the 1430s to command the Pevensey levels. There Sir Roger Fiennes lived as a prominent county gentleman. His brother James's career, however, spread the family influence through Sussex, Surrey, and Kent. In Kent James accumulated through royal grants the manors of Monkecourt (later exchanged for Witley in south-west Surrey), Capel, Huntingfield, Shorne, and Tracy, and land in Chelsfield.[67] In Surrey in 1439 he gained interests at Camberwell through the grant of a wardship and marriage and that same year acted as sheriff of Surrey and Sussex.[68] Other offices came his way, continually strengthening his connection with the South-East, only the occasional gift coming from outside the region. In 1442 he was constable of Rochester castle for a spell; in 1443 he was appointed bailiff of Otford and Ukfield Stonham with the hundred of Loxfield in Kent and Sussex; in 1446 he became steward of all the late duke of Warwick's Sussex and Kentish lands and lordships.[69] Beginning as an esquire of the body he had made himself so invaluable as a royal servant within the household and in the counties (he acted as a justice on every commission of the peace appointed in Kent between 1436 and 1447)[70] that by 1447 he enjoyed the offices of chamberlain of Henry's household, constable of Dover castle, warden of the Cinque Ports, and a place in the king's council as Lord Saye and Sele. In September 1449 he reached the height of the office of lord treasurer, a precipitous height as it soon emerged.

As for his conduct within the offices he held, presentments made in 1450 before a commission investigating offences and malpractices committed by the recent county administration in Kent revealed him to be pre-eminent amongst the group of parvenus intruding themselves into Kentish society. In 1447 he and Stephen Slegge, sheriff of Kent 1448–9, had allegedly expelled a man violently from his 250 acres in Elmley on the marshy flats of the Isle of Sheppey and forcibly kept him from it right up until July 1450.[71] Again, in 1448, so it was said, he, his wife, and Slegge had so threatened a Reginald Peckham with imprisonment, death, drawing, and hanging that he had given up to

---

[67] *CPR*, 1436–41, 77–8, 93, 100, 428, 471, 493; *CPR*, 1441–6, 140, 296.
[68] *CPR*, 1436–41, 245, 248.   [69] *CPR*, 1441–6, 83, 160, 445.
[70] *CPR*, 1436–41, 584; *CPR*, 1441–6, 472; *CPR*, 1446–52, 590.
[71] Virgoe, 'Ancient Indictments', 225–6.

Fiennes his own property in the parish of Seal (hard by Fiennes's seat at Knole) in exchange for a lesser property belonging to Fiennes. Although Peckham enfeoffed Fiennes in Fiennes's newly acquired property, Fiennes, on his side of this fraudulent bargain, made no such security for Peckham for whom the transaction altogether amounted to a loss of a £100.[72] And again at Michaelmas 1449, as lord of the manor at Seal and Kemsing, Fiennes, once more abetted by Slegge, had distrained tenants in their lands so obliging them to pay an additional 50 per cent and more per acre than was their annual due, and this was from small men who felt the increase badly.[73]

If our source is to be trusted—and it is the view of a contemporary ecclesiastic, Thomas Gascoigne—it would appear that Fiennes, fully aware of his own notoriety and that of his colleagues in the royal household, was one of several who took it upon themselves to censor preachers coming before the king. Echoing closely allegations made by Thomas Brunton, bishop of Rochester, of similar censoring at the end of the fourteenth century, Gascoigne reports that there were those, especially among the London clergy, going about denouncing the vices of the time and that Fiennes and others would let no one preach in front of the king unless the sermon had first been written and submitted to them or unless the preacher had promised on oath that his sermon would not attack the king's household, the king's own conduct, or the conduct of his privy council (which Gascoigne prefers to call his 'depraved council').[74] Likewise a popular poem had it that as far as the commons were concerned,

> The lorde Say biddeth holde hem downe,
> That worthy dastarde of renowne,
> He techithe a fals loore.[75]

Both these accounts of him suggest that there was a good deal of truth in the picture offered by the rebels' complaint in 1450 that men below the rank of hereditary peers had been exalted to amongst the chief of Henry's privy council 'the which stoppeth matters of wrongs done in the realme from his excellent audience', with the result that such wrongs could not be remedied without the use of bribes among the council members.[76]

---

[72] Virgoe, 'Ancient Indictments', 234.   [73] Ibid. 233–4.
[74] G. R. Owst, *Preaching in Medieval England* (Cambridge, 1926), 40; Thomas Gascoigne, *Loci e libro veritatum*, pp. xlvi, 191.   [75] *Political Poems*, ii. 230.
[76] J. Stow, *Annales, or a Generall Chronicle of England* (1631), 389.

The Stephen Slegge, gentleman, mentioned above as acting in conjunction with Saye, is likewise revealed by the 1450 indictments to be amongst the most notorious office-holders in Kent during the 1440s, abusing his position again and again by extortion and the violent taking of land and property.[77] Under-sheriff to Saye in 1436–7, under-sheriff to John Warner 1441–2, escheator of the county 1442–3, and sheriff in 1448–9, he also acted as MP for Dover in 1449.[78] It was usual for sheriffs to fail to recover and answer for all the revenue due from their respective counties, but after Slegge's term of office expired in 1449 the exchequer was suing him for a debt of £4,078 10*s.* 5*d.* and finding him difficult to bring to book.[79] Slegge was not a man to waste the advantages of being sheriff of the county. In October 1449 he and Robert Est, a gentleman from Maidstone, together with a great gang, allegedly 200 strong, broke into the close of Edward Neville, Lord Abergavenny, at Singlewell, two miles south of Gravesend, looted his granary, and assaulted his servants. And this was not, the allegation revealed, the first time he had raided Lord Abergavenny in this way.[80] Throughout the 1440s Slegge had stood witness to Saye in his transactions, acted as his co-feoffee, collaborated with him in crime, and was generally one of his most frequent associates.[81] He was lucky to survive him.

William Crowmer, like James Fiennes, was a recent incomer to Kentish society. His father, a London alderman, had come from Norfolk and then like so many other prosperous Londoners bought some property in Kent.[82] A king's squire, William was given the office of sheriff of Kent in 1444–5 and again, significantly, in December 1449. The only kind of details known of his terms of office are of an unremarkable kind: in August 1445 eleven prisoners escaped his custody in the gaol of Canterbury castle, and in the Easter term of 1450 he was fined for insufficient returns.[83] This belies the kind of corrupt and malevolent administrator he was. In the summer of 1450 he was revealed to be one of the most hated men in Kent, explicitly named by rebels as one of the county's four great extortioners, alongside Stephen Slegge, William Isle, and Robert Est. Even his own

[77] Virgoe, 'Ancient Indictments', 223, 225–6, 227–8, 233–4, 239.
[78] Griffiths, *Henry VI*, 633, 660; *CFR*, 1437–45, 241.
[79] E368/222 *Adhuc precepta* Michaelmas 28H6.
[80] KB9/267, m. 71; KB27/765 *rex* side, m. 23ᵛ.
[81] *CCLR*, 1441–7, 440–1; *CCLR*, 1447–54, 54, 68.
[82] Griffiths, *Henry VI*, 630–1.
[83] *CPR*, 1441–6, 372; E368/222 *Adhuc communia* Easter 28H6.

stepbrother, Robert Poynings, seems to have sided with the rebels of 1450 as part of a quarrel against him. But for most men it was hatred for Crowmer as an administrator and as son-in-law to Lord Saye which fired their action.[84]

Crowmer's character may be deduced from the well-documented behaviour attributed to those acting directly under his authority in Kent during the 1440s (attributed again by the commission of 1450). John Alpheigh, a gentleman from Chiddingstone, a Wealden village west of Tonbridge, acted as under-sheriff to both Slegge and Crowmer. By colour of his office he extorted sums of money from the inhabitants of the county and joined raiding parties taking livestock and household goods. His was a lawlessness so habitual that it apparently went unchastened even by the loss of some of his closest protectors. Likewise, another of Crowmer's henchmen, John Watte of Sandhurst, a bailiff during his (and also Slegge's) shrievalty, extorted, oppressed, and defrauded those with whom he dealt in the Weald.[85] Again, another of Crowmer's bailiffs, Richard Snelgare of Boxley, north-east of Maidstone, was similarly a 'common extortioner and oppressor of the people' as an indictment of August 1450 was to describe him.[86]

William Isle, a gentleman from Sundridge in the Weald west of Sevenoaks, was another associate of Saye's, representing Kent alongside him in parliament in 1441–2 and acting as witness to his business transactions.[87] As part of this same network to which Saye, Slegge, and Crowmer belonged, his regular appearance on commissions of the peace in Kent throughout the 1440s must have been helpful to his colleagues. In addition to which he had a term as sheriff in 1446–7 and again represented the county in the parliament of 1449–50 along with John Warner.[88]

Robert Est, the Maidstone gentleman mentioned above as an accomplice of Stephen Slegge in his autumn raid on Edward Neville's property in 1449, has an ample dossier on his doings in Kent during the 1440s. The commission of 1450 would bring charges against him on no fewer than eleven separate counts. He kept much the same

---

[84] Stow, *Annales*, 389; R. M. Jeffs, 'The Poynings–Percy Dispute', *BIHR* 34 (1961), 148–64.　　　　　　　　　　　　　　[85] Virgoe, 'Ancient Indictments', 224, 239–40.
[86] Ibid. 223.　　　　　　　　　　　　　[87] For example, *CCLR*, 1441–7, 440–1.
[88] *CPR*, 1441–6, 422, 472; *CPR*, 1446–52, 382, 590; E. Hasted, *The History and Topographical Survey of the County of Kent* (reprint of 2nd edn., 12 vols., Wakefield, 1972), iii. 129.

company as the rest of the Saye connection and was, for instance, a member of a raiding party of July 1449 at Ash in which Stephen Slegge and John Alpheigh also took part.[89] In 1441 in his home town of Maidstone he expelled a Thomas Hilles from some property and nine years later Thomas had still been unable to regain possession.[90] The next year it was money he obtained by fraudulent means, persuading a debtor in Maidstone that he was the creditor's appointed attorney and then making off with the 15*s.* debt himself. Est's complete disregard for the possible consequences of his conduct on this and no doubt many other occasions explains well why he should have engendered such hatred in Kent, for the creditor considering the debt to have been unpaid then took the debtor to court. As a result the debtor was outlawed and his goods forfeited to the king, so that finally through Est's cruel chicanery he lost not only the original 15*s.* but £30 worth of animals, goods, and chattels.[91]

Est used another, this time more elaborate, ploy in 1449 when, together with a John Brok, he entirely fraudulently and without any royal writ drew up and sealed warrants to attach and seize tenants of the archbishop of Canterbury at Wingham, and using these fabricated warrants extracted considerable sums from three tenants there.[92] Est was an employee of the archbishop during the second half of the 1440s, acting as his receiver in his bailiwick of Otford, a job which would have taken him about the roads of a largish district of western Kent and opened up considerable opportunities for extortion.[93]

However, as keeper of Maidstone gaol his most effective lever for extracting monies, and the one he most frequently employed, was imprisonment. In 1444, for example, he forcibly seized a man at Maidstone and kept him in prison for a day and night until his victim paid a fine to have his release.[94] Again, in 1448, he and John Brok forcibly imprisoned a man at Maidstone, on this occasion for almost a week, until he paid for his freedom.[95] This, it might be observed, happened whilst Est was holding one of the more prominent county offices: from November 1447 to November 1448 he was escheator for Kent and Middlesex. Like John Alpheigh, he would be apparently undeterred from his old ways by the seeming overthrow in 1450 of the court party with whom he was connected through Saye.

---

[89] Virgoe, 'Ancient Indictments', 227–8. [90] Ibid. 234.
[91] Ibid. 235. [92] Ibid. 240–1.
[93] Du Boulay, *The Lordship of Canterbury*, 272–3, 400.
[94] Virgoe, 'Ancient Indictments', 236. [95] Ibid. 236–7.

Est and his kind were able to carry on as they did unchecked because they were never brought to court during the 1440s, despite their patently criminal activities. The presence of such fellow criminals as Saye and William Isle on the commissions of the peace must have been of assistance in this matter. If the allegations made by the commons of Kent in 1450 concerning the activities of the king's bench are accurate, then the royal courts of law were used as vehicles of exploitation in the county. They alleged that in cases of treason defendants' lands were granted away before any conviction was made, these grants adversely prejudicing their chances of ever standing a fair trial. Indictments were feigned by sheriffs, under-sheriffs, and others in hunting cases just to generate income from fines. Justice was held in such contempt by its protectors that when certain of the king's household chose to make false claims to property in Kent (so the allegations continued) there was no way in which the true owners could claim their rights in it.[96]

Office-holders in Kent were hated and distrusted in all their activities. They were suspected—probably rightly, as is suggested by the case of Est mentioned above—of making extortionate use of the so-called summonses of the Green Wax, that is, mandates issued to county officers under the exchequer seal authorizing the taking of fines. Summonses of the Green Wax were always associated with the grasping hand of government and had been a major target of the looters and burners of the 1381 rising in the South-East.[97] More money was raised in the county by means of the Green Wax, the ominous rumour ran, than was ever recorded in the books of the king's exchequer.

In view of the fact that the county returning officer for parliamentary elections was the sheriff himself, an allegation which suggested that the elections of county members during the 1440s had been rigged is likely to have had a good deal of truth in it. This was after all a decade which saw sheriffs such as John Warner (1441–2)—a relation of William Isle—William Crowmer (1444–5), Stephen Slegge (1448–9), and Crowmer again (1449–50).[98] There was a close connection between the facts that 'all four sheriffs who had responsibility for

[96] Stow, *The Chronicles of England, from Brute unto this Present Yeare of Christ, 1580* (1580), 654–5.
[97] N. Brooks, 'The Organization and Achievements of the Peasants of Kent and Essex in 1381', in H. M. R. E. Mayr-Harting and R. I. Moore (eds.), *Studies in Medieval History Presented to R. H. C. Davis* (London, 1985), 260.
[98] Griffiths, *Henry VI*, 633.

making the returns for the five parliaments immediately preceding Cade's rebellion came from Saye's charmed, but unpopular, circle' and the 'near-monopoly of representation of the county and its major towns by a small group of men closely connected with Saye, the household circle, or government service'.[99] Hence in the parliament of 1442 Isle, Warner, and Saye represented the county; in 1445–6 Saye (again); in 1447 Saye (once more) and Crowmer; and in 1449–50 Isle again and Crowmer again.

And if the sheriffs and their underlings were corrupt, the choice of county MPs managed, and the operation of the JPs grossly partial, royal purveyance made yet another Kentish grievance during the 1440s. The beef, mutton, cereals, and other goods taken were not paid for. Needless to say such matters rarely reached the courts, so we must take the word of the men of Kent when they complained of this in 1450. The 'kynges taker' was of course not a nuisance confined to Kent by any means. However, Henry's tendency to keep himself and his household in the South, and the creation of a special zone around the coast of Kent for the purveyance of goods may explain why Kent felt so especially victimized.[100] It was also a rich county. The fact that there were local con men trying their hand at purveyance around the Sussex and Kentish coast speaks for the predatory and lucrative nature of the practice: such a man as James Bowelond of Romney who successfully passed himself off as victualler of the king's kitchen and so was able to go out into the Channel with his men and bring back to Winchelsea a Hansard ship he had spotted 'saillyng upon the See charged with hamburgh Byer and Bacon'.[101]

The influence of Suffolk's affinity in Kent was perhaps all the more conspicuous because the county had not been accustomed to the dominance of any particular great magnate. Christ Church Canterbury owned extensive property in Kent, and Lord Cobham, the duke of Buckingham, Edward, Lord Ferrers of Groby, and Edward, Lord Abergavenny, owned land in Kent, but no great family clan dominated county life. This was true also of Middlesex and Surrey. Among those lords summoned to parliament in January 1449 one earl and two barons had their seats in Sussex: William Fitzalan, earl of Arundel, Thomas Hoo, Lord Hoo and Hastings, and Reynold West of

---

[99] Ibid. 633, 634.
[100] See ch. 1, above. The expression 'kynges taker' is found, for example, in an indictment of 1444, KB9/246, m. 27.   [101] C1/17/418.

Broadwater, Lord Delawarr.[102] No lords resided principally in Surrey or Middlesex, and the one baron to have his seat in Kent was of course James Fiennes of Knole, the recently created Lord Saye and Sele. More characteristic of Kentishmen in central government perhaps were men like John Prisot of Ruckinge (a village six miles from Ashford), chief justice of the common pleas, who also had land in Hertfordshire; Walter Moyle of Eastwell not far from Ashford, serjeant-at-law; or descendants of former sheriffs like the Septvans family.

Suffolk's predominance in East Anglia by the late 1440s formed a special case. There Suffolk supplanted John Mowbray, the third duke of Norfolk, the greatest landowner and natural leader of the region.[103] It was an irksome position for Norfolk to be in, with the duke of Suffolk based at Wingfield castle only a few miles from his own seat at Framlingham. Throughout the 1430s and 1440s the rivalry of the two magnates was played out in East Anglia by their respective affinities, on occasion seriously threatening the region's stability.[104] Apart from the duke of Norfolk, his relative the duke of York was another major East Anglian and Essex magnate with his combined properties of the Honour of Clare, the Essex lands of the House of York, and the Holand manors (which went down into Surrey, Sussex, and Kent).[105] The county of Essex also had John de Vere, earl of Oxford, at Earl's Colne, and Henry Bourchier, Viscount Bourchier, at Stansted, whilst Thomas, Lord Scales, was up in Norfolk at Middleton.

During the 1440s, then, both Norfolk and Suffolk were in the grip of adherents of the duke of Suffolk. Under their administration Norfolk and Suffolk saw the kind of violent corruption and injustice which was characterizing Kentish society at that time. The sufferings of the counties of Norfolk, Suffolk, and the city of Norwich at the hands of Suffolk's clients is especially well recorded in the records of commissions which sat during the last four months of 1450. These hearings give a retrospective view of persistent bullying, extortion, and harmful interference in county life and government by a small group of men headed by Thomas Tuddenham, John Heydon, and John

[102] Wedgwood, *Register*, 97 ff.

[103] Virgoe, 'The Murder of James Andrew: Suffolk Faction in the 1430s', *Proceedings of the Suffolk Institute of Archaeology and History*, 34 (1980), 263.

[104] Ibid. 263–8.

[105] For details of York's extensive lands, see J. T. Rosenthal, 'The Estates and Finances of Richard, Duke of York (1411–1460)', in W. M. Bowsky (ed.), *Studies in Medieval and Renaissance History*, 2 (Lincoln, Nebr., 1965), 115–204.

Ulveston. Their careers in East Anglia during the 1440s were a matter for scandal. Of course, such evidence offered by victims during an eclipse of the influence of their persecutors is heavily partial, but with the exception of one or two improbable stories such as a patently unjust charge concerning Suffolk's alleged allegiance to the king of France, there is nothing implausible about them, and every good reason why they had not been heard publicly before. These malefactors were, after all, the law enforcers themselves.

The notorious Sir Thomas Tuddenham of Oxburgh acted as MP for Suffolk in 1431 and thenceforward for Norfolk in three parliaments during the 1430s, and again in 1442 and 1443–4.[106] During 1432–3 he was sheriff of Norfolk and Suffolk. In 1447 he was entrusted with the custody of the Great Wardrobe, and so flaunted the law in the provinces from the doubly safe vantage of household man at court and of Suffolk's adherent in Norfolk. John Heydon from Baconsthorpe in Norfolk was a lawyer and JP for the county 1441–50 who acted as MP for Norfolk 1445–6.[107] John Ulveston of Debenham in Suffolk was a lawyer-JP in Suffolk 1443–50. He was escheator for Norfolk and Suffolk 1442–4 and MP for Yarmouth in 1447 and 1449–50; he was also dignified during the 1440s with the office of receiver of Eton College, and in 1444 became keeper of the writs and rolls of the common bench.[108]

Those were their official positions. As for their unofficial, but no less public, activities, according to the several sets of jurors presenting indictments late in 1450, Tuddenham, Heydon, Ulveston, and others of Suffolk's clients such as John Belley of Wingfield, Suffolk, gentleman, and Thomas Brigge of Eggfield, Norfolk, gentleman, had leagued, sworn, and combined together to pursue each other's quarrels in Norfolk, Suffolk, and Norwich, taking goods, lands, and sometimes lives.[109] Their intention was to maintain one another and to ensure that the men of these counties should know the might of the earl of Suffolk. In 1436 Tuddenham, Heydon, and Thomas Brigge allegedly tried to elect their own candidate as mayor of Norwich against the wishes of the Norwich electors, but failed in the attempt.[110] So perhaps it is not surprising to hear that in 1438 these men

[106] Wedgwood, *Biographies*, 880–1.   [107] Ibid. 452–3.
[108] Ibid. 895.
[109] KB9/267, m. 25; KB27/767 *rex* side, m. 7; KB27/792 *rex* side, m. 2; KB27/793 *rex* side, m. 6; KB27/795 *rex* side, mm. 8, 8/2; KB27/798 *rex* side, mm. 9, 26; it is a reiterated charge with various dates being offered from the 1430s and early 1440s.
[110] KB27/795 *rex* side, m. 8.

threatened the city that they would inform the earl of Suffolk that the citizens of Norwich intended to rise against the king in order that Suffolk might turn against them and inform Henry. Under the pressure of such intimidation the city, anxious for Suffolk's goodwill, paid a sum of over £80 to Tuddenham in September 1441 in the hope that in return he would incline his lord in its favour.[111] The gamble did not come off. As the city saw it, Tuddenham merely turned Suffolk against them all. Individual citizens too were harassed for sums of money by Tuddenham and Heydon under threat of having all their goods distrained through rigged suits or of being indicted for treason and felony and so hanged. Coming from men who were JPs in the county this was not an idle threat.

The list of their misdoings covers membrane after membrane among the records of the king's bench. It was in Norwich that they also falsified returns from the sheriff's tourn; were behind the formation of an illicit and disruptive gild of St George; helped in the destruction of a city water-mill; and colluded in the appropriation of city tolls by the prior of Holy Trinity. Beyond the city in the two counties they so intimidated some men that they dared not go about their business openly; rustled flocks of sheep in their hundreds; concocted judicial records (something which required the forging of thirteen signatures); threatened individuals into writing obligations for sums like £100; and interfered with other men's views of frankpledge. These are just some examples of their activities.[112]

Among this East Anglian affinity Heydon may have been the most violent. A man as rich as Sir John Fastolf admitted to a correspondent in the spring of 1450 that he had not taken up pleas against Heydon 'because the world was alway set after his rule'.[113] Fastolf lost possession of four valuable manors through Suffolk and his associates but he (realistically) had thought it futile to challenge the earl at common law or through a suit in chancery. Instead he sought a negotiated private settlement with Suffolk and his advisers.[114]

---

[111] KB27/767 *rex* side, m. 7; KB27/798 *rex* side, m. 26; KB27/795 *rex* side, m. 8ᵛ.

[112] KB27/793 *rex* side, m. 6; KB27/798 *rex* side, m. 9; KB27/758 *rex* side, m. 9; KB27/759 *rex* side, m. 33; KB27/762 *rex* side, mm. 1ᵛ, 29; KB27/763 *rex* side, m. 21; KB27/767 *rex* side, m. 7; KB9/267, mm. 25, 64ᵃ; KB9/272, mm. 2–5. G. Johnson, 'Extract from the Books of the Corporation of Norwich, relative to the injuries done to the city by Sir Thomas Tuddenham and others; the offence given to Alice, countess of Suffolk; and the real History of Gladman's Insurrection', *Norfolk Archaeology*, 1 (1847), 294–9.   [113] *PL*, ii. 137.

[114] A. R. Smith, 'Aspects of the Career of Sir John Fastolf (1380–1459)', D.Phil. thesis (Oxford, 1982), 127, 142; *Catalogue of Ancient Deeds*, i. (HMSO, 1890), 74.

Heydon had a running feud with Norwich, which may have dated from his dismissal some time in the mid-1430s from the office of recorder of the city by the mayor and commons.[115] His methods included the use—in conjunction with the prior of Holy Trinity—of gangs which on at least four separate occasions during the 1440s prevented coroners from their duties of conducting inquisitions into various deaths.[116] No motive is offered for this action. His intimidatory tactics were notorious: in October 1440 he took fifty marks each off four men in Norwich.[117] Perhaps the best-recorded example of his heavy-handed use of force comes in January 1449 when he and Lord Moleyns backed and incited the attack and seizure by a large gang comprising several hundred armed men of John Paston's manor at Gresham, smashing gates and doors, rifling possessions in the house; and, with the manor taken, combing the countryside in pursuit of Paston's friends, tenants, and servants through houses and barns, stabbing into sheaves and straw after their quarry.[118] Poor tenants of the manor were intimidated into making false plaints in the hundred courts against these associates of Paston who naturally dared not appear in public to defend themselves in court, nor could they even obtain copies of the plaints to answer them by law because the keeper of the court was in league with Lord Moleyns and Tuddenham. It is a picture of a complete breakdown of effective law and order although the processes and functions of the law continued as a charade played out by its misusers.

There are also well-documented examples of a similar misuse of government and law by associates of the regime in other parts of the country that do not closely concern us. In Cornwall, for example, favoured servants of the king were active participants in piracy.[119] The principal owner of the Edward of Polruan which in November 1449 robbed a Spanish ship anchoring off Plymouth of £12,000 of goods was John Trevilian, yeoman of the Crown.[120]

V

Yet for all the perversion of justice and entrenched favouritism which Suffolk's regime represented in the South-East and East Anglia, it was

[115] P. C. Maddern, 'Violence, Crime and Public Disorder in East Anglia, 1422–1442', D.Phil. thesis (Oxford, 1984), 176.   [116] KB27/795 *rex* side, mm. 8, 8ᵛ.
[117] KB27/767 *rex* side, m. 7; KB27/798 *rex* side, m. 26.
[118] KB27/762 *rex* side, m. 29; KB27/763 *rex* side, m. 21; *PL*, ii. 127–30.
[119] C. L. Kingsford, *Prejudice and Promise in Fifteenth-Century England* (Oxford, 1925; repr. London, 1962), 78–106.   [120] Ibid. 94–6.

in connection with his foreign dealings that his enemies hoped to bring about his downfall. The oppression of its local officials was perhaps a sufficiently common phenomenon as to be regarded as an inadequate pretext for ousting any clique, but the matter of France and of the movement of an enemy army towards the French ports of the Channel coast was an issue of life and death which affected all of southern England. It was certainly on this matter that popular opinion swung most strongly against the duke, although just how manipulated this popular opinion was it is very hard to say.

The great preoccupation of the royal council during the 1440s was the search for peace with France, a search in which Suffolk took a leading role.[121] The decade saw a perpetual toing and froing of embassies across the Channel, amicable relations reaching their height in 1444–5 with the sealing of a marriage alliance but sliding off sharply at the end of the decade as open hostilities resumed in 1449. The deep animosity shown towards Suffolk and his 'false progeny' during the second half of the decade was in significant part based upon what was seen as Suffolk's disastrous mishandling of negotiations with France. In early 1450 when Suffolk was first denounced in parliament it was in the guise of a volley of accusations about his duplicity in the Anglo-French negotiations and his alleged work on behalf of the French in bringing about the loss of Normandy. Topical poems and songs made obsessive repetition of the idea that 'Suffolk normandy hath swold'[122] and that it was through his fault that able captains, exemplified above all by John Talbot, earl of Shrewsbury, taken as hostage by the French after the surrender of Rouen in 1449, were kept from a proper defence of France.

> And he is bownden that oure dore shuld kepe,
> That is Talbott oure goode dogge,

and again,

> Jack Napys [Suffolk], with his clogge,
> Hath tiede Talbot oure gentille dogge.[123]

As has already been noted, other individuals besides Suffolk who

---

[121] For a survey of Anglo-French diplomacy during the 1440s, see Griffiths, *Henry VI*, chs. 17 and 18.

[122] R. H. Robbins (ed.), *Historical Poems of the Fourteenth and Fifteenth Centuries* (New York, 1959), 204.

[123] *Political Poems*, ii. 222, 224; Suffolk is referred to in this way because his badge was an ape's clog, just as Talbot's was a dog.

were also involved in these bargainings became objects of popular contempt. It was in large degree in this connection that the names of Adam Moleyns, bishop of Chichester, Walter Lyhert, bishop of Norwich, and Reginald Boulers, abbot of St Peter's Gloucester, gained the reputations that had them lampooned in popular verse by the end of the 1440s. In contrast, Humphrey duke of Gloucester's consistent defence of the need to pursue and uphold what he saw as England's just claims to sovereignty in France gave him his popular estimation as 'Good Duke Humphrey', 'verray fader and protectour of the land'.[124]

Despite his uncle Gloucester's opinion, Henry VI himself had long been anxious to end what he saw as the wasteful loss of property and money which the war entailed. It was he who in 1440 had decided— against Gloucester's advice—to release England's most prized French prisoner, the duke of Orleans, and a strong card in diplomatic manœuvres with France, in the hope that he would promote the cause of peace between the two countries. It was a card which, as it turned out, was thrown away to no benefit. By 1440 Henry and his councillors were taking up a new line of approach to what they hoped would be reconciliation with France: a truce to be sealed by a marriage alliance with a French princess. Suffolk was decided upon as the leader of the embassy to go over to negotiate the matter with the French, a role, it is worth noting, that he was reluctant to take up. He saw himself as an inappropriate candidate for the job since not only had the French asked for him but Orleans had been his guest and he had other friendships amongst the French aristocracy. Also on Suffolk's mind was the kind of popular odium which had greeted the return of earlier ambassadors to France in the cause of peace. None the less, at royal command he went on an initial embassy in the spring of 1444 accompanied by Adam Moleyns, then dean of Salisbury, the new keeper of the privy seal. Following another grander embassy of the autumn of 1444 Suffolk returned to Henry with an Angevin bride, the second daughter of Rene of Anjou, king of Naples (until 1442), count of Anjou and of Provence and brother-in-law to Charles VII of France. Margaret of Anjou did not bring with her a substantial dowry, and the truce terms accompanying this alliance, admittedly the first general truce for twenty-four years, were given a cautious two years.[125]

[124] Robbins, *Historical Poems of the Fourteenth and Fifteenth Centuries*, 183.
[125] For these matters in greater detail, see E. F. Jacob, *The Fifteenth Century, 1399– 1485* (Oxford, 1961), 475–81; Griffiths, *Henry VI*, chs. 17 and 18.

Much time and thought was given to making a permanent truce between the countries and for months the possibility of a meeting of the two kings in person was mooted amongst the negotiators. In the mean time the truce of Tours, initially due to expire in April 1446, was given short-term extensions. A final peace settlement, however, evaded the ambassadors despite their continual consultations. So impatient became Henry's desire for peace that in the last days of 1445 he signed an agreement ceding the county of Maine to the French. This opened up the entire southern border of Normandy to attack. Not surprisingly he was to find his soldiery there obstructive and full of delays when it came to implementing the agreement. In retrospect this event was seen, rightly, as the beginning of the fall of Lancastrian France: to his enemies in parliament Suffolk's complicity was central. He had promised Maine to Rene 'above his Instruction and power to hym by you [Henry] committed' to Henry's 'over grete disheritaunce and losse irrecuperable, enforsyng and enrichyng of your seid Enemyes, and grettest mean of the losse of youre seid Duchie of Normandie'.[126]

Early in 1447 the pace and temper of events moved up another gear. Humphrey, duke of Gloucester, the leading opponent of Henry's peace-seeking policies died suddenly in very suspicious circumstances at the parliament held in Suffolk at Bury St Edmunds in the heart of de la Pole country. The rumour was soon about that Gloucester had been murdered. The fact that forty-two of his retinue were seized at Bury and imprisoned in castles throughout the south of England increases the likelihood that this was a deliberate attack upon the duke.[127] Five months later the keeper of Gloucester castle allegedly said that the king had killed the duke of Gloucester and that the duke was more fit to be king than Henry. Whether this was actually spoken by the keeper cannot be proven, but it is significant that the idea was already current by the second half of 1447 when the case came to court.[128] Chroniclers, too, were ready to interpret Gloucester's death as murder. The crime was laid at the door of Suffolk and his associates. According to one chronicler the Bury parliament,

was maad only for to sle the noble duke of Gloucestre, whose deth the fals duke of Suffolk William de la Pole, and ser James Fynes lord Say, and othir of thair assent, hadde longe tyme conspired and ymagyned.[129]

---

[126] *RP*, v. 178.
[127] H. Ellis (ed.), *Original Letters Illustrative of English History*, 2nd series, i. (London, 1827), 108–9.   [128] KB9/256, m. 13.   [129] *Davies Chron.*, 62.

James Fiennes certainly reaped benefit from Gloucester's death. Immediately after the duke's death he petitioned for some of Gloucester's offices and was successful in receiving the constableship of Dover castle and wardenship of the Cinque Ports. It was at this time too that he was made Lord Saye and Sele. Indeed, the death of the duke was followed by a fairly extensive use of the Crown's recently introduced power to create additional lords temporal by patent.[130] Not all chronicle accounts took the line that Gloucester had been murdered; some did not even intimate that there had been foul play. However, this was undoubtedly the version which caught the popular imagination and became crucial to the reputation of the duke of Suffolk. Indeed, it was perhaps for his death that Gloucester was best remembered: 'To dine with Duke Humphrey' was to become a wry euphemism for going hungry.[131]

In 1447 three important figures disappeared from the political scene. Following Gloucester's death in February, Cardinal Beaufort, uncle of Henry V and elder statesman of Henry VI's minority, died on 11 April.[132] The death of Beaufort left Suffolk as unquestioned chief councillor in the royal council. The third magnate to die that year was John Holand, the duke of Exeter. Custody of his young heir, Henry Holand, was granted to Richard, duke of York.

The gaining of this custody was one small sign of recognition and favour granted to York during the late 1440s amidst others to the contrary. For this second half of the decade saw—under Suffolk's ascendancy—York's virtual political eclipse. The government owed him huge sums of money, unpaid arrears of his wages and expenses which caused him real financial embarrassment. Despite his position as lieutenant-general in France, John Beaufort, earl of Somerset, had been given the government of Gascony in 1443, and had been given preferential treatment by the exchequer. In December 1446 Edmund Beaufort, the late John's brother, was appointed as lieutenant-general in France in place of York. By the late 1440s, more especially after the death of Gloucester and Beaufort, York lacked powerful friends at court to speak for him. Bishop Aiscough, Sir John Beauchamp, and James Fiennes had all been annuitants earlier in the 1440s, but by 1447 these household men were unlikely to gain the king's ear on

---

[130] J. E. Powell and K. Wallis, *The House of Lords in the Middle Ages* (London, 1968), 481–2.   [131] Anon., *A Compleat History of Suffolk* (1730), 258.
[132] Wolffe, *Henry VI*, 108.

York's behalf, they were now too much the king's men.[133] In June 1449 York would sail for Ireland.

Meanwhile so obdurate were Henry's commanders in Maine in their stalling tactics over the county's surrender that the French in March 1448 after months of waiting resumed hostilities with the siege of Le Mans. Adam Moleyns and Sir Robert Roos, already on their way to France, hastened to reaffirm an earlier agreement for the surrender of Le Mans and other fortresses in Maine. And so Maine was finally ceded. Henry's captains there asked for indemnities to declare that this had been a performance of their duty and not (as it seemed to them) a desertion of it. For all that, the handing over of Maine failed to make surer the prospect of a final peace as Henry had hoped. The English soldiers had retreated to garrisons in the disputed territory on the Breton–Norman frontier and for the time being an uneasy truce prevailed. That winter of 1448–9 the quarries of Caen, the source of some of the finest building stone for the king's new college under construction at Eton, ceased their regular export to England.[134] The master of the works responsible deemed it time to look for substitutes in Yorkshire and Oxfordshire. His timing was apt, for the truce ended in March 1449 after which there were no more truces in Normandy.

---

[133] Griffiths, *Henry VI*, 673–6.

[134] R. Allen Brown, H. M. Colvin, and A. J. Taylor (eds.), *The History of the King's Works*, i. *The Middle Ages* (London, 1963), 281–2.

3

CRISIS COMES, 1449–1450

DURING 1449–50 there came a crisis which laid bare 'the political, military, and financial bankruptcy of Henry VI's government'.[1] These years saw, in France and at home, the outcome of years of cumulative mismanagement so disastrous that the people of whole regions of England were finally provoked into a demonstration of protest and hostility.

The government's financial difficulties came to an impasse. Throughout the 1440s parliament had reacted reliably but not over-generously to the government's requests for money. In every year but one during the decade the exchequer could be sure of the income from a half lay subsidy, and, apart from the exchequer years 1440–1 and 1448–9, it received a half clerical tenth from the southern province.[2] However, when grants were made they could not be exploited to the full; the number of towns and communities who pleaded poverty and an inability to pay the required tenth and fifteenth in 1446 led to a further reduction of the yield from this tax beyond previous abatements. From now on the income from this source was reduced by some £6,000. The revenue was further undercut by numbers of individual exemptions that were quite likely to have been made by the king in his characteristic open-handedness to people with government connections. The customs on foreign trade were the other form of parliamentary taxation; the rate of poundage charged on imports and exports of general merchandise was increased in 1440, but two years later this higher rate was abandoned. Indeed, for the 1440s as a whole it has been calculated that revenue from the customs was less than it had been during the two preceding decades.[3] The drop in the government's income from direct and indirect taxation came at a time

---

[1] G. L. Harriss, 'Marmaduke Lumley and the Exchequer Crisis of 1446–9', in J. G. Rowe (ed.), *Aspects of Late Medieval Government and Society* (Toronto, 1986), 143.

[2] Ibid. 144.

[3] As quoted by R. A. Griffiths, *The Reign of Henry VI: The Exercise of Royal Authority, 1422–1461* (London, 1981), 379.

when the important Crown revenues of the duchy estates were withdrawn for the funding of the royal foundations at Eton and Cambridge and for the queen's dower. And since the royal patrimony could no longer support the increasing costs of the household it became the exchequer's task to meet them from taxation. This combination of declining receipts and enlarged expenditure precipitated a crisis of credit in the exchequer which so preoccupied Marmaduke Lumley, bishop of Carlisle, appointed treasurer in December 1446, that no provision was made for the defence of Normandy in the event of renewed hostilities. His remedial policies depended for their success upon the maintenance of the truce: so that when in 1449 the truce did collapse there was 'neither the money nor the mechanism, nor the will to fight a war'.[4] It is just possible that MPs, for all their grumbling about the king's subjects being unable to bear the burden of repeated taxation, might have granted the government's requests for money more freely had they been more fully informed of the seriousness of the English position in France. However, when parliament convened for its first session at Westminster in February 1449 (with some lords instructed to stay away and keep guard on the troublesome Scottish border),[5] it was as loath as ever to meet Henry's demands for taxation. So the Commons granted no more than the usual half of a tenth and fifteenth to be paid in two parts at Martinmas of 1449 and 1450, and they took the unusual step of obliging the king to cancel those assignments on it which he had already made in anticipation of the income of the subsidy. Thus the provisioning of Normandy at this crucial time suffered because the Commons could not trust those who were in favour around the king to make proper use of the taxation of the people of the realm.

Parliament had its own financial worries that spring concerning the health of the country's most important exported manufacture, woollen cloth. In March it complained about the official exclusion of English cloth from one of its major European markets in Holland, Brabant, and Flanders and asked for reprisals to be taken.[6] It was decided that goods from these countries should not be allowed into England unless the matter was resolved before the end of the forthcoming September. As it happened no redress was to be forthcoming and so the retaliatory

---

[4] Harriss, 'Marmaduke Lumley and the Exchequer Crisis', 171.

[5] *PPC*, 1443–61, 65–6.

[6] E. Power and M. M. Postan (eds.), *Studies in English Trade in the Fifteenth Century* (London, 1933), 27.

action was to continue into 1450. The official closing of this market to English cloth is the probable explanation behind the figures for the denizen export of cloth from London during the late 1440s which dropped from 8,827 cloths for ten months of the year Michaelmas 1446 to Michaelmas 1447 down to a mere 4,413 in the period 1447–8, rising to only about 6,000 annually during the following two years.[7] In 1449 there was also a collapse of the Hanseatic exports from England for reasons which will be discussed presently. During 1449 feelings in England naturally ran high against the subjects of the duke of Burgundy. In June the king was to issue a writ to the mayor and sheriffs of London ordering the issuing of proclamations in the capital prohibiting the spate of molestations of this foreign group, citizens having been provoked by stories that the duke was going to attack Calais.[8]

Meanwhile, as parliament discussed the cloth export business, developments were taking place in France. On 24 March 1449 an English mercenary, François de Surienne, a knight of the Garter and royal pensioner, took the Breton town of Fougères in a surprise attack and in contravention of the existing Anglo-French truce.[9] The dukes of Suffolk and Somerset were both at work behind this incident. The taking of Fougères was by no means the first, but it was perhaps the most provoking of several infractions of the truce that the duke of Somerset, now the king's lieutenant in France following York's transferral to Ireland, appeared to tolerate. It is traditionally cited as the incident which provoked Charles VII's invasion of Normandy that summer. It would appear that the attack was a reckless move by Suffolk to try to regain some of the public stature which he had so signally lost in his connection with the cession of Maine. But apparently altogether more disturbing to Charles VII was a wider issue of an alleged English plot to remove the duke of Brittany and his brother from their allegiance to the king of France, an allegiance the English now claimed was owed to them. For prior to the capture of Fougères Suffolk had covered himself technically from the accusation of breaking the truce with France. He had done this in 1448 when, as the Anglo-French truce was once again renewed, he had taken the inconspicuous but certainly not innocuous measure of listing the duke

---

[7] Ibid. 28.   [8] *PPC*, 1443–61, 74–5.
[9] For this incident see A. Bossuat, *Perrinet Gressart et François de Surienne, agents de l'Angleterre* (Paris, 1936), chs. 10–13; M. G. A. Vale, *Charles VII* (London, 1974), 116–18; J. Ferguson, *English Diplomacy, 1422–1461* (Oxford, 1972), 30–2.

of Brittany amongst the English allies instead of amongst the French allies. This of course meant that Charles VII was excluded from any interference in the relations of Brittany and England since these were now supposedly the relations of liegeman to overlord.[10] The French themselves claimed later that they had not regarded the Fougères incident as being nearly as crucial to the reopening of hostilities as the English diplomatic schemes to alienate the duke of Brittany and his brother from their allegiance to their overlord the king of France.[11] None the less, the attack on Fougères provided the French with a useful pretext both to perpetuate further infractions of the truce that spring and to draw closer to the Bretons again, since, with the English taking only half-hearted steps to restore the town to Brittany, Charles VII made an alliance with Duke Francis to help him to regain it.

Normandy that spring was in a very uncertain state, stricken with financial and military problems. The Norman Estates, however, were increasingly reluctant to finance even the reduced numbers of the peacetime military occupation.[12] The duchy was therefore quite unprepared for the reopening of full-scale hostilities which the English leaders seemed prepared to risk. Edmund Beaufort, duke of Somerset, had not been a happy choice in some respects as the king's lieutenant-general and governor in France, although as the most important English landowner in France, and a man who had spent much of his career there, his appointment in December 1446 to replace the duke of York had not been an incongruous one.[13] His popularity among the English notables in Normandy had not increased when, following the long-delayed cession of Maine in 1448, he had been recompensed for his losses there with lands in the bailliages of Caen and Cotentin whilst they demanded compensation for their own losses in Maine to no avail.[14] The months of refusal to surrender Le Mans and the bitterness which followed the cession of Maine illuminate the mood of grim determination among the English in Normandy and northern France to hold on to the lands and property for which they had fought.

By May 1449 parliament would have been aware of the ill-timed

---

[10] Griffiths, *Henry VI*, 510–13; M. H. Keen, *England in the Later Middle Ages* (London, 1973), 401–3. [11] Vale, *Charles VII*, 116.

[12] M. K. Jones, 'Somerset, York and the Wars of the Roses', *EHR* 104 (1989), 297–300.

[13] Despite the appointment there followed a period of some months of confusion when it was unclear whether York would return for another term of office. Ibid. 291–3.

[14] Ibid. 293; C. T. Allmand, 'The Lancastrian Land Settlement in Normandy, 1417–50', *Econ. HR*, 2nd ser., 21 (1968), 479.

action of Surienne, yet any apprehension on this score may have paled beside the shocking news that arrived just before parliament was prorogued for Whitsun on 30 May. Reports came in of the capture by English privateers in the Channel on 23 May of the annual convoy known as the Bay Fleet as it was on its return journey north from buying salt and other goods in the great salt works of Bourgneuf Bay, just south of the mouth of the Loire.[15] One hundred and ten ships were taken in this spectacular coup and were driven off the high seas to the Isle of Wight. Fifty of them belonged to merchants of the Hanse, the remaining sixty belonged to Flemings and Dutchmen who had joined the protection of the convoy. Unlike those of the Hanse, the Flemish and Dutch ships were later released with their cargoes by their captors. As an unprovoked peacetime attack on maritime trade it was a scandalous act even by the deplorable standards of Henry VI's reign, a time when the government rejected Henry V's policy of maintaining royal ships and 'the English pirate had his last most perfect, and probably most successful, freedom'.[16] As their captor, Robert Winnington, enthusiastically described it,

ye sawe never suche a syght of schyppys take in to Englond this c. wynter . . . for I der well sey that I have her at this tyme all the cheff schyppys of Duchelond, Holond, Selond, and Flaundrys.[17]

According to the report of a Prussian agent in London, the Kentish rebels marched up to London in 1450 calling for the restoration of Hanseatic trade and for the punishment of the pirates involved.[18] There is no corroboration of this report, but it is known that the rebels would call for the downfall of those men, particularly Daniel, Trevilian, and Say, who were implicated in the incident: because the capture of the Bay Fleet profited—and this was about the most disgraceful aspect of the entire affair—some of the most influential men in the realm.

Relations between England and the Hanse had been fraught and difficult for years, more especially between England and the Prussian branch of the Hanse with whom England had long been agitating for

[15] A. R. Bridbury, *England and the Salt Trade in the Later Middle Ages* (Oxford, 1955), 76–8, 80–1, 90.
[16] C. F. Richmond, 'Royal Administration and the Keeping of the Seas, 1422–1485', D.Phil. thesis (Oxford, 1962), 93–4. Not only was there no Crown naval force but for naval defence the Cinque Ports service was now obsolete. Ibid. 170.
[17] *PL*, ii. 105.
[18] Power and Postan, *Studies in English Trade in the Fifteenth Century*, 129.

parity between the English merchants in Danzig and the privileged Hansards of London. Up until the late 1430s England had emerged more or less in the stronger position from her various offensives against the Hansards, but from the 1440s onwards the strength of the English position deteriorated badly. Much of the responsibility for this decay can be put upon the issuing in 1442 of an act of parliament for the keeping of the seas that did away with the previous restrictions regarding safe conducts and truce on the high seas and in effect replaced them with what was an organized system of privateering. The ordinance provided that English shipping was to be policed and protected from attack by a fleet of twenty-eight ships. This fleet was given a more or less free hand to make capture at sea and the masters and owners of the ships were offered the incentive of generous terms in the sharing out of the captured goods and cargoes. It was this fleet that captured the Hanseatic convoy. Since the boats were provided by powerful individuals closely connected with certain members of the king's council, men such as William, Lord Bonville, Sir Philip Courtenay, John Howard, John Church, and Hugh Taverner, the act effectively authorized some of the highest men in the land to draw income from the profits of privateering.[19]

The leader of the English privateers who captured the Bay Fleet in 1450, Robert Winnington, had been employed by the king in 1449, 'to do us service in the see, for the clensing of the same and rebukyng of the robbeurs, and pirates therof'.[20] Some of the boats of his fleet belonged to Thomas Daniel, noted in the previous chapter as one of the more hated members of Henry VI's court circle during the 1440s.[21] It would seem likely from the rashness of the action that Winnington was not acting in his own capacity but as Daniel's lieutenant and agent. Indeed, he knew his need for friends in high places, and upon making the capture he wrote to another member of Daniel's circle, John Trevilian, telling him of what had happened and seeking his support. Word soon got about that lords of the king's council were implicated in the raid. The Hanse merchants in London and Londoners themselves placed the blame for involvement with all Suffolk's clique and especially with John Trevilian, Thomas Daniel, and Lord Saye.

[19] Power and Postan, *Studies in English Trade in the Fifteenth Century*, 126.
[20] Stevenson, i. 489. In May payment was made to Gervase Clifton and Alexander Eden for doing similar work. F. Devon (ed.), *Issues of the Exchequer* (Record Commission, 1837), 463.
[21] Power and Postan, *Studies in English Trade in the Fifteenth Century*, 128.

Prior to the capture customs officials in England had been trying in 1449 to collect from merchants of the Hanse the newly raised subsidy of tonnage and poundage from which they were supposed to be exempt. At their refusal to pay their goods had been sequestrated and this had caused the Hanse to answer in kind.[22] The capture is seen now, as no doubt it was by many then, as perhaps one of the most glaring symptoms of the demoralized state into which the Lancastrian government had fallen by the late 1440s. It also goes a good way, although previous uncompromising and obstructive negotiating by the English played its part, towards explaining why Hanse exports of cloth from England dropped by more than a half between 1446–8 and 1448–50.[23]

On 16 June parliament reassembled at Winchester and sat until 16 July. It is perhaps a measure of the domestic instability felt at the time that in a debate in council during this parliament concerning the problem of how to supply the French possessions sufficiently with men and ordnance the lords first of all discussed measures for dealing with disorder at home. It was proposed that commissions of oyer and terminer should be appointed to establish better order before anything could be done.[24] The Isle of Wight, only just to the south of where they sat in Winchester, offered an example of such lack of order. There John Newport, a former steward of the duke of York, who also went under the self-aggrandizing titles of 'Newport the Gallant' or 'Newport the Rich', so terrorized the inhabitants of the island and practised such piracy that the people were deserting for the mainland, leaving the island without proper defence.[25] In this parliament Henry managed to extract only a further half of a tenth and a fifteenth to be paid in two instalments by the Martinmas of 1449 and 1451.[26] The wool subsidy was renewed but most of its income was assigned to the defence of Calais and maintenance of fortifications, and authorization was given to officials to investigate and make sure that the money was spent according to parliament's decrees.[27] At the time of the dissolution of this parliament the king's current charges and debts were running, it was said, at the level of £372,000.[28]

---

[22] Ferguson, *English Diplomacy, 1422–1461*, 100–1. For a complaint by Hanse merchants concerning the undue levying of the subsidy at Sandwich, see C1/19/386.
[23] Power and Postan, *Studies in English Trade in the Fifteenth Century*, 401.
[24] A. R. Myers, 'A Parliamentary Debate of the Mid-Fifteenth Century', *BJRL* 22 (1938), 403.   [25] *RP*, v. 204–5.
[26] R. Virgoe, 'The Parliamentary Subsidy of 1450', *BIHR* 55 (1982), 128.
[27] Griffiths, *Henry VI*, 380.   [28] Ibid. 377.

It is likely that MPs left Winchester that July bitter about the financial incompetence of the government. Their bitterness can only have increased when some time in early August the news filtered through that on 31 July Charles VII had abrogated the truce and was once more officially at war with the English. None the less, few of them would have foreseen at that point just how catastrophic and final a change this was going to bring about in northern France. Months of negotiations had gone on since Surienne's attack in March, but neither the French nor the Bretons had been able to obtain any satisfactory reparations from the English who were taking the intractable line that the duke of Brittany was England's liegeman. By July Charles VII was not only in the right temper for war, but he was equipped for it militarily, having used the time since the 1444 truce to reorganize his army. Not only did he have more men than the English but he had a good supply of artillery which he was to put to effective use. He also had the advantage of being on the attack, with a manœuvrable field army, against the garrison-bound English troops. Moreover, unlike in any previous campaign, ample financial supplies were assured by the French royal banker, Jacques Cœur. That August Charles's soldiery swept into Normandy: a dozen or so castles and towns were all regained by the French in just over a month.[29] Autumn with its likelihood of less-clement weather saw no slowing of the French advance. On 12 September Coutances capitulated to Duke Francis's army, three days later St Lo fell; throughout the month more and more castles and towns were regained, concluding on 29 September with Carentan. Many fortresses surrendered without a fight, some betrayed by the French inhabitants or naturalized British soldiers. The French enjoyed telling the malicious and highly improbable story that the castle of Essay had been taken when the duke of Alençon heard that the English garrison of the town and castle were out fishing a pond some distance from the town and took them prisoner on their day off.[30]

The difficulty was that Somerset was short of men and many of them were ill-disciplined. To put an army of sufficient size in the field would have meant the use of garrison troops and the opening up of garrison positions to attack. At about this time an anonymous soldier in France vented his feelings against Somerset in a series of rhetorical

---

[29] W. Hardy and E. L. C. P. Hardy (eds.), *Recueil des croniques et anchiennes istories de la Grant Bretaigne par Jehan de Waurin*, v. (Rolls Series, 1891), 126 ff.

[30] Stevenson (ed.), *Narratives of the Expulsion of the English from Normandy, 1449–1450* (RS, 1863), 272.

questions (the document remained amongst those of Sir John Fastolf's secretary, William Worcester).[31] Had Somerset been bribed to take Fougères? And why with English soldiery plundering the countryside for food and turning the population against them did he not pay his officers and soldiers properly? Moreover, why did he not see to the repair of the fortifications of towns and castles and to their proper supply with artillery and provisions? The matter of compensating those who had lost their property in Maine had still not been attended to: was it because he had pocketed the proceeds?

News from across the Channel gave Henry every cause for alarm. Early in September he ordered a commission of array for Hampshire and the setting up of beacons in the usual places there; preparations were put under way for sending reinforcements to Normandy from Portsmouth; and later in the month he was sending commissioners about the counties to raise loans for the maintenance of the war.[32] But all this was rather too little and too late.

A sense of impending disaster began to disturb the departments of state. On 17 September Bishop Lumley resigned his office as treasurer with a balance in the treasury of a mere £480 5s. 3d.[33] He was replaced by James Fiennes, Lord Saye and Sele. On 11 October the French took Gavray, and by 16 October Charles VII was at the gates of Rouen to confront Somerset's army. After a short and, as some saw it, token engagement, Somerset was persuaded by the archbishop and citizens to negotiate with the French, and on 29 October the capital of Lancastrian France surrendered without a siege. It was an agreement which affronted the sensibilities of the English nobility and which would be castigated by the duke of York for its dishonourable and treasonable nature. This failure even to attempt a defence of Rouen, the town of which York had remained captain, was perhaps the core of the feud between himself and Somerset which would occupy so much of English political life in the following five years.[34] Meanwhile October was nearly out and still the relieving army had not been sent from England. Following Bishop Lumley's example, Adam Moleyns, the keeper of the privy seal, asked to be allowed to retreat from office. With tragic consequences for himself, he was not allowed to do so immediately.

---

[31] Stevenson, ii. pt. ii. 718–22; Griffiths, *Henry VI*, 514.
[32] *CPR*, 1446–52, 297–9, 316–17.
[33] Harriss, 'Marmaduke Lumley and the Exchequer Crisis', 169.
[34] Jones, 'Somerset, York and the Wars of the Roses', 302–7.

On 5 November 1449, as parliament was assembling for the new session to begin the next day, Fougères, where Surienne's force had occupied the citadel for over seven months, finally surrendered to Duke Francis.[35] On 10 November Charles VII, accompanied by his banker Jacques Cœur, entered Rouen with all the trappings of sumptuous propaganda. The veteran soldier Lord Talbot was there, detained as one of the English hostages, a cheerless onlooker to a bright pageant of horses decked in velvet and mechanized symbolic devices set up in the canopied streets: here an *Agnus Dei* running drink by its horns, and there a winged stag wearing a crown on its neck which knelt as Charles passed by.[36]

In the circumstances, the Commons might have been expected to make some immediate provision for the defence of Normandy and relief of the garrisons there. Indeed, this was the intention of the new parliament, reassembling as it was so soon after the ending of the previous one in July. Yet this parliament, which was to last through from November to June 1450, and which has been described as 'one of the most dramatic and contentious of the whole medieval period', was also remarkable for its parsimony and financial inaction.[37] Normandy was slipping out of English hands but the Commons would not accept any proposals for further direct taxation. They had already made a grant that year and it would be collected over the next two years. They were agreeable to discussing other means of raising money, but these discussions produced no grants of money for the war that year.

Arising out of the defeats in France an incident took place during the parliament that November which in its way was to spell the turning of the tide against Suffolk.[38] Despite the duke's dominance of the council there were yet a small number of its members who were willing to voice their indignation at the catalogue of disasters going on in France. Among these was Ralph, Lord Cromwell, a long-standing royal councillor and servant who had resigned as treasurer in 1443. It was

[35] Griffiths, *Henry VI*, 511.

[36] Stevenson, *Narratives of the Expulsion of the English from Normandy, 1449–50*, 309–20.

[37] Virgoe, 'The Parliamentary Subsidy of 1450', 125. It is suggested that the lack of will displayed by parliament in the face of the military disasters of 1449–50 stemmed from a perception of Lancastrian Normandy as a separate entity from Lancastrian England, and one whose difficulties and expenses were not the responsibility of the Commons in England. M. H. Keen, 'The End of the Hundred Years War: Lancastrian France and Lancastrian England', in *England and her Neighbours 1066–1453: Essays in Honour of Pierre Chaplais*, ed. M. Jones and M. Vale (London, 1989), 297–311.

[38] See Griffiths, *Henry VI*, 286–8.

therefore most ominous that a lawless esquire of the household, known to have been patronized by Suffolk, William Tailboys, should make an attempt to assassinate him.[39] On 28 November with extraordinary brazenness Tailboys attacked Cromwell outside the Star Chamber in the palace of Westminster itself. Tailboys had been perpetrating outrages throughout the 1440s under the protection of his patrons Suffolk and Viscount Beaumont but this particularly vicious incident was to stand out in his career not only for its unpleasantness but for its important repercussions. Because of it Cromwell, who believed Suffolk to be the instigator behind the outrage, became completely hardened in his antipathy towards him and was soon to encourage the Commons in their bid to impeach him.

By November 1449 the preparations for the sending of troops over to Normandy by a fleet from Portsmouth were slightly further ahead. Shipping was being arrested for this purpose in the ports of London, East Anglia, Lincolnshire, and the North-East, and soldiers were being mustered in readiness at Portsmouth.[40] Sir Thomas Kyriell was assigned to the command of this army of some four and a half thousand men and in November to December up to £9,000 was assigned for the payment of wages.[41] Yet November went by and still the troops were in Portsmouth waiting in a dangerous state of unemployment. During December as the French pushed on through Upper Normandy the government was on a desperate hunt for money. It was unable to make any adequate supply of cash to Somerset whose soldiers were already in a demoralized state.

It was not until early in the new year that Bishop Moleyns was sent down to Portsmouth to take to the force awaiting shipment to Normandy the first, long-overdue, instalment of their wages. Accusations were subsequently made that he withheld some of this money from the troops.[42] In all events, his escort could not save him from a mob of furious sailors and soldiers, said to number over 300 men, who on 9 January dragged him out of his lodgings to a field and killed him. According to one source, a confession was extracted from him before his death in which he made charges not only against himself but also against Suffolk and other 'traitors' of the Crown.[43] Chroniclers agree that Moleyns died 'for hys covetysse'.[44] More especially, he was hated as one of the best-known figures of Suffolk's faction at whose door the

[39] Ibid. 580–1. [40] *CPR*, 1446–52, 317–18. [41] Griffiths, *Henry VI*, 519.
[42] *Davies Chron.*, 64. [43] *Benet's Chron.*, 196.
[44] *Gregory's Chron.*, 189; *Davies Chron.*, 64.

responsibility was being laid for the chain of defeats in France over the past six months.[45] Harfleur had fallen nine days previously; the Channel was now the border with enemy France. Invasion, it seemed, could come at any time.

II

In such an atmosphere of uncertainty about defence, trouble was also beginning early in the year further along the Channel coast in Kent where in the last week of January 1450 there was an attempted uprising. This rising led by a Thomas Cheyne came to nothing, but it was a demonstration which revived the notion, put into effect in 1381, of addressing complaints to the king by raising the south-eastern counties into a mass demonstration converging upon London.[46] On Saturday, 24 January rebels gathered in the villages of the stretch of countryside which lies between Sandwich and Dover, making up the extreme south-eastern corner of Kent. They had a list of those whom they wanted to see beheaded (heartened possibly by the example of the troops at Portsmouth). The list comprised William Aiscough, bishop of Salisbury, William, duke of Suffolk, James, Lord Saye, and the abbot of Gloucester. The rebels hoped to draw upon support from Kent, Essex, Hertfordshire, Surrey, Sussex, and the city of London.[47] The rebels' targets further extended to religious houses. They had in mind particular valuables which they wanted to take from the prior of Christ Church, Canterbury.[48]

[45] In Mar. 1450 a John Asteley, esq., who had gone down to Portsmouth with the bishop to ensure the safe conduct of the money, was rewarded for what had turned out to be such an uncongenial task with the not ungenerous sum of £6 13s. 4d., E403/778. m. 13.

[46] The main sources for Cheyne's rising are: KB27/755 *rex* side, m. 4; /756 *rex* side, m. 2; /786 *rex* side, m. 2ᵛ; /790 *rex* side, mm. 1ᵛ, 45; KB9/263, mm. 56, 57, 58; *PPC*, 1443–61, 107–9; C. L. Kingsford, 'An Historical Collection of the Fifteenth Century', *EHR* 29 (1914), 513–15; *Benet's Chron.*, 197. Other chroniclers make passing references to this rising as the rising of the hermit Bluebeard, servant of the queen of the fairies, although Bale identifies the leader as the queen of the fairies. *Bale's Chron.*, 127. The *Great Chron.*, 181, and *Brut*, 516, would seem to place the rising out of its true sequence, identifying it as one of the protests against Suffolk's release from custody in Mar. 1450.

[47] KB27/755 *rex* side, m. 4; /756 *rex* side, m. 2; KB9/263, mm. 56, 57, 58.

[48] KB27/786 *rex* side, m. 2ᵛ; /790 *rex* side, m. 1ᵛ. The rebels name a chair of silver and gold worth £100 which they would have liked to have carried off. This is very likely to have been the chair given to the priory by Cardinal Beaufort in the late 1440s which had involved the cost of £12 in transporting it from Winchester to Canterbury. C. Eveleigh Woodruff, 'Notes on the Inner Life and Domestic Economy of the Priory of Christ Church, Canterbury, in the Fifteenth Century', *Arch. Cant.*, 53 (1940), 9.

They marshalled themselves into some kind of military array, appointing captains to order their ranks. These leaders hid their identities behind names such as 'King of the Fairies', 'Queen of the Fairies', and 'Robin Hood', a trick used by poachers.[49] Thomas Cheyne, the captain in chief, went under the name of 'the hermit Blewbeard'. Several of the leaders involved were perhaps not local to east Kent. Cheyne was a labourer from Newington by Southwark in Surrey, another ringleader was, significantly, a soldier from Warwickshire, and another was a yeoman from Cheshire, although they were at the head of a gathering of men from this hinterland of Sandwich and Dover, from villages such as Temple Ewell, River, Eastry, and Northbourne, as well as from Sandwich itself.

Having congregated and made their plans on the Saturday, the rebels took action the following Monday, 26 January. Some two hundred or so rose up in rebellion at Eastry under Cheyne that day, the numbers joining him later on in the week allegedly swelling into the thousands. What the men actually did is unclear, but word went about that besides attacking local religious houses Cheyne intended taking the castle at Dover. However, it was at Canterbury, perhaps *en route* to London, that the rebellion ended and where the anti-clerical element in the rising was manifested in an attack on St Radegund's abbey hospice just outside the city walls on Canterbury's northern boundary. This was the town house of the abbey of St Radegund at Bradsole near Dover, situated close to the villages of Temple Ewell and River from which some of these rioters came. It may well have been they who inspired the assault on this particular building as a means of attacking their own local religious house.[50]

Cheyne was captured with the aid of some of the citizens of Canterbury on Saturday, 31 January, just a week after the rising had begun.[51] The government's response was prompt. On 2 February a commission led by the earl of Wiltshire was sent into Kent with the task of dealing with the offences recently committed there, and so by the end of the first week of February proceedings were in progress at

---

[49] KB9/263, mm. 56, 57, 58; KB27/755 *rex* side, m. 4.

[50] *CCR*, 1427–1516, 123. It is recorded in a cartulary in Bodleian MS Rawl. B 336 that St Radegund's abbey at Bradsole was given land at Froxpole just outside the northern wall of the city of Canterbury at some date around 1230. I am most grateful to Margaret Sparks of Canterbury for this information: she and the late James Jobbs located and traced the history of this hospice which survives now only in the name of St Radegund's street.

[51] *CCR*, 1427–1516, 123; *Benet's Chron.*, 197; HMC, ix. (1883), 140.

Greenwich and Canterbury to charge the ringleaders with treason. Cheyne was sent to Westminster to be judged and was subsequently hanged, drawn, and quartered at Tyburn, west of the city walls.[52] His head was sent to London Bridge and his quarters were distributed between London, Norwich, and two of the Cinque Ports; although not without some difficulty, since no one was willing for fear of their lives to take on themselves the job of transporting the dismembered corpse to its several destinations.[53] Such, evidently, was the general pitch of support felt for the uprising in the South-East.

Cheyne was apparently the only figure from the disturbances in eastern Kent to be executed. But during the brief period of his rising another man had been executed in the suburbs of London for his alleged intentions towards prominent courtiers. In the very last days of January, before Cheyne's rising had been quelled, there had been the threat of an uprising at Westminster led by a yeoman of the town, Nicholas Jakes. It is interesting that he is described by one contemporary author as a servant of one of the late duke of Gloucester's squires, Bassingbourne, and that among his fellow plotters was a servant of the duke of Buckingham: these were men associated with some of the great figures of the realm.[54] Chroniclers describe Jakes as being executed for treasonable language, since his conspiracy was detected before it could develop into action. A jury assembling on Friday 30 January presented that Jakes and others had been plotting to behead the bishop of Salisbury, Lords Saye and Dudley, and the abbot of Gloucester, and to take the government of the country upon themselves that very day. This plotting had, allegedly, gone on the previous day, 29 January, the day on which the impeached duke of Suffolk was committed to the Tower. Found guilty of these high ambitions, Jakes was hanged and quartered at Tyburn. His quarters were sent to Chichester, Rochester, Colchester, and Portsmouth—this last was not a surprising choice.

---

[52] *Benet's Chron.*, 197; Kingsford, 'An Historical Collection of the Fifteenth Century', 514–15.

[53] *PPC*, 1443–61, 107–9; this evidence is confused as to whether Cheyne's head went to Canterbury or to London, first saying one, then the other. A chronicle source reports that Cheyne's head went to London Bridge. Kingsford, 'An Historical Collection of the Fifteenth Century', 514–15.

[54] KB27/755 *rex* side, m. 3; KB9/263, m. 64; KB29/81 Hilary term m. 12; HMC, ix. pt. 1 (1883), 140; Kingsford, 'An Historical Collection of the Fifteenth Century', 514. Jakes is probably the anonymous person alluded to as 'a man [who] was jugged and hanged and drawen for woordes that he said ageinst the rule of the lordes'. *Bale's Chron.*, 128. Similarly in *Benet's Chron.*, 197.

It is possible that it was this very action which provoked the renewed disturbances which then broke out in Hampshire on 1 February. At Bishop's Waltham, nine and a half miles south-east of Winchester, an ex-soldier marshalled an army together appointing captains and officers, flying a red flag of defiance and threatening war against the king. According to later indictments these were the same troops as those which had recently turned upon Adam Moleyns and murdered him.[55] It is this incident which is behind the cryptic statement in one chronicle, 'And in the same day [9 March] was broughte from Portesmouthe to London a man called Holand, a Sowdiour, for setting up of a baner at Portesmouthe'.[56] One wonders why both accounts of the incident found the rebels' red flag or banner a sufficiently significant detail to give it mention. Displayed like a mock Oriflamme, the red battle flag of the French, flown at Agincourt,[57] it evidently shocked and disturbed the authorities as a symbol of deep disaffection amongst their own troops.

Although Cheyne and Jakes were both agitating during the last week of January there is no evidence to suggest that they were in collusion. Ferment was perhaps to be expected at Westminster at this time, moreover, since the second session of parliament had begun there on 22 January with the Commons seeking vengeance upon the duke of Suffolk.

III

The timing of the next outbreak of trouble in Kent following Cheyne's attempted rising was in response to a further, and, in this case, final, development in Suffolk's doings. The duke, evidently foreseeing a confrontation and under the strong impression that 'odious and horrible language' about him had reached alarming proportions, used the very first day of the new session to ask the king if he could offer a statement to parliament. He was willing, he said, to answer whatever accusations might be made against him. The Commons for their part felt that the vigorous rumours going about concerning him were in themselves sufficient ground for having the duke arrested and put to

---

[55] KB27/774 *rex* side, m. 29. (KB9/109, mm. 16, 25, are poorly legible.)

[56] Kingsford, 'An Historical Collection of the Fifteenth Century', 515.

[57] H. Nicolas, *History of the Battle of Agincourt, and of the Expedition of Henry the Fifth into France in 1415* (London, 1833), 85, 115.

law. The lords, however, rejected such reasoning and so prompted the Commons into a more formal series of accusations presented on 28 January before the chancellor and a group of lords. It was of course the issue of the war on which they wanted to make him answerable. The duke they said was intending to aid their enemy France by surrendering Wallingford castle (of which he was constable) to Charles VII, a treasonable charge which had Suffolk placed in the Tower on 29 January.[58] Two days later the long-serving chancellor, Archbishop Stafford, resigned. He may have felt it proper that in a month which had seen the murder of the keeper of the privy seal and the arrest of Suffolk he, as their associate and part of their collapsing regime, should also go. Certainly in retrospect and probably at the time he was popularly regarded as corrupt, as one of those preventing freedom of speech to preachers and trying to circumscribe criticism of the court:

> Trowthe in no wise he wille not teche;
> He is the devels sheparde.[59]

London and the southern counties were in such a state of tension that February and March that further uprising · was feared. On 14 February yet another man was arrested for treasonable language against the king, William Raulyns of London, a woolpacker turned soldier.[60] As a soldier it is possible that he was either like those fomenting rebellion in Hampshire at the beginning of the month, a man cheated of employment, or perhaps he had recently returned from Normandy. The troops streaming back across the Channel were certainly heightening the unrest in the South-East, coming as they did 'in great mysery and poverte' so that 'many of them drewe to theft and misrule and noyed sore the cominalte of this land'.[61] They were an element likely to express themselves forcibly about the government which had put them where they were.

On 20 February the king sent out an order to the sheriffs of London and Middlesex, Kent, Surrey, and Sussex to make proclamation against the carrying of arms in their counties. Those going against the proclamation were to be arrested and imprisoned.[62]

In the mean time the more Suffolk came under attack the better the populace were liking it. By late February or March the chanting in the streets seems to have become positively gleeful.

---

[58] *RP*, v. 177.
[59] *Political Poems*, ii. 231.
[60] KB29/81 Hilary term m. 12.
[61] *Bale's Chron.*, 128.
[62] T. Rymer (ed.), *Foedera, conventiones, literae* . . . (London, 1704–35), xi. 262.

Now is tyme of Lent, the Fox is in the Towre;
Therfore sende hym Salesbury to be his confessoure,
Many mo ther bene, and we kowde hem knowe;
But wonne most begynne the daunce, and all come arowe.[63]

'Fox' here being, of course, Suffolk, and 'Salesbury' being Bishop Aiscough, the bishop of Salisbury, popularly regarded, as we have seen in the previous chapter, as one of the duke of Suffolk's closest allies.

Contributing to the excitement of the people in the streets was the Commons' decision in parliament to try to obtain Suffolk's impeachment; they now saw their chance to have him dislodged from power. The Tailboys incident of the previous November ensured that they had the weight of Lord Cromwell's encouragement behind them, and he may have helped to draw up the lists of charges made against his fellow royal councillor. With French raiding parties taking men for ransom from the Norfolk coast and disporting themselves on Caister Sands, parliament cast two groups of accusations against the duke on 7 February and 9 March to do with alleged treachery in negotiations with France and embezzlement of royal funds and the perversion of justice at home.[64] He had plotted, they said, in July 1447 with the French for an invasion of England and the replacing of Henry VI by Suffolk's own son, John, whose queen was to be Margaret Beaufort, of royal descent; he had independently promised the delivery of Maine to the French without consultation with the other English ambassadors; he had revealed confidential matters of the council and of the English defences to the enemy; he had controlled the appointment of sheriffs for many years; he was responsible for great extortions and murders; owing to his great might homicides, rioters, and notorious misdoers had been upheld in their flagrant disregard of the law. On the first group of charges, largely to do with Suffolk's foreign dealings, the king found no case against him. On the second group, recognizing the temper of the Commons, he exercised his prerogative to save his favoured minister and on 17 March declared him banished from his realms as from 1 May, imposing a five-year exile upon him.[65]

That evening as Suffolk fled the capital for his manor of Eastthorp in Suffolk a crowd of angry Londoners gave chase and managed to set upon some of his party, although the duke himself got clear.[66] East

[63] *Political Poems*, ii. 224.   [64] *PL*, ii. 136; *RP*, v. 177–82.
[65] *RP*, v. 183.
[66] Stevenson, ii. 767; *Bale's Chron.*, 128–9; *Benet's Chron.*, 198; Kingsford, 'An Historical Collection of the Fifteenth Century', 515; *EHL*, 344.

Anglia was in an unsettled way itself with the French worrying away at the Norfolk coast. Only the day before Suffolk's departure from London a commission had been appointed to set up watches and wards and erect beacons on the coasts there in tardy response to the situation.[67]

There is no suggestion that Suffolk's disappearance from London defused the atmosphere there in any way. On 21 March, four days after he had quit the capital, John Frammesley, or Ramsey, a London wine merchant, called by one chronicler 'an olde poure man' went about the streets of Dowgate ward chanting, 'By this toun, by this toun, for this array the kyng shall lose his Croune'.[68] For this his head joined Jakes's and Cheyne's on London Bridge, and just as Jakes's and likewise Cheyne's quarters had been used as warning messages to towns in Kent, Essex, Sussex, Hampshire, and Norfolk, so Frammesley's own, dispatched to Winchester, Newbury, Coventry, and Stamford, went out to quell possible disaffection in the cloth towns of southern and central England.[69]

It is a measure of the unusually menacing mood about in the south of England that parliament left Westminster on 30 March for Leicester, a centre of the king's hereditary lands. On his way northward Henry was met in Stony Stratford by a Yorkshire shipman who threshed the earth of the road before him with a flail, saying that this was how the duke of York should deal with the traitors. For this he was led off to Northampton castle, later to be hanged, drawn, and quartered, Thomas Daniel taking charge of the matter.[70] That April the abandoned capital seethed dangerously with popular ferment. Church doors everywhere were posted with schedules and bills freely advertising opinions on the maladies of the realm, so much so that the sheriffs were asked to put a stop to the billsticking.[71] For Suffolk the writing was, quite literally, on the wall.

The fading of Suffolk's regime over the winter and spring of 1449–50 can be traced also in individual fortunes whose movement reflected this realignment of political power. Thomas Kemp, nephew of the archbishop of York, for example, had been provided in 1448 to

[67] *CPR*, 1446–52, 378.
[68] KB9/73, m. 1; *CPR*, 1446–52, 320; *PPC*, 1443–61, 107–9; Kingsford, 'An Historical Collection of the Fifteenth Century', 515; *Bale's Chron.*, 129.
[69] KB9/73, m. 1.
[70] *EHL*, 371.
[71] T. Rymer (ed.), *Foedera, conventiones, literae*, xi. 268.

the see of London but remained unconsecrated probably because he lacked Suffolk's favour. However, with events proceeding as they were in parliament early in 1450, Kemp was given licence on 4 February to accept provision.[72] Likewise with Sir John Fastolf, disapproved of by Suffolk, whose official employment increased quite suddenly from November 1449 onwards and through 1450. He even took up duties briefly as a royal councillor from April 1450 to January 1451,[73] whilst up in Essex he was able after three years of its forcible disseisin to retrieve his manor of Dedham in the spring of 1450 merely through the duke's political decline.[74] The Commons, too, were emboldened to petition at Leicester in the spring of 1450 for an Act of Resumption. They pointed out how deeply the king was in debt and asked him, albeit with a list of exemptions, to take back and resume all land and property which he had granted since the first day of his reign— 1 September 1422. (The common rumour which put the king's debts at a scandalous 40,000 marks was, had it been known, far short of the actual figure[75]). Henry ostensibly agreed to this but qualified his assent by reserving the right to add any provisos of exemptions he thought were necessary. So although this act was passed on 6 May 1450 it became in effect almost powerless owing to 186 provisos which Henry then appended to it before parliament was dissolved in early June. Nor would a copy of the act reach the exchequer until October of that year, so that the exchequer did not begin to send out writs to the sheriffs to order local inquiries concerning holders of Crown lands until the spring of 1451.[76]

The months of 1449 to the May of 1450 were fraught and disturbing ones. The slipping away of England's French possessions and the disarray of the country's important trade with the Low Countries were having lively repercussions at home. The Commons in parliament saw this as a time when the government should be made answerable for events abroad, and besides toppling Henry's chief minister, the duke of Suffolk, they had hopes of changing the outlay of the king's patronage. Moreover, the murder of another chief minister, the bishop

---

[72] P. A. Johnson, 'The Political Career of Richard, Duke of York, to 1456', D.Phil. thesis (Oxford, 1981), 131–2.

[73] A. R. Smith, 'Aspects of the Career of Sir John Fastolf (1380–1459)', D.Phil. thesis (Oxford, 1982), 120–2.　　　[74] Ibid. 126.

[75] J. A. Giles (ed.), *Incerti Scriptoris Chronicon Angliae de Regnis Trium Regum Lancastrensium Henrici IV, Henrici V, et Henrici VI* (London, 1848), 38.

[76] *RP*, v. 183–99; B. P. Wolffe, 'Acts of Resumption in the Lancastrian Parliaments, 1399–1456', *EHR* 73 (1958), 598–9, 601.

of Chichester, by troops, and abortive risings in southern England showed that the commons of the realm, too, were seeking to make their voice heard in events. But it was not until June 1450 that they found a proper mouthpiece in the form of a regional uprising.

4

CADE'S REBELLION IN KENT
AND MIDDLESEX

I T was the circumstances of the duke of Suffolk's death, which occurred whilst he was travelling out of the country into exile by ship, which caused such alarm in Kent as to turn discontent into open action.[1]

On 1 May the vessel transporting Suffolk across the Channel from Ipswich was intercepted by a ship called the 'Nicholas of the Tower'. The unknown master of this ship had Suffolk taken aboard and, according to report, gave him some form of trial before having him beheaded the following day, 2 May, in a small boat in Dover Road.[2] The duke's head was stuck on a pole and his body was flung up the high strand with the pebbles on Dover Beach. Who masterminded the plot is unknown. It certainly occurred to some that the shipmen could have been acting at the instigation of one of Suffolk's influential enemies.[3] By whosever design, the action caused the frightening rumour to go about Kent that the king intended to take retribution by turning the county into a wild forest, a threat believed to have been made by the king's treasurer, Lord Saye, a former sheriff of Kent.[4] This fear appears to have been the spark which set alight the already evident discontent in Kent and drew the county together into rebellion.

What is more, the news of Suffolk's death was coming not long after

---

[1] R. Virgoe, 'The Death of William de la Pole, Duke of Suffolk', *BJRL* 47 (1965), 489–502. For two letters reporting this incident on 5 and 6 May, see *PL*, ii. 146–8.

[2] 'The Nicholas of the Tower' was associated with Bristol. In Jan. 1450 a dispute brought before the exchequer concerning a Bristol merchant exporting uncustomed cloth in her suggests that up until quite close to the timing of the duke's capture her activities had been of an unremarkable kind. E207/16/4.

[3] By the seventeenth century an edition of Stow would state (improbably) that Henry Holand (who was granted livery of his patrimony as duke of Exeter in July 1450) owned the ship in question. J. Stow, *Annales, or a Generall Chronicle of England* (1631), 388a. No mention is made of this in Stow's edition of his *Chronicles* in 1580.

[4] Ibid. 389a.

news that the army which had eventually set off in March under Sir Thomas Kyriell had met a terrible defeat in battle at Formigny north-west of Bayeux on 15 April where the French had used cannon fire against the English archers to devastating effect. The small force, which, it might be noted, included many Beaufort followers in Kent, had set off with all the signs of being a half-hearted affair: only one other knight, the traditional captains of English armies, could be troubled to accompany Kyriell, and insufficient numbers of men at arms could be found to bring up the proper ratio with archers.[5] Rumour had it that four thousand English had been lost in the fight.[6] These men would have been seen as the victims of Suffolk's treacherous dealings with the French. The war was in effect drawing to a close in northern France. The French had recovered Normandy: their next move could well be over the Channel to England. On 21 April Queenborough, on the Isle of Sheppey on the north coast of Kent, had had to resist an enemy raid, and had only just succeeded in doing so.[7]

Rebellion was under way by at least the second half of May.[8] From 18 May onwards (for many months to come as it turned out) no consistories were held in the diocese of Rochester because of the serious insurrection in Kent.[9] It is perhaps no coincidence that it was on 18, 19, and 20 May that Rochester held its annual three-day fair, attracting in crowds from all over Kent and beyond, and providing natural means for the fast distribution of news and opinions over a whole region. It is noteworthy that in the following year Rochester's privilege of holding a fair would be resumed by the Crown and the fair abolished.[10] Other towns whose annual fairs took place during the period of the rebellion were, for example, Heathfield in Sussex on 15–17 June and Sevenoaks in Kent on 29 June.[11] Obviously, news of insurrection or the plotting of insurgents could be disseminated in an

---

[5] G. L. Harriss, *Cardinal Beaufort: A Study of Lancastrian Ascendancy and Decline* (Oxford, 1988), 382; M. R. Powicke, 'Lancastrian Captains', in T. A. Sandquist and M. R. Powicke (eds.), *Essays in Medieval History Presented to Bertie Wilkinson* (Toronto, 1969), 382.

[6] Stevenson, ii. pt. ii. 767; I do not suggest that this was the actual figure.

[7] *Bale's Chron.*, 129.

[8] R. A. Griffiths, *The Reign of King Henry VI: The Exercise of Royal Authority, 1422–1461* (London, 1981), ch. 21: 'Cade's Rebellion, 1450' (pp. 610–65) is an excellent, and the best, account of the rebellion. I am very much indebted to it.

[9] Kent Archive Office DRb/Pa; *Davies Chron.*, 64.   [10] E101/330/7.

[11] *VCH* Sussex, ix. 201; D. Clarke and A. Stoyel, *Otford in Kent: A History* (Otford and District Historical Society, 1975), 70.

informal way by traders and fair-goers, but there must also have been a planned course of action behind the marshalling of the county. It is not known from whereabouts in Kent the rising was masterminded (or even, indeed, whether it was masterminded within Kent); but there can be some certainty that a good deal of reading and riding went on in the county that May. Nearly every rebel leader of the period had his scribe or secretary and a messenger service. Thomas Cheyne, the leader of the rising in eastern Kent in January 1450 had had a scrivener amongst his supporters and had sent messengers about the county.[12] The rebels of May 1450 had at least one secretary, Henry Wilkhous, a notary from Dartford.[13] William Petur, a notary from Strood, may well have been another such secretary. He was an associate of Wilkhous and would seek a pardon after the rebellion.[14] Such evidence as there is suggests that scribes and messengers mobilized the county through the usual system of muster: the arrangement of the subsequent pardons to the insurgents would be based upon the county muster units of parish and hundred. By this system parishioners were summoned to gather in their church or churchyard by the ringing of the church bells; the men of the parish would then move off to congregate under their parish and hundred constables at the traditional meeting-places—very often at crosses or on an open common—of their respective hundreds.[15] At this juncture, gathered in their ranks with men of the same hundred, it is possible that the rebels of May 1450 may have sworn oaths of allegiance binding themselves to one another in their shared cause. Certainly at a later point in the rising a visitor to the rebel army was obliged to swear to the captain and his followers as a guarantee that he would act on their behalf.[16]

Earlier in May Suffolk's body had been taken to St Martin's, Dover, where masses had been said for the duke. Now late in May the corpse was carried in procession through eastern and northern Kent via Canterbury and Rochester, stopping at Canterbury on 22 May where a

---

[12] KB29/81 Easter term m. 19; KB27/786 *rex* side, m. 2ᵛ.

[13] Virgoe, 'Ancient Indictments', 236, 255–6.

[14] *CPR*, 1446–52, 339. He had been involved in the theft of a church document together with Henry Wilkhous and the vicars of Dartford and Westerham in Dec. 1443, KB9/245, m. 89.

[15] For the parish as a convenient framework for corporate action, see R. H. Hilton, *A Medieval Society* (Cambridge, 1983), 149. The ringing of bells to gather parishioners is mentioned in an account of an array at Boston, Lincolnshire, in 1449, KB9/265, m. 83.

[16] *PL*, ii. 153–6.

service in the cathedral brought in 40s. in offerings. But outside
Canterbury the sight of the funeral cortège acted, contrary to all
intention, as a catalyst to revolt in the areas through which it passed.[17]
Already satirical verses were going about making mock lamentation of
Suffolk's death: 'For Jake Napes Sowle, *Placebo* and *Dirige*'.[18]

> Monkes, chanons, and prestis, with al ye clergy,
> Prayeth for hym that he may com to blys,
> And that nevar such Anothar come aftar this!
> His interfectures blessid mot they be.

In a parody of the service for the dead the duke's 'mourners' formed a
catalogue of those most despised men of his circle. It was a poem
which showed a clear knowledge of who precisely were the most
objectionable individuals at court. A clutch of bishops were named,
including Hereford, Chester (that is, Coventry and Lichfield), and
Salisbury, and also certain courtiers such as Daniel, Trevilian,
Hungerford, Say, Slegge, Hoo, Hampton, and Tuddenham. The
rhymer saw these men as having come to the end of their time of
influence,

> *In memoria eterna*, seyth Mayster Thomas Kent,
> now schall owre treson be cornicled for evar;
> *patar nostar*, seyd mayster Gerveyse,[19] we be all shent,
> for so fals A company in englond was nevar.

So if there was fear going about Kent that May there was also a strong

---

[17] W. G. Searle (ed.), *The Chronicle of John Stone Monk of Christ Church 1415–1471*
(Cambridge Antiquarian Society, 1902), 49. Library of the Dean and Chapter,
Canterbury, Sacrist Roll 37. Curiously, during excavations of the market-place at Dover
in 1810 near St Peter's church a chalk coffin was discovered containing only a head.
This was incorrectly thought to be that of Suffolk. C. R. Haines, *Dover Priory: A History
of the Priory of St Mary the Virgin, and St Martin of the New Work* (Cambridge, 1930), 286
n. 2.

[18] Printed in F. J. Furnivall (ed.), *Political, Religious, and Love Poems* (EETS, OS 15,
1866), 6–11; also in *Historical Memoranda in the Handwriting of John Stowe* (Camden
Soc., NS 28, 1880), 99–103. Both of these use a text from MS Lambeth 306, fo. 51.
All the following quotations are from this text. The same poem but in a shorter
version and with slight variants appears in BL MS Cott. Vesp. B xvi fo. 1 and is edited in
Political Poems, ii. 232–4 and in R. H. Robbins (ed.), *Historical Poems of the Fourteenth and
Fifteenth Centuries* (New York, 1959), 187–9. This latter version reads 'this pascall tyme'
for the Lambeth text's 'this Ioyfull tyme', so putting the dating of the poem firmly in the
month of May and certainly no later: since that year Easter fell on 5 Apr. making 3 May
already the fourth Sunday after Easter.

[19] Presumably John Gerveys of Bury St Edmunds, a gentleman of ill repute, outlawed
during the 1430s for his activities. *CPR*, 1436–41, 358–9, 389; he would be sought again
for arrest in the mid-1450s *CPR*, 1452–61, 225, 344.

sense of rejoicing in Suffolk's death and the possibility it brought of a change for the better in 'this Ioyfull tyme'.

Such political poetry or doggerel as remains from this period is now a close gauge of how events were popularly viewed there and then. In some cases this can be detected month by month, since these unliterary productions came out in quick succession, soon to be superseded, and so the progress of the duke of Suffolk can be charted from the Tower to his funeral service. Whether they were an appeal to popular opinion rather than its expression it is hard to say.[20] Certainly this was a recognized way of moving opinion. Much of the rising of 1431 was, as we have seen, built upon a wide-reaching campaign of billsticking through the southern Midlands and West Country.[21] It was a device used, too, more parochially in local differences. In 1424 Wiliam Aslak during the session of the county court at Norwich put about on gates around the city 'certeyns Englische billes rymed in partye' threatening Judge William Paston.[22] All that can be said with much certainty for 1450 is that such rhymes about Suffolk and his circle would be on doors and windows around the South-East for passers-by to read and that some men and women may have been singing or dancing to these refrains.[23]

The inflammatory preaching of friars, the popular itinerant preachers, had played its part in moving opinion before the outbreak of the Great Revolt of 1381 and other earlier risings. And it was to be heard again after 1450, as, for example, in August 1452 when a Dominican friar from Stamford allegedly excited his congregation in Boston to support the duke of York.[24] Whether such preaching affected the events of 1450 it is not easy to say. The royal pardon obtained by a Franciscan in May 1451 for his adherence to Cade, however, suggests that preaching may have played some part in stirring the insurgents of 1450.[25]

It seems likely that by early June insurgents were gathering themselves together at hundred meeting-places such as Somerden Green in Chiddingstone in the hundred of Somerden, Calehill Heath

---

[20] C. D. Ross, 'Rumour, Propaganda and Popular Opinion during the Wars of the Roses', in R. A. Griffiths (ed.), *Patronage, the Crown and the Provinces in Later Medieval England* (Gloucester, 1981), 16. In this quotation Ross is expressing the opinion of V. J. Scattergood, *Politics and Poetry in the Fifteenth Century* (London, 1971).

[21] *PPC*, 1430–6, 99–100. [22] *PL*, ii. 13.

[23] The suggestion of dancing is, for example, offered in a line such as 'But wonne most begynne the daunce, and alle come arowe'. *Political Poems*, ii. 224.

[24] KB9/65A, m. 1. [25] *CPR*, 1446–52, 426.

north-west of Ashford in the hundred of Calehill, and on Blackheath in the hundred of Blackheath in Kent's far north-western corner.[26] They had elected themselves a leader: Jack Cade was being designated as 'the Capitayne of the oste'.[27] Just who this Cade was is uncertain. The government believed him to be called John Mortimer which was one of the names he assumed—John Amendalle was another.[28] That they took the Mortimer connection seriously almost certainly means that during the course of the rising at least the king and his ministers chose to believe that the duke of York with his Mortimer ancestry (his mother, Anne, was heiress of the Mortimer earls of March) was involved in some way in the revolt. And although the rebels themselves would explicitly deny it, a rumour did go about during the rising that the insurgents were intending to do away with Henry's favourites and with the king himself so that they might replace him with the duke of York.[29] The king and his advisers believed Cade to have come from Ireland, the home of some Mortimer lands and the country in which York was then posted as the king's lieutenant. Chroniclers shared this notion.[30] Speculation led to various tales circulating about Cade. One suggestion was that he was a physician, John Aylemere, married to a squire's daughter from Tandridge, Surrey, remembered as decking himself out in scarlet.[31] There was another story that he was a sorcerer of the black arts, capable of summoning up the Devil in animal guise, and that during 1449, whilst living in Sussex in the household of Sir Thomas Dacre, he had murdered a pregnant woman and had had to flee the country. To top it all, he was also alleged to be an ex-partisan of the French.[32] At least a portion of this may have been true: between December 1448 and December 1449 a John Cade, yeoman, of Hurstpierpoint in mid-Sussex, did abjure the realm, the escheator for Surrey and Sussex taking 20s. from the profits of Cade's horse, gown,

---

[26] J. K. Wallenberg, *The Place-Names of Kent* (Uppsala, 1934), 1, 77, 387.

[27] HMC, v. (1876), 520 (Lydd Corporation Archives).

[28] It was the discovery shortly after 6 July that this was not his true name that led to his pardon being declared invalid. *Short English Chron.*, 68. Even subsequent to this discovery a writ of 12 July was still calling him 'a certain man calling himself John Mortymer'. E101/336/5. That he called himself John Amendalle is recorded in *Davies Chron.*, 64.

[29] The rebels themselves would protest their innocence of this slander, claiming it to be mere defamation to turn the king against them. HMC, viii. (1881), 267.

[30] Stow, *The Chronicles of England, from Brute unto this Present Yeare of Christ, 1580* (1580), 662; *Short English Chron.*, 66; *Davies Chron.*, 64; E403/779, m. 9.

[31] *EHL*, 365.

[32] *Literae Cantuarienses*, iii. (RS, 1889), 207–9; Stow, *The Chronicles of England*, 662–3.

and bed.[33] The manor of Hurstpierpoint was held at this date by Sir Thomas Dacre.[34] He was son of Lord Dacre of the North but he himself made his links among the most prominent families of the South-East. Indeed, his son-in-law was the very Sir Richard Fiennes, future first Lord Dacre of the South, whose uncle was the notorious Lord Saye and whose cousin's husband was William Crowmer, sheriff of Kent in 1450.[35] From this it seems reasonable to infer that if the Hurstpierpoint Cade was the rebel captain he received no backing or support from Sir Thomas after he had fled his employ in 1449.

Kent did not rise that late spring of 1450 with one accord. When on 8 June Cade advanced on the western suburbs of Canterbury, with what one citizen there at the time estimated to be a host of four thousand men, they waited three hours in the great field which then existed between St Michael's Harbledown and St Dunstan's in the hope of some positive response from the city. Finally they gave up and took the road to London.[36] Warily towns near the coast, Lydd, Rye, and Romney, sent out lookouts on horseback to Ashford and Appleford to report back on the progress of the captain and his army.[37] Cade was sending out written appeals for support, but places such as these held back from giving him their whole-hearted backing, although quite possibly in these three mentioned instances the reason may have been the quite legitimate one of fear of French attack. After all, Winchelsea not far away on the Sussex coast had been attacked by the French the previous year.[38]

Insurgents from different parts of Kent were moving in separate groups. On the day that men from eastern Kent were gathered outside Canterbury, men from districts nearer London had already reached Middlesex. At Westminster John Sawyer, a fruiterer alias yeoman from St Mary Cray in north-western Kent, led a gang in an attack on a royal servant, Thomas Walter, and carried him off hostage to Staines and

---

[33] E136/212/11, m. 7.

[34] *VCH Sussex*, vii. 175. Inexplicably he is described as Thomas Dacre of Bailey Park, Heathfield, by W. D. Cooper, in 'Participation of Sussex in Cade's Rising, 1450', *Sussex Archaeological Collections*, 18 (1866), 18. I find no other reference to support this. *VCH Sussex*, i. 513 apparently follows Cooper.

[35] *CPR*, 1452–61, 460; Griffiths, *Henry VI*, 339–40.

[36] W. G. Searle (ed.), *The Chronicle of John Stone Monk of Christ Church 1415–1471* (Cambridge Antiquarian Society, 1902), 49.

[37] HMC, v. (1876), 520 (Lydd Corporation Archives); ibid. 490 (Rye Corporation Archives); ibid. 543 (New Romney Corporation Archives).

[38] Ibid. 520; W. D. Cooper, 'Notices of Winchelsea in and after the Fifteenth Century', *Sussex Archaeological Collections*, 8 (1856), 207.

then through the woods and villages of Middlesex for the next six days until he paid a ransom of £10.[39] During this time the whole county must have been buzzing with rumours about the size of Cade's advancing army.

The grievances and fears behind the uprising were drawn up into written bills of complaint at varying stages of the revolt: three different petitions from the rising remain today. The bill with the most strongly Kentish concerns may date from the earliest stages of events, perhaps circulating during May, its purpose being to galvanize the men of Kent into action. Not only were the compilers of this bill disturbed about the rumour that Kent should be destroyed by royal power and made into a wild forest, but they wanted something done about the inconvenience and nuisance caused to the tax collectors in Kent by the requirement that they sue out writs of exemption for the barons of the Cinque Ports (the Cinque Ports having to provide properly manned vessels were exempt from subsidies but the people of Kent thought that the ports should claim such exemption at their own cost). Another issue was the way in which the officials of the court of Dover outstepped their jurisdiction; others, the rigging of the elections of the knights of the shire in Kent and the need for the holding of the sessions of the peace in two separate ends of the county so as to save the inordinately long journeys some men were obliged at present to make.[40] Alongside these county issues they were complaining that the king should restore to himself the Crown revenues he had granted away, that his natural counsellors among the aristocracy should be restored to their proper ascendancy in the king's council, and that inquiry should be made throughout the land to find out who the traitors were who caused the French possessions to be lost so that they might be punished without pardon. The remaining complaints concerned the extortions and grave abuses of office of royal household men and their colleagues holding positions in the county administration. Such grievances were comprehensive enough in scope to affect at some level every man and woman in the county.

News of serious trouble in Kent was sent up to Leicester where parliament was in session. On 6 June parliament was adjourned, the Commons having granted a subsidy on income in a much delayed response to the Crown's financial needs.[41] On the day of the adjournment the duke of Buckingham and the earls of Oxford, Devon,

---

[39] KB27/762 *rex* side, m. 8ᵛ.   [40] Stow, *The Chronicles of England*, 656.
[41] Virgoe, 'The Parliamentary Subsidy of 1450', *BIHR* 55 (1982), 125.

and Arundel were commissioned by the king to go 'against the traitors and rebels in Kent and to punish and arrest the same'.[42] Soon afterwards the king himself set off southwards for London and four days later was in Buckinghamshire at Newport Pagnell where he strengthened the force moving against the rebels by commissioning Viscount Beaumont and Lords Lovel, Scales, Rivers, and Dudley to share in the task.[43]

This commission came too late to nip the rising in the bud. Kentishmen were already well on the road to London and by 11 June they were encamped on Blackheath, a fine natural vantage-point south of the river looking down at the capital.[44] There they secured their site with stakes and ditches and Cade sent a written order to the Italian merchants in London to supply him with certain specified quantities of arms and money; if they failed him in this, he added, they would forfeit their heads.[45] Whether rebels from eastern Surrey and Sussex were here at this encampment it is not possible to say.[46]

Londoners were unhappily placed during these developments of the second week of June. They had as much to fear from the royalist nobles and their armed retainers as from the rebels marching upon them from the south.[47] The Common Council of the city took various precautions: the gates of the city were to be fortified and to be guarded twenty-four hours a day; the armed retainers of the nobles were to be admitted to the city only on specific errands and were not to be quartered there; and armourers were not to sell their goods outside the city.[48] The reason for this last injunction was obvious, and indeed two days after it on 10 June the Court of Aldermen heard that men had

---

[42] *CPR*, 1446–52, 385. [43] Ibid. 385.

[44] Gough, 153; *Benet's Chron.*, 198; *Bale's Chron.*, 129 gives the date of the assembling on Blackheath as 12 June.

[45] *Gregory's Chron.*, 190; Gough, 153; *Bale's Chron.*, 129–30; *Great Chron.*, 181. For the written command from Cade to the Italians, see Stow, *The Chronicles of England*, 653.

[46] This was the opinion of the Tudor historian, Hall, whose work at times includes independent material absent in other chronicles and apparently furnished by oral tradition. E. Hall, *The Union of the two noble and illustre fameilies of Lancastre and Yorke* (1550), fo. 77ᵛ.

[47] From Stafford over 70 yeomen were on their way to London to join the duke of Buckingham. K. B. McFarlane, 'The Wars of the Roses', *Proceedings of the British Academy*, 50 (1964), 91; C. Rawcliffe, *The Staffords, Earls of Stafford and Dukes of Buckingham, 1394–1521* (Cambridge, 1978), 47, 77.

[48] C. Barron, 'The Government of London and its Relations with the Crown, 1400–1450', Ph.D. thesis (London, 1970), 484–5. Ch. 9 of Dr Barron's thesis ('London and the Revolt of Jack Cade in 1450', 479–540), is such a comprehensive account of events that I have used it extensively for this part of the story.

been seen travelling by barge down river towards Gravesend with bundles of arms, no doubt to supply the insurgents.[49] Londoners could also fear the outbreak of mob violence within their own walls. As far as is known the civic community was not troubled by extreme divisions within itself but hatred of Suffolk and what he represented had been as widespread here as elsewhere.

The first sign of the king's return to the vicinity of London was the arrival of the duke of Buckingham and Lord Rivers with a large armed company, and by 13 June Henry was staying at St John's Priory, Clerkenwell.[50] This was the day on which the Court of Aldermen appointed a London merchant and a common councilman to act as captains of two barges which the city had provided in order to make sure that food supplies got through to London and also to defend the city by water against the rebels and their craft.[51] On 15 June the king sent messengers over the river to Blackheath to order the Kentishmen to disband. Later the same day the earl of Northumberland, Lord Scales, and Lord Lisle rode over to the heath with an armed company, perhaps with the idea of forcibly dispersing the Kentishmen. It may well be that seeing the size of the rebel camp they decided not to act without reinforcements to their numbers. The king had thought to go himself the following day accompanied by magnates and an armed force to see the rebels off (perhaps he had in mind the stories of how the young Richard II had courageously ridden out to meet the rebellious peasantry in 1381), but he was persuaded to adopt another plan. Instead, a prestigious delegation was sent, several of whose major members could be regarded as interested parties to the well-being of the county of Kent: the archbishops of Canterbury and York, the duke of Buckingham, the bishop of Winchester, and Viscount Beaumont. Archbishop Stafford was the county's largest landowner; Cardinal Kemp, himself born at Wye in Kent, was a former bishop of Rochester, of Chichester, and of London; Buckingham was another important landowner in Kent; the bishop of Winchester came from a near neighbouring diocese, and Viscount Beaumont was the constable of England.[52] Their mission, apparently, was to persuade Cade of the wisdom of withdrawing all his men from the heath and returning home

[49] C. Barron, 485.

[50] *Bale's Chron.*, 129; Stevenson, ii. pt. ii. 767; *Benet's Chron.*, 198; *EHL*, 371–2; *Great Chron.*, 181, to the contrary, says that the king lodged in the Tower.

[51] Barron, 'The Government of London and its Relations with the Crown', 486.

[52] *Bale's Chron.*, 129–30; *Gregory's Chron.*, 190; *Benet's Chron.*, 198–9; *English Chron.*, 65; Griffiths, *Henry VI*, 611.

with a royal pardon. In this they failed, but they were able to discover more about the insurgents' real motives for their action, and they returned to the king with a bill of petition from them.

The petition which the royal delegation took away may well have been that version of the rebels' petitions which is printed as Appendix A (iii), below—the shortest of the three versions and that carrying the greatest urgency.[53] The items of this petition appear originally to have been incorporated in an earlier and longer version dated 4 June which, in the manner of a document looking to make converts, offered explanation, defence, and assurances about the rebels' behaviour and future conduct.[54] That longer petition appears to have been reworked into two separate petitions, so that the king was presented not with lengthy apologetics but a short list of demands. The direct tone of the petition—here Henry, just once, was addressed as 'you' instead of being alluded to in the standard third person—reinforces the probability that this was the document sent to the king. First the captain assured Henry of his concern for his welfare and the welfare of all his true lords spiritual and temporal, and then went on to suggest that Henry take back all his demesnes so that he might reign like a 'Kyng Riall'. The king's true commons also asked that he might rid himself of all the false progeny and affinity of the duke of Suffolk 'the whiche ben opynly knowyn traitours' and that he should punish them. In their place he should bring the dukes of York, Exeter, Buckingham, and Norfolk. The commons desired, too, the punishment of the murderers of the duke of Gloucester and of those who had contrived and imagined the deaths of the duke of Exeter, of the bishop of Winchester, the duke of Somerset, and the duke of Warwick (the suggestion here that these last four deaths might have been sought after is extraordinary). The same traitors who perpetrated these crimes were also responsible for the loss of France, that is to say, Normandy, Gascony, Guienne, Anjou, and Maine. The commons of Kent here again made mention of their particular grievance of the abuse by county officials of the writs sealed under the green wax of the exchequer. And the document ended with three other Kentish grievances: purveyance, the troublesome statute of labourers, and

---

[53] *EHL*, 360–2; a sixteenth-century copy of this version appears in Stow, *The Chronicles of England*, 656–8.

[54] This longer document exists only in a sixteenth-century copy, Lambeth MS 306, printed in *Three Fifteenth-Century Chronicles*, ed. J. Gairdner (Camden Soc., NS 28, 1880), 94–9.

Kent's 'grete extorcioners', named here as Slegge, Crowmer, Isle, and Est.

Henry's response was to go in force against the Kentishmen. On the morning of Thursday 18 June he arrived at Blackheath from Clerkenwell with an impressive array of military strength which included, besides numerous lords and their retainers, carts of guns for firing lead and stone.[55] He found the heath empty. Cade and his men, who had had no positive response to their petition and who had perhaps heard word of the king's intention to go against them with arms, had gone away in the darkness of the previous night.[56] There was little point in the king and his large force chasing a disbanding party of rebels, so as the king moved down to Greenwich a smaller posse was sent into Kent to see them off led by Sir Humphrey and William Stafford. As it happened Sir Humphrey was no friend of Suffolk himself, having suffered from his associates.[57] It would appear that they took on this task too lightly and did not expect any offensive from this retreating army, because when later that same day they encountered some of the rebels near Sevenoaks (perhaps Cade's men had been making for Lord Saye's seat at Knole) both the Staffords and some forty of their men were killed in an ensuing fight.[58]

On the same day, 18 June, as jurors would allege the following autumn, Lords Dudley and Rivers, Sir Thomas Stanley, and Thomas Daniel rode into north-western Kent with a force said to number over two thousand, alluded to later by local Kentishmen as 'the Chesscher men'.[59] They first headed to the south of the main Deptford–Dartford road to Foots Cray and then to St Mary Cray where they stole eighteen horses; then they turned south down the Darent valley in the general direction of Sevenoaks, stopping at Eynsford to beat up badly and rob at least one individual and going a few more miles further south to the archbishop of Canterbury's park at Otford where they took sixteen

---

[55] E28/80/65 giving the date as 20 June, which looks like a slip. In 1459 the king granted a pardon for debt to a William Stanley of Hooton, Cheshire, esq., 'who took the field with the king against the traitor, Cade of Kent', *CPR*, 1452–61, 570.

[56] *Bale's Chron.*, 130–1; Gough, 154; *Benet's Chron.*, 199; *Gregory's Chron.*, 191; *Short English Chron.*, 67; *PPC*, 1443–61, 94.

[57] Through his court connections with Suffolk's circle Sir Robert Harcourt, who had slain Sir Humphrey's son, was able to get the king to stay the proceedings which had been initiated against him for this murder. B. Wolffe, *Henry VI* (London, 1981), 120–1. Following upon Suffolk's exile the violence of the Harcourt–Stafford feud had escalated. R. L. Storey, *The End of the House of Lancaster* (London, 1966), 57–8.

[58] *Benet's Chron.*, p. 199; *Short English Chron.*, 67; *Gregory's Chron.*, 191; *Bale's Chron.*, 131; *Davies Chron.*, 66; Gough, 154.   [59] C1/19/501.

horses. Not much further along their route they came to Chipstead where they stole silver spoons and linen sheets from one man, merchandise of saffron, pepper, and spices from another, and cash from them both.[60] The following day they were at Sevenoaks robbing and intimidating there, and on 20 June at Tonbridge.[61] This episode with its rapacious violence throws extraordinary light on the king's adherents. Their intention was apparently mere indiscriminate terrorization. After the events of these few days the aspect of the rising changed. They appear to have given a new resolve to the men of Kent and emboldened others to rally to them. It may well have been at this point that the men of Essex, East Surrey, and East Sussex began to join the rising.[62]

Another even more important development of these few days was that on Friday 19 June some of the retainers of the king and of his lords quartered at Blackheath began to agree among themselves that Cade had a genuine cause, and to threaten that unless the king did execution upon the 'traitors' about him they themselves would go over to Cade's side. They named among these traitors Lord Saye, the bishop of Salisbury, Lord Dudley, the abbot of Gloucester, Thomas Daniel, and John Trevilian. This was the grim news that the duke of Buckingham took to the king at Greenwich.[63] Clearly he could not rely on the assembled forces to support him. Henry was left with little choice: he had Henry Holand detain James Fiennes, Lord Saye, the lord treasurer and until recently the king's chamberlain, and place him in the Tower, probably privately viewing this ostensibly concessionary gesture as a measure to preserve his minister. Moreover he made proclamation that all traitors should be taken wherever they might be found. So it was as well for Thomas Daniel that he was away from the capital in Kent in the company of an armed troop. Yet the king was not abandoning his friends; on 20 June he went over the river from Greenwich back to Westminster and that night summoned Saye in secret from his confinement. His intention was in all likelihood to provide him with some means of escape, but Henry Holand as

---

[60] Virgoe, 'Ancient Indictments', 223, 232, 241, 241–2, 243; KB27/765 *rex* side, m. 26; KB9/226, m. 84; Dudley was pardoned for all this a couple of years later.

[61] Virgoe, 'Ancient Indictments', 224–5, 232.

[62] E. Hall, *The Union of the Two Noble and Illustre Famelies of Lancastre and Yorke* (1550), fo. 77ᵛ.

[63] *Short English Chron.*, 67; *Bale's Chron.*, 131–2; Gough, 154; *Benet's Chron.*, 199; *Brut*, 517; *Great Chron.*, 182.

constable of the Tower would not co-operate with the king and refused to release his prisoner.[64]

The events of the last few days were revealing to Henry uncertain loyalties in unexpected places, and by 23 June the decision appears to have been taken that he should leave London again.[65] It had been decided, much to the discomfiture of the mayor and aldermen, to garrison the Tower well, leave it in the keeping of Lord Scales, and to let the city look to its own devices in the event of any trouble from insurgents.[66] Meanwhile as Henry was retreating from his capital, so across the Channel the English surrendered possession of Caen on 24 June, continuing a line of defeats which all spectators could see had not much longer to run. The king left London on 25 June, going first to Berkhamsted castle in Hertfordshire and from there to Kenilworth in Warwickshire, a hundred miles or so from London, the safest hereditary castle of his family.[67] With him went courtiers, lords, justices, and government personnel. This action naturally aroused considerable dismay and rancour amongst the citizens of London: the atmosphere in the capital was one of great apprehension.[68] In such circumstances they had every reason to fear that the men of Kent would reassemble and take the road back to London. This was just what occurred. On 27 June the Common Council was sending out spies to discover which route Cade was taking, and these returned to report that he was coming straight towards the city. London Bridge, the only bridge crossing of the Thames to the city, and therefore a main route for traffic and trade, was drawn up. It was not to resume its normal operation until the second half of July.[69]

Troubles were arising in other parts of the south of England. On 29 June William Aiscough, bishop of Salisbury, was murdered by rebels at Edington in Wiltshire as he fled London. It was probably on this day that Cade and his men began arriving back on Blackheath.[70] They came as a military force: later that summer a royal writ to the

---

[64] *Benet's Chron.*, 199.   [65] Griffiths, *Henry VI*, 613.

[66] On 30 June he had ordered his treasurer, now Lord Beauchamp, to release £100 to pay for all provisions necessary for the safeguarding of the Tower of London. E404/66, m. 186.

[67] *Short English Chron.*, 67; Gough, 154; *Benet's Chron.*, 199; *Brut*, 518.

[68] It was the custom of the Mercers' Company to hold a feast on 25 June, but that year festivities were felt to be out of order and the Mercers merely attended to business. Barron, 'The Government of London and its Relations with the Crown', 493.

[69] There were no Bridge house receipts from 28 June until 18 July. Ibid. 499.

[70] There is some difference of opinion amongst chroniclers over which day the rebels returned to the heath. *Benet's Chron.*, 199, gives 29 June, as does *Great Chron.*, 182.

exchequer would allude to Cade as having made insurrection 'with gret Power of Men of Armes and Archiers Arraised'.[71] They came, at least some of them, on horseback.[72] Cade may have been the captain in chief of this host, but he created other captains to order the ranks of his men. One such under-captain may have been Michael Skellys, a leech or treacler from Scarborough—that is, if we are to believe him when in 1453 at Norwich, arrested and brought before an alderman and a JP, he boasted that he had been an under-captain to John Cade on Blackheath.[73] Of Cade he claimed, 'Y was of his counsell and knewe his secretnes'. If this was the case, Cade tolerated men of dubious reputation among his henchmen. In 1447 Skellys had been imprisoned in Winchester gaol on charges of thefts committed at Beverley in Yorkshire the previous year.[74]

We have a vivid picture of a visit made to the rebel army recorded in a letter written in 1465 to John Paston, executor of Sir John Fastolf's will, by Fastolf's former servant John Payn in which Payn recalls what was a very perilous escapade made at his master's instruction. Payn had been told to take a man and two of Fastolf's best horses to go to the commons and obtain a copy of their articles of petition.[75] His report conveys the impression of a force marshalled and disciplined in military manner, but edgy and aggressive. Straight away upon his arrival there he was apprehended in a manner such as to make him decide to dismiss his companion and both their horses for their better safety. As an unknown intruder he was led before Cade the captain of the host. When it was spotted that he was one of Fastolf's men he was taken to the four parts of the field led by a herald dressed in the duke of Exeter's livery (who appears to have been pressed into the rebels' service) and announced as a spy, out to assess their manpower and weaponry. The leaders of the host were very hostile to Fastolf whom they regarded—as they announced to the rebel army by means of the herald—as having 'mynnysshed all the garrisons of Normaundy, and Manns, and Mayn, the whech was the cause of the lesyng of all the Kyngs tytyll and ryght of an herytaunce that he had by yonde see'.[76] Moreover, the herald broadcast that Fastolf had in his house in

Gough, 154 gives 30 June, as does *Bale's Chron.*, 132, if one reads 'the Satirday folowyng' as 27 June; *Gregory's Chron.*, 191 gives the date as 1 July.

[71] T. Rymer (ed.), *Foedera, conventiones, literae* ... (1704–35), xi. 275.
[72] E28/80/73.   [73] KB27/778 *rex* side, m. 26.
[74] KB9/257, m. 70; KB9/997, m. 31.   [75] *PL*, ii. 153–6.
[76] Ibid. 154.

Southwark old soldiers out of Normandy armed at the ready to attack the rebel host if it should enter Southwark. Payn, as Fastolf's servant, was, in the light of his connection, declared a traitor. He would have been executed there and then had not Robert Poynings, sword-bearer and carver to Cade, with other of Payn's friends, argued against it.

The petition which Payn took away with him is very likely to have been the same copy as that which still exists among the manuscripts of Magdalen College, Oxford.[77] Although apparently originally drawn up as part of a lengthy petition dated 4 June which incorporated the demands which were redrafted as the short petition offered to the king, it became a manifesto in its own right, of which more copies remain than of any other rebel document. Couched in the language of petitioners and of reasonable, responsible men, not rebels, this document sought to attract support from the whole of the South-East, perhaps particularly from its upper strata. Its concerns were with the relationship of the king to his commons and the manner in which this relationship had been destroyed by the circle of 'false traytours': traitors who should have suffered from the recent act of resumption but had not done so; who had prevented access to the king's presence except by the use of bribes; and who had corrupted the law to their own profit, falsely declaring innocent men traitors just in order to take their forfeited goods. Couldn't the king see how he was suffering from this false counsel?

ffor his lordez ern lost, his marchundize is lost, his comyns destroyed, the see is lost, ffraunse his lost, hymself so pore that he may not [pay] for his mete nor drynk; he oweth more than evur dyd kynge in Inglond.[78]

It may have been during this second encampment on the heath that the town of Lydd on the Kent coast sent an entire porpoise up to Cade. This was a highly complimentary gesture. Porpoise—this one almost the value of a brace of swans—was the food of aristocrats, something which in certain parts of the country lords chose to reserve to themselves among their demesne possessions.[79] Later in the 1450s Rye would present Lord Fauconberg with porpoise, although he was apportioned only a piece of this delicacy.[80]

In London further precautions were being taken against the host's

---

[77] Magdalen College, Oxford, MS Misc. 306, printed in HMC, viii. (1881), 266–7.
[78] Ibid. 267.
[79] HMC, v. (1876), 520; ibid. 521 (for price of swans); R. R. Davies, *Lordship and Society in the March of Wales, 1282–1400* (Oxford, 1978), 107.
[80] HMC, v. (1876), 491.

imminent attempt at entry. Four citizens were chosen in every ward to help their aldermen. These aldermen were now empowered to inflict summary punishment upon anyone who did not do their share in the vigil rota, and it was arranged that men from wards in the inner part of the city should help relieve those outer wards which were burdened with the responsibility of guarding the city gates.[81]

On 1 or 2 July, as the duke of Somerset was taking his leave of Normandy and setting sail for Calais, Cade led his men down into closer proximity to the city and into more congenial accommodation at Southwark. There they took up lodgings in inns and hostelries and quite possibly in private houses too.[82] Cade took up his lodgings in the tavern of the White Hart.[83] The mayor was refusing to permit him or any of his men into London, and not without reason, for the rebels had set about looting in Southwark.[84] Fastolf and his men, warned by Payn of the host's vehement opinions, had fled to the Tower leaving Payn in Southwark to guard his master's property. Payn, despite managing to prevent the rebels from burning down Fastolf's house, was unable to save his own belongings: the brigandine and gown he was wearing were taken from his back and in his lodging his chest was ransacked of its valuables.[85]

It was probably after the revolt of the retainers in London on 19 June, which had led to the arrest of Lord Saye, and amongst growing signs of government inability to handle the situation, that Cade had sent messengers into Essex to widen the area of his support. On Friday 26 June, the day after the king had retreated from London, there had come the first show of response from Colchester with a rising in the town, orchestrated by a certain John Gibbes, gentleman, sent down by Cade for that purpose—or so it would be alleged a couple of years later in 1453.[86] Gibbes, it would be said, had remained in the town for

---

[81] Barron, 'The Government of London and its Relations with the Crown', 500–1.

[82] *Benet's Chron.*, 200; *Gregory's Chron.*, 191; *Bale's Chron.*, 132; Gough, 154. That private houses were billeted is hinted at by the fact that amongst the 62 men known to be from Southwark who obtained a royal pardon when the revolt was over, 2 yeomen and 2 husbandmen took the unusual step of including their wives' names alongside their own, and, moreover, by the fact that two widows and a wife of the town had pardons made out in their own names, among the very few women to do so. *CPR, 1446–52*, 351, 352, 366, 370. There is also a list of names on the pardon of no given location which includes the names of 105 women and which could well be from Southwark. Ibid. 357–8.

[83] *Gregory's Chron.*, 191; *Davies Chron.*, 66; *PL*, ii. 155.

[84] Gough, 154–5; *Great Chron.*, 183; *Benet's Chron.*, 200.

[85] *PL*, ii. 153–6.

[86] KB9/271, m. 46; /26/1, m. 1; /273, m. 86; KB27/770 *rex* side, m. 31'; /774 *rex* side, m. 9.

several days, doubtless arguing the rebels' cause to the inhabitants and infecting them with his enthusiasm. Since the second uprising at Colchester was on 1 July, five days after the initial demonstration, it seems possible that Gibbes was instructed to wait until Cade's army had reached the southern outskirts of London before setting off.[87] There were, too, other Essex men already gathered on the eastern outskirts of London at Mile End. For villages throughout southern and central Essex were now afoot: this was the alarming news which John Hillesdon, a yeoman of the Crown, had taken to the king at Berkhamsted before Henry had left there on 1 July for Kenilworth, and which had caused the king to employ him as a spy to live in London and keep an eye on what was going on in Essex.[88] So, as Cade had entered Southwark, Essex men had been coming into the eastern suburbs of London and pitching camp on the field at Mile End.[89] It would be these Essex men, from parishes such as East Ham, Barking, Dagenham, and Brentwood, similarly roused by Cade's lieutenants,[90] whom the Colchester group set out to join.[91] Numbers snowballed as the body of Essex insurgents passed through settlements on the main road to London. On 2 July they were joined by men from the parish of St Mary Matfelon outside Aldgate, one of the cloth-manufacturing districts of London and a place of somewhat insalubrious reputation.[92]

In the mean time south of the city walls Cade was finding difficulties in keeping order among so many men and holding to the ostensible purpose of the rising—that of petition and reform. On 30 June he had had one of his under-captains, Parys, executed at Blackheath for disciplinary reasons.[93] To emphasize that theirs was a demonstration of loyal subjects Cade proclaimed his ordinances in the name of the king.[94] Yet even on the very day on which he was executing Parys for breaking one of these ordinances some of his followers were down in Southwark on the lookout for plunder. Ralph Harries, a London skinner, with a gang of some forty others attacked and took captive a man there whom they accused of being a servant of Lord Saye and

---

[87] KB9/26, mm. 16, 17; /279, mm. 5, 92; KB27/778 *rex* side, mm. 8, 43. *London Chrons.*, 160.   [88] E404/67/170.
[89] Gough, 155; *Benet's Chron.*, 200 says that 6,000 Essex men went to Mile End; Stow, *The Chronicles of England* (1580), 659; *Great Chron.*, 183.
[90] *Bale's Chron.*, 132 describes them as 'a great ffelawship out of Essex ordeined by the seid capitaigne'.   [91] *CPR*, 1446–52, 350, 343, 355.
[92] KB9/270A, m. 45; Barron, 'The Government of London and its Relations with the Crown', 506; weavers from this parish are mentioned, for example, in KB9/958, mm. 27, 28; /249, m. 52; /996, m. 49; /259, m. 4; and a fuller in /996, m. 9.
[93] Gough, 154 n. 2; *Great Chron.*, 182.   [94] *Great Chron.*, 182.

therefore regarded as necessarily a traitor.[95] They held him to ransom for a sizeable £20. On the same day Lawrence Hope, a yeoman from Molasshe in Kent, and another gang robbed a Southwark man (of no obvious significance) of two horses worth 100s. and a bag of money.[96]

On 3 July with London almost in a state of siege, flanked to the south by Cade's army in Southwark and to the east by his followers recently arrived out of Essex, a county now engendering its own captains, a commission of oyer and terminer got under way at the Guildhall.[97] The commission had been appointed by Henry on 1 July to examine all treasons, felonies, and insurrections in London and the suburbs and was presumably intended by him to be a conciliatory gesture to help the authorities left with the task of keeping order in the city.[98] It turned out to be rather different in nature than that, however, since in the afternoon of that same day on which proceedings began something went amiss with the city defences on the bridge. After some fighting, Cade cut the ropes of the drawbridge on the bridge's southern end so that it might not be drawn up again and accepted the keys of the gate which blocked his path beyond the drawbridge, having first threatened to fire the whole bridge (which would have meant the city too). He was then free to lead his men across into the city.[99] At St Magnus's church and at Leadenhall he proclaimed that the punishment for anyone found robbing in the city would be death.[100] Cade had had problems disciplining his followers earlier, as has been seen, but now the success of having forced their way into the city intoxicated them, and they entered, as one London chronicler later observed, as men half out of their wits.[101] They turned upon the house of alderman Malpas, the 'Green Gate' in Lime Street,[102] and despoiled it, carrying

---

[95] KB9/226, m. 67; regarding Harries, see Barron, 'The Government of London and its Relations with the Crown', 501.

[96] KB9/275, m. 136. Hope is not explicitly named as a follower of Cade, as Harries is, but the probability that he was is very strong.

[97] William Tyrell, junior, of Rawreth was later to be indicted, and acquitted, on the charge of having set himself up to be a captain in Essex and of having made an uprising at Stratford Langthorn on the main London to Colchester road on 3 July 1450. KB9/273, m. 26; KB27/772 *rex* side, m. 31ᵛ.

[98] *CPR*, 1446–52, 388; Barron, 'The Government of London and its Relations with the Crown', 504–5.

[99] *Great Chron.*, 183; *Gregory's Chron.*, 191; W. G. Searle (ed.), *Chronicle of John Stone Monk of Christ Church, Canterbury* (Cambridge Antiquarian Society, 1902), 50; Barron, 'The Government of London and its Relations with the Crown', 510–11.

[100] *Bale's Chron.*, 133; *Great Chron.*, 184; Gough, 155.

[101] *Gregory's Chron.*, 191.

[102] Barron, 'The Government of London and its Relations with the Crown', 519.

off quantities of valuables, household goods, and merchandise such as woollen cloth, tin, wood, madder, and alum.[103] The name is known of at least one of these looters, a Thomas Walker, a soldier who had recently come out of Normandy. He came out on to the street his arms full of cloth and three silver dishes only to have them stolen in turn from the woman to whom he gave them for safe keeping.[104] Philip Malpas was an unpopular figure. He had been at one time sheriff and MP for London, but on 26 June he had been demoted from his office as alderman of Lime Street ward, a position he held by virtue of a royal command which had overridden the Court of Aldermen's rejection of him.[105]

Cade retired over the bridge back to his lodgings for the night, but in the morning of Saturday, 4 July he was in the city again. Through the influence of his presence and that of his followers the Guildhall sessions turned into a commission to indict and condemn traitors and extortioners. Some of the eleven judges named in the commission of 1 July had made themselves scarce upon the entry of the rebel army, but Thomas, Lord Scales, Thomas Charlton the mayor, and six other justices remained to preside over the proceedings. Amongst those indicted in their absence were Thomas Kent, clerk to the Council, under-constable of England, and also acting keeper of the privy seal after Moleyns's death until 1 February, when Andrew Holes took over.[106] Another was Edward Grimston, treasurer of the chamber and keeper of the king's jewels. Both of these men were accused of having plotted in London in the parish of St Sepulchre on 20 July 1447 to overthrow the king and replace him by John, son of the duke of Suffolk, to whom they had planned to marry Margaret, daughter of the duke of Somerset. This was the repetition of a charge which had been levelled against the duke of Suffolk.[107] Mention was also made in the indictments of the way in which the duke of Suffolk and 'several other enemies and traitors of the king' had accepted from the king goods, castles, lordships, manors, and other commodities pertaining to the Crown and had sought to expel Henry from his realm of England and France. Others indicted at this hearing, and they may have totalled up to ten persons, were John Say, John Trevilian, and Thomas Daniel, the notorious courtiers described in Chapter 2.[108] These men were

[103] *Gregory's Chron.*, 191–2; *Bale's Chron.*, 133.   [104] C1/19/30.
[105] Griffiths, *Henry VI*, 626.   [106] E28/80/19, 21.
[107] KB9/265, mm. 120, 121, 144, 145.
[108] Barron, 'The Government of London and its Relations with the Crown', 515.

not on hand to receive their allotted punishment, but Lord Saye, the treasurer, was. He was brought out of the Tower, where Henry had sent him fifteen days previously (perhaps Lord Scales felt unequal to the outcry of the mob if he failed to release his prisoner), and taken to the Guildhall. There he was charged with various treasons including being party to the death of the duke of Gloucester. Then he was taken to the Standard in the Cheap and beheaded.[109] Saye met with this act of vengeance not merely as a treasurer to a corrupt and incompetent regime and as one of Suffolk's allies, but also as a previous sheriff of Kent and constable of Dover castle. Also to be executed that day was, another figure of public odium among the men of Kent: William Crowmer, sheriff of Kent that year and son-in-law to Lord Saye. During the morning, whilst the session was in progress at the Guildhall, Cade had ridden at the head of his foot army across the bridge from Southwark bedecked in improvised regalia, stripped from one of the slain Staffords, of gilt spurs and a blue velvet coat furred with sable, a drawn sword in his hand and another sword borne before him like an aristocrat. He progressed to St Paul's before returning to Southwark.[110]

In the afternoon Cade again rode into the city, drank at a tavern in the Cheap, then moved on towards the east of the city, first collecting Crowmer from the Fleet prison. How Crowmer found himself there is unknown. He was taken outside the city walls to the men at Mile End where Cade had him beheaded.[111] On his return into London Cade waited at the Standard in the Cheap where Lord Saye was brought from the Guildhall and there saw him not only beheaded but despoiled and publicly degraded by having his naked corpse dragged by a horse through the streets.[112]

Hawarden, a common thief and murderer who had lived for a long while in the shelter of the sanctuary of St Martin le Grand, also fell victim to this general purging and was beheaded that day.[113] Another victim was William Bailly who was executed along with Crowmer at Mile End, presumably as a measure to satisfy the Essex followers.[114]

[109] *Gregory's Chron.*, 192–3; *Great Chron.*, 184.
[110] *Bale's Chron.*, 133; *Davies Chron.*, 66.
[111] At an inquest held on 8 Feb. 1451 before the sheriffs of London a jury declared that Crowmer died on 3 July 1450, and not on 4 July, as most chroniclers infer. E199/20/16 Middlesex and London.
[112] *Bale's Chron.*, 133; Gough, 156; *Benet's Chron.*, 200–1.
[113] *Benet's Chron.*, 201; *Gregory's Chron.*, 193.
[114] *Bale's Chron.*, 133; Gough, 155.

Who he was is unknown, but he was evidently of significance to the men gathered at Mile End. This was the case with the man executed the following day under Cade's auspices. There had been looting and violence in Colchester before the rebels took the road to Mile End. Their main victim had been Thomas Mayn, servant of John Hampton, an unpopular royal official who since 1447 had enjoyed the profits of the office of constable of Colchester castle.[115] The rebels had stolen goods and written deeds from Hampton and carried Mayn off to their leader in Southwark where Cade now, on Sunday, 5 July, gave his assent to Mayn's execution.[116]

Alongside these killings in London a deal of further looting went on. A certain John Gest, a citizen and gentleman of London, whom Cade regarded as a traitor and extortioner, entertained Cade to a meal, doubtless in the hope of averting Malpas's fate, but he too was plundered.[117] At the house of John Judde a gang of Cade's men threatened his wife that unless she paid them a ransom 'they should leave no peny worth good in the house', so she was forced to a fine in order that her house should not be despoiled. Judde was picked on as an act of revenge because he and Richard Horne had been sent out of London with barges to ensure the city's food supply and defence.[118] Main mover behind the attacks on Judde and Horne was a Lawrence Stockwood, a London salter, who called them traitors and incited others to do the same and declared that they should hang. Stockwood was created an 'alderman' by Cade, and he with Simon Shipton, John Billyngdon, John Frenssh, and Henry Capron were identified as captains among the rebel host during this misrule in London. They were described as 'the greatest rulers that were about the traitour John Cade in ransoming of their neighbours'.[119] Another Horne, alderman Robert Horne, a target of the rebels probably on account of his resistance to their entry into the city in his capacity as alderman of Bridge ward, had also to reach into his purse to evade the anger of the mob.[120]

---

[115] *CPR*, 1446–52, 33.

[116] KB9/26/1, m. 16; *Gregory's Chron.*, 193; *Bale's Chron.*, 133; *Benet's Chron.*, 201 (where the chronicler confuses Mayn with his master, Hampton, and calls Mayn himself keeper of Colchester castle).

[117] *Bale's Chron.*, 132; *Great Chron.*, 184; Gough, 156; *London Chrons.*, 161; see Barron, 'The Government of London and its Relations with the Crown', 519–20.

[118] C1/19/134.

[119] Ibid.

[120] Barron, 'The Government of London and its Relations with the Crown', 507–8.

Looting by Cade's men was not confined to the city alone. On 4 July a group whose composition suggests that Cade's followers from the different counties were mixing well among themselves, took the initiative, or perhaps were instructed, to strike southwards from Southwark further into Surrey instead of going with the main numbers into London. The group comprised a husbandman from Goudhurst and a parish clerk from Cranbrook, both in Kent, a yeoman from Fulscot in Berkshire, and another yeoman from Walden in Essex.[121] They made their way to Beddington, just north of Croydon, where they broke into and robbed the house of Nicholas Carew, a Surrey JP, three times sheriff of Surrey and Sussex during the 1440s, the last of these terms being 1448–9, and a man of close connections with the Fiennes family.[122]

By Sunday 5 July Cade's men had been loose in the city for two days, during which time there had been uncontrolled pillaging and the execution of at least five men there and in the suburbs. Not surprisingly there was now a body of citizens who wanted Cade and his men out, a body which may have exceeded in size the large number who had not wanted him in the first place.[123] The obvious thing to do was to wait until the rebels were in their Southwark lodgings for the night, attack those of Cade's men who were holding the bridge and then bar the bridge against their re-entry. Cade, however, got wind of this development and mustered all his men late that evening in Southwark calling them to make an armed assault on the city because he had heard that the mayor and aldermen were trying to lock them out.[124] To swell the ranks of his attacking force he opened the Marshalsea prison in Southwark so that its inmates might assist him.[125] An armed confrontation was more or less inevitable with Cade's men massed on the Southwark bank and the Londoners and royal troops from the Tower led by Lord Scales, the veteran royal captain Matthew Gough, and several aldermen, gathered on the bridge.

Fighting began some time around 9 o'clock in the evening and did

---

[121] KB9/273, m. 89; KB27/789 *rex* side, m. 31. That they were based in Southwark with the rest of Cade's men and were not a roving band who had left the uprising and gone their own way is suggested by the fact that they were received back from their expedition on 6 July in Southwark.

[122] Griffiths, *Henry VI*, 340; Wedgwood, *Biographies*, 155–6.

[123] See Barron, 'The Government of London and its Relations with the Crown', 509.

[124] Gough, 156.

[125] *Gregory's Chron.*, 193.

not end until daybreak.[126] The battle was perhaps a surprisingly long-drawn-out affair considering how well stocked the Tower had been with rebawkins, serpentines, stones, lead, bows, arrows, and other arms upon Henry's withdrawal from London, and which ordnance was now put to use.[127] The Londoners had got as far as closing the gates of the bridge but they could not keep Cade's men off its southernmost section. Failing to force his way forward across the bridge, Cade eventually set this drawbridge section of it alight. It had been a hard-fought struggle, however, before this happened. As the sun rose over the Thames that Monday morning the bridge must have been a dismal sight, charred and smoking with dead bodies strewn about it and floating in the river below. We know no names or precise numbers of those who died among Cade's ranks, but among the several hundred casualties there were from the Londoners' side an alderman, John Sutton, and also Matthew Gough, the celebrated soldier so feared and hated among the French that in 1449 he had been burnt in effigy by the local inhabitants as he had left Perche.[128] For many Londoners the main memory of the rising must have been of its pillaging and slaughter. One London note of the revolt, jotted as marginalia at the top of a document, records only the horrible conflict of the rebels and the beheading of Lord Saye and of Crowmer, the plundering of Alderman Malpas and the killing of Matthew Gough, Alderman John Sutton, and William and Humphrey Stafford (although these last two had been killed, of course, out near Sevenoaks).[129]

In the morning after the battle a truce of a few hours' duration was agreed upon with either side promising to keep to their respective sides of the bridge. This time was used by the representatives of the government still in the capital to negotiate with the insurgents about a general withdrawal. It was a matter of importance to the city and to the

---

[126] Not all the chronicles agree upon the duration of the fight although there is a complete consensus about its intensity and destructiveness. *Bale's Chron.*, 133–4 says it continued until four of the bell; *Benet's Chron.*, 201 says the battle began at about 10 o'clock and continued until 8 o'clock in the morning; *Gregory's Chron.*, 193 agrees with this account; Gough, 156 says it went on from about 9 o'clock until 8 o'clock in the morning.

[127] *PPC*, vi. 94. In a commission of 5 Aug. 1450 the constable of the Tower was to be instructed to inquire in London and Middlesex concerning all the arms which had been taken from the Tower by lieges from the city and county, presumably on this above-mentioned occasion. *CPR*, 1446–52, 388.

[128] *Gregory's Chron.*, 193; *Bale's Chron.*, 134; *Benet's Chron.*, 201; A. D. Carr, 'Welshmen and the Hundred Years War', *Welsh History Review*, 4 (1968), 39–41.

[129] Muniments of the Dean and Chapter of Westminster Abbey, MS 12239.

government authorities to make full use of the opportunity since the movement still had plenty of life left in it. That very day followers of Cade in Essex were making some sort of demonstration out in Blackmore, south-west of Chelmsford, rousing more men to rise up and support Cade's followers at Mile End.[130] There were too still rumblings of support for Cade in Suffolk.[131]

It would add greatly to our understanding of the rebellion to know just what happened at these negotiations between Cade and the prelates in Southwark. Cade and his men had been ejected from London, but they were still a force to be reckoned with, and satellite risings in the shires must have been seen as potential reinforcements to the men in Southwark, so it is hard to guess which party saw themselves as possessing the upper hand in the bargaining. As the numbers enrolled demonstrated, the terms of the pardon were attractive and favourable to Cade's followers, which raises the question why Cade made such a hasty departure from the scene. Perhaps he saw the archbishops and the bishop as more inclined to clemency than their royal master. Yet if he himself did not trust the pardon, and · maybe interpreted it as the government's means of defusing the situation before proper action could be taken, the great mass of insurgents appear to have enrolled their names in good faith. In the years which followed they would feel bitterly angry about the way they had been cheated by the royal negotiators. It is impossible to say with how much good faith the negotiators themselves acted.

The outcome of these negotiations held in St Margaret's church, Southwark, between Cade and the archbishops of Canterbury and York and the bishop of Winchester was that on that day and on the following day, Tuesday, 7 July, a general pardon was offered to Cade and his followers without payment.[132] The pardon extended to all transgressions committed prior to 8 July 1450 and guaranteed that anyone holding such a pardon would go unmolested by the king's justices, escheators, sheriffs, coroners, or bailiffs.[133] Cade was enrolled under the date of 6 July on the pardon roll begun that day. This roll, over the following day, ran to many hundreds of names. Cade was named as John Mortimer who, the pardon stated, was

[130] KB9/26, m. 2; /270A, m. 62; KB27/769 *rex* side, m. 8; /798 *rex* side, m. 30.
[131] KB9/118, m. 6; /271, m. 67. For a discussion of these indictments of 1453, see Ch. 6, below.   [132] *Benet's Chron.*, 201; *Gregory's Chron.*, 193.
[133] Kent Archives Office Fa/Z3 (pardon to the inhabitants of Faversham). HMC, v. (1876), 455 (copy of the king's proclamation of pardon held by the dean and chapter at Canterbury cathedral).

granted a general pardon at the request of the queen.[134] The public disclosure shortly afterwards that this was not his true name led to the pardon being declared invalid.[135] And, indeed, Cade acted as a man who did not trust his pardon. With a small band of followers and a good portion of booty he made off for northern Kent.

On 9 July, with his army of supporters now straggling home in a not always well-conducted fashion along the roads into Surrey,[136] Sussex, Kent, and Essex, Cade passed through Dartford *en route* to Rochester, from where, perhaps hoping for a strong position from which to hold out, he made an attack on Queenborough castle.[137] This attempt of Cade's failed, whilst earning the castle's captain, Sir Roger Chamberlain, a reward for his successful defence of it. He would also be rewarded for the capture of some of Cade's henchmen, one of whom went by the name of 'the Captain's bucher'.[138] But Cade was conspicuously still on the offensive. Since 7 July a hard core of his followers who had refused to disperse quietly had been agitating at Blackheath, Rochester, and near Gravesend at Singlewell where Robert Poynings made some kind of demonstration on 9 July.[139] On 10 July a Faversham soapmaker, Robert Spenser, was one of the main figures in a demonstration of support for Cade which took place at Rochester. He was later hanged and quartered for this action.[140] That day the exchequer issued a writ declaring Cade to be a traitor who 'laboureth now of newe to assemble the Kings people againe', putting a reward of 1,000 marks on his head and broadcasting tales of his past history of necromancy, murder, and allegiance to the French: 500 marks were offered to anyone bringing in one of Cade's chief councillors, and ten marks were offered for the taking of any of his followers. In his turn Cade was reputed to be saying that the royal pardons were invalid without the authority of parliament.[141]

---

[134] *CPR*, 1446–52, 338.
[135] *Short English Chron.*, 68. Yet even subsequent to this discovery a writ of 12 July was still calling him 'a certain man calling himself John Mortymer'. E101/336, m. 5.
[136] Three Sussex men robbed a house at Walkhampstead near Godstone, Surrey, of clothes, arms, and money on the road home to East Grinstead and Mayfield, KB9/271, m. 96; /270A, m. 8.   [137] *RP*, v. 224.   [138] E404/66/202.
[139] Virgoe, 'Ancient Indictments', 257, a rising against the king at Blackheath and Rochester on 7 and 8 July. Ibid. 252–3, a rising at Rochester on 9 July. KB27/789 *rex* side, m. 2ᵛ, the demonstration at Singlewell.
[140] KB27/759 *rex* side, m. 5; KB29/82, m. 15.
[141] *Gregory's Chron.*, 194; J. Brigstocke Sheppard (ed.), *Literae Cantuarienses*, iii. (RS, 1889), 207–9; Stow, *The Chronicles of England*, 662–3; *Short English Chron.*, 68, which mistakenly dates the writ to 12 July.

The authorities were in pursuit in earnest. From his position in Rochester Cade in full flight doubled back through the Weald into Sussex, perhaps, if he was from Hurstpierpoint, fleeing for refuge to the landscape whose byways and back lanes he knew best. According to one tradition he fled in disguise.[142] He left behind him in Kent some of his closest followers to continue his fight. One source (of autumn 1450) reports that on 11 July a posse of men led by Alexander Iden, the man who had replaced Crowmer as sheriff of Kent, caught up with Cade's secretary, Henry Wilkhous, in the parish of Little Chart, north-west of Ashford, arresting Wilkhous and despoiling him of his purse and other valuables.[143] Another source (of the summer of 1451) reports that on the following day, 12 July, Wilkhous was at Langley, just south-east of Maidstone and some ten miles or so to the west of Little Chart, gathering some forty men who rallied round declaring that they could call upon the support of 4,000 armed men to join Cade's cause.[144] Whether or not either of these conflicting accounts is accurate, both suggest the picture of Iden harrying Cade's supporters westwards across Kent towards the Sussex border. And indeed, on 12 July he finally caught up with Cade himself down in Sussex at Heathfield, badly injuring him as he captured him.[145]

It was also on 12 July that William Appultrefeld and Robert Shamell arrived in Rochester, having been sent down by the treasury to collect together and take back all Cade's loot.[146] Sir Thomas Tyrell and Richard Waller who had been nominated as two of the four treasurers of the recently granted subsidy were likewise sent down to Rochester to receive these goods and monies and to use them for the capture of Cade's adherents.[147] They were not the only people with an interest in these goods. Even whilst some of them were being stored in Rochester by Stephen Knight, the escheator for Kent, his premises were broken

---

[142] Hall, *The Union of the Two Noble and Illustre Famelies of Lancastre and Yorke*, fo. 79.
[143] Virgoe, 'Ancient Indictments', 236. Iden was found not guilty upon this charge.
[144] Ibid. 255–6.
[145] See Griffiths, *Henry VI*, 653 n. 45, for the chronicle variants of the place where Cade was finally apprehended. The Christ Church chronicle reports that Cade was killed on 12 July in the county of Sussex in the parish of 'Hethfeld'. Searle, *The Chronicle of John Stone Monk of Christ Church*, 50. For the extraordinary fascination the actual place of Cade's capture, whether it was Heathfield, Sussex, or Hothfield, Kent, held for local historians and antiquarians of the last century, see R. Furley, *A History of the Weald of Kent*, ii. pt. ii. (London, 1874), 386–98, where over 9 authorities on the subject are cited.
[146] E403/779/8; E28/80/70, 74, 84.
[147] Virgoe, 'The Parliamentary Subsidy of 1450', *BIHR* 55 (1982), 130–1.

into by a Rochester barber and some of the valuables stolen.[148] John
Kemp, the chancellor, was also sent to Rochester to try to calm the
atmosphere there and to help with the retrieval of the goods.[149]

By the time Iden had brought Cade back to London the rebel
captain had died from his injuries. The corpse was taken to Southwark
where the wife of the innkeeper of the White Hart identified that it was
indeed that of Cade. It then underwent a ritual beheading at Newgate
a few days later, the head being placed aloft over the scene of the
rising's most violent episode on London Bridge.[150] The remainder of
the body was then dragged over the bridge from Southwark through
London to Newgate where it was quartered. On 17 July the mayor and
sheriffs of Norwich were sent a quarter to place on their city gate in a
way which strongly suggests that there had been some sympathy for the
rising there.[151] Blackheath (the rebel encampment), Salisbury (the late
Bishop Aiscough's cathedral city), and Gloucester (home of Abbot
Reginald Boulers) were the other three places chosen for the display of
these retaliatory warnings.[152]

On 21 July an indenture was delivered into the exchequer itemizing
the goods, jewels, and money taken off Cade and his followers in Kent
on their retreat from Southwark: silver dishes and spoons, purses,
girdles, a gold salver garnished with sapphires and pearls, silver pots,
silver salt cellars, precious stones, cups, collars—over a hundred and
fifteen items in all, in addition to a massive £105 15s. in ready money.
Yet this was by no means all the rebels' takings.[153] It is telling evidence
as to what the rising had turned into inside the city walls and in
Southwark too. Most of these valuables look to have come from the
robbing of private houses such as that of Philip Malpas, where the
duke of York had been storing some of his possessions, but the
presence here of a golden chalice and paten and a paxbred of silver and
gilt suggests that churches were pillaged too. During the next month
the citizens of Rochester were granted £40 from Cade's goods at

---

[148] KB9/284, m. 50; KB27/783 *rex* side, m. 1ᵛ; this indictment gives the date of the arrest of the goods as 3 July 1450, an error which can be accounted for by faulty memory, since the indictment was presented in 1457.   [149] E404/67/16.

[150] *Gregory's Chron.*, 194.   [151] KB27/758 *rex* side, m. 9.

[152] *PPC*, 1443–61, 107; the city of Salisbury paid 20s. to Geoffrey Ponyng for his expenses riding to London for the quarter and 3s. 4d. to a man carrying it. Muniments of the Corporation of Salisbury (Trowbridge Record Office), Chamberlains Accounts 1449–50. Gough, 157 has the idea that Cade's quarters were distributed in Kent. This may be in error for the quarters of some of his followers which certainly were.

[153] E101/336/5 and E357/40 which differs slightly in its inventory. John Payn is an example of someone whose stolen valuables are not included in this list. *PL*, i. 134.

Rochester for the mending of their Eastgate, and in July Iden collected his 1,000 marks reward from the profits of the sale of the goods. Those who had been robbed had to go to the exchequer and there all they received was first preference in buying back their belongings for somewhat less than they were worth.[154]

[154] *PPC*, 1443–61, 101; E28/80/71, 84.

5

REBELLION THROUGHOUT SOUTHERN
ENGLAND IN 1450

WITH the death of Cade in the middle week of July the central events
of the rising of 1450 were over, although activities associated with it
would continue sporadically for years. This, then, seems an appropriate
point at which to consider just who these rebels were who had followed
Cade and who had shared those grievances for which he had been
spokesman.

Until quite recently a picture of the participants, their origins and
occupations, has been constructed quite simply by abstracting
information from the long list enrolled among the Patent Rolls of some
3,300 names, many of them accompanied by occupations and place of
origin, of those persons who received a pardon on 6 and 7 July at
Southwark. However, in 1981 Professor Griffiths established without
any doubt that the roll was no mere list of rebels and that the document
requires a much more subtle interpretation.[1] He drew attention to the
way in which these numerous pardons with their promises that the
recipients should thereby gain immunity from any future actions of
royal officials of any kind had the effect of a great screen coming down
over the details of the insurgents from these south-eastern counties.
An offer of a pardon such as this, available to anyone, free of payment,
was, quite naturally, taken advantage of by men other than the rebels
themselves, bearing in mind the complete uncertainty which then hung
in the air as to whether future proceedings would go against the rebels
or against those of whom the rebels complained. No one knew in the
first week of July just how the tide of events would swing.

Thus the notorious Robert Est, the gentleman from Maidstone
named in one of the rebel petitions as a great oppressor in Kent, is to
be found on the pardon roll. Likewise with William Isle, named
alongside Est as another of the four great oppressors.[2] There too is

---

[1]See R. A. Griffiths, *The Reign of King Henry VI: The Exercise of Royal Authority, 1422–
1461* (London, 1981), 619–23. I have not counted the names, but take this figure from
B. P. Wolffe, *Henry VI* (London, 1981), 233 n. 43.   [2] *CPR*, 1446–52, 343, 356.

John Watte of Sandhurst, the corrupt bailiff of the late William Crowmer.[3] A similar character was John Ram of Halstow, under-steward to Lord Cromwell's steward, Richard Bruyn, in his lordship of Hoo, Bruyn being 'a great supporter and maintainer of the said John'. Yet Ram too is on the pardon roll.[4] Katharine de la Pole, abbess of St Mary's, Barking, in Essex, as sister of the murdered duke of Suffolk is likely to be on the pardon roll only as a measure of defence against the possibility of some anti-Suffolk backlash occurring in the courts after the rebellion. Such was the intensity of the odium connected with that name that men were apparently made fearful by their association with her. Four of the five men named on the roll from Barking and at least four of the eight men coming from unnamed locations within Becontree hundred turn out to be her tenants.[5]

Names such as those of Est, Isle, and the abbess, however, stand out conspicuously amidst a sea of unknowns: numerous hundred constables and lists of village and town inhabitants. It would seem entirely plausible to suspect that some of these names could represent those cautious and law-abiding people who did not rise behind Cade but took the precaution of having their hundred protected in this way by the representation of the constables and a few other inhabitants. The city of Canterbury offers an example of such cautious tactics. Twenty-nine people, at least three of whom were gentlemen, are named on the pardon roll from the city. They are wine, paper, and livestock merchants, former and future members of parliament, and mayors: a close-knit group from the city's ruling faction who married one another's widows and took up offices from one other.[6] In January 1450 their city had vigorously withstood the insurgents who had risen up in the villages of the countryside between Sandwich and Dover under the leadership of Thomas Cheyne, the hermit Bluebeard, and, indeed, had helped in Cheyne's capture. The city had been equally resistant to Cade himself six months later when on 8 June the rebel host had advanced on the western suburbs of Canterbury. Come November 1450 the royal exchequer would be found issuing a £10 reward to ten

---

[3] Ibid. 341: here he is named as coming from Hawkhurst.
[4] Ibid. 352, 370; Virgoe, 'Ancient Indictments', 226, 227, 229, 230.
[5] *CPR*, 1446–52, 355; Essex Record Office (Chelmsford) T/A 206/1.
[6] HMC, ix. report (1883), 140, where Simon Morley and William Bryan (*CPR*, 1446–52, 338, 362) are mentioned. Charles Cotton (ed.), 'Churchwardens' Accounts of the Parish of St Andrew, Canterbury Part I: 1485–1509', *Arch. Cant.*, 32 (1917), 191–2; the John Fremingham and John Swann both mentioned here are on the pardon roll (*CPR*, 1446–52, 338, 354).

Canterbury men for their great labour and costs in taking and bringing unto the king's presence one Simon Scryven of the parish of Herne who had been active in stirring up insurrection and rebellion. Four of these ten zealous Canterbury citizens are to be found on the July pardon roll; Simon Scryven the rebel is not.[7] Evidently then, the men on the pardon roll for Canterbury are there as representatives of their community, not as any kind of rebels, as men of substance who could command respect.

Scrutiny of the names on the pardon roll is a most interesting exercise, but since it can contribute little to the question in hand here as to who the rebels were I have placed it in an appendix where the matter can be given fuller treatment.[8] Rejecting, however, the list as direct evidence for the participants in the rising means that extremely little evidence of any kind remains to help answer the question. As far as is known at present, indictments brought against alleged insurgents exist only for the counties of Suffolk, Essex, and Wiltshire. No indictments remain from Kent, Sussex, Surrey, or Middlesex— although judicial proceedings certainly took place against insurgents in Kent and Sussex.

Perhaps the best evidence as to what manner of insurgents these were lies in the petitions mentioned in the previous chapter. Three separate bills were circulated during the rebellion.[9] The petition produced by Cade's followers, a copy of which one of Sir John Fastolf's men retrieved for him from Blackheath during June 1450, combines tones of anger and restraint.[10] This fluently, if very inelegantly, written document recites the evil consequences of the presence of a circle of 'false traytours' around the king and its pernicious effects at national and county level in condemnations which are trenchant but not indiscriminate. The petitioners do not blame all lords, all gentlemen, all lawyers, nor all clergy, but only such as might be found guilty by due process of law—something these men claim to have been denied at the hands of corrupt county officials. They press the point that this is a peaceful demonstration of responsible petitioners. The evil councillors 'calle us risers and treyturs and the kynges enymys, but we schalle be ffounde his trew lege mene and his best freendnus'.[11] And again, 'we wulle that alle men know that we wulle

---

[7] E404/67/94; *CPR*, 1446–52, 338, 344, 350, 351, 354, 362, 373.

[8] See App. B, below.   [9] See App. A, below for a discussion of the petitions.

[10] Magdalen College, Oxford, MS Misc. 306 (printed in HMC, viii. report (1881), 266–7); an earlier and much longer version of this bill is printed in *Short English Chron.*, 94–9.   [11] Magdalen College, Oxford, MS. Misc. 306.

neythur robbe nor stele, but these fawtes amendid we schall go hoom'. These sound the sentiments of men rather loath to rise. But on the other hand they are risers who once roused could organize a county-wide and wider than county demonstration and offer a coherent programme of proposed reform.

The evidence of this and of the other two petitions suggests that the drafters of these petitions and those acting at the centre of events were neither illiterate nor uninformed. Indeed, they may be defined quite closely by means of their own grievances. Whoever drew up the bills of complaint understood and were agitated about anomalies in the system of tax collection in Kent whereby the exemptions of the barons of the Cinque Ports created greater labour for the tax collector; about the way in which sheriffs, under-sheriffs, and bailiffs might line their own pockets in the name of the exchequer using summonses under its green wax seals; about the recently renewed statute of labourers which placed further duties upon the constables whose task it was to enforce it; about special jurisdictions in Kent such as the Court of Dover; about the selling by knights of the shire of the office of tax collector; about the farming of offices by sheriffs and under-sheriffs; and about the lack of free election in the choosing of the knights of the shire. These complaints identify the petitioners as administrators in county life below the level of the major offices: the forty-shilling freeholders. A statute of 1429–30 had set the right to vote at elections of knights of the shire at the level of freeholders holding land with a net revenue of at least forty shillings a year. It was the same property qualification as governed grand jury services in the county court. This definition of the franchise in 1429–30 has been seen to reflect a growing sense of community within the counties among a stratum of county society that included more than the gentry class.[12] With a gentleman's annual landed income standing somewhere between £10 to £20, and an esquire's between £20 to £40, the £2 level of the forty-shilling freeholder admitted of a large sector of a county's population: merchants, well-to-do artisans, and the up-and-coming yeomen who formed a group so characteristic of fifteenth-century Kentish society.

The voice of this county community can be heard in the rebels' bills.

---

[12] S. J. Payling, 'The Widening Franchise—Parliamentary Elections in Lancastrian Nottinghamshire', in D. Williams (ed.), *England in the Fifteenth Century: Proceedings of the 1986 Harlaxton Symposium* (Woodbridge, 1987), 167–85. The suggestion that the rebels' call for the repeal of the labour laws could reflect the discontent of the constables was made by B. H. Putnam (ed.), *Proceedings before the Justices of the Peace in the Fourteenth and Fifteenth Centuries: Edward III to Richard III* (London, 1938), p. cxxvi.

They are the grievances of a group who although not of that select band of gentry who dominated the offices of MP, sheriff,[13] under-sheriff, or JP, none the less had a political stake in the county and took an active role in its administration as collectors of parliamentary subsidies, as local jurors, as constables, and bailiffs of local hundreds. Theirs is the concern for the king's thrift, good management, and availability to hear his subjects' wrongs; theirs too the anxiety for security of title in land and the bitterness against the corruption both of the men of the royal household and of the sheriffs, under-sheriffs, and knights of the shire. For nothing was more important to this moderately landed, literate, and litigious group than the establishment and consolidation of their family holdings, an activity for which some level of honesty in county administration was imperative. Active and acquisitive, they had experienced the frustration of living in counties where the administration and operation of justice were exercised in a highly partial manner by an 'in' group to which they were not allied. Their literacy meant that their concern with national and local politics could be endlessly discussed. As C. L. Kingsford has pointed out, 'The Paston Letters have been too often quoted as if they were a unique phenomenon instead of a happy survival'.[14] All over the South-East during the ill-governed years before 1450 these men and their wives would be writing to one another gossip-laden letters about the latest scandals of Robert Est in Kent or Thomas Tuddenham in Norfolk.

As hundred jurors they had been observing the figures they condemned as extortioners—Isle, Est, Crowmer, and Slegge—at close quarters for years: seven members of a twelve-man jury which offered presentments before William Isle and his fellow JPs at an inquest at Tonbridge in 1442 are to be found on the pardon roll of 1450.[15] The pardon roll, not to be used as sole guide as to who the rebels were, does, however, lend this kind of corroboration of the picture offered by the three rebel bills. Here are tax collectors,[16] local hundred jurors,[17]

---

[13] A mere 14 families provided half of the sheriffs appointed in Kent between 1422 and 1509. P. W. Fleming, 'The Character and Private Concerns of the Gentry of Kent 1422–1509', Ph.D. thesis (Swansea, 1985), 77.   [14] Kingsford, *EHL*, 10–11.

[15] KB9/241, m. 24; *CPR*, 1446–52, 351, 352.

[16] For example, Richard Lovelace of Kingsdown, gent., Thomas Petsmyth of East Farleigh, mason, William Spert of High Halden, gent., and William Wynterbourne of Ashford. E159/226 *De visu* Kent and *Adhuc Communia* Michaelmas term; E372/295 *Item* Kent; *CPR*, 1446–52, 338, 341, 351, 364.

[17] For example, for the town of Dartford. KB9/255/2, m. 10; *CPR*, 1446–52, 346, 350, 363. And for the hundred of Axton. KB9/255/2, m. 17; *CPR*, 1446–52, 346, 363, 364.

constables, and former constables;[18] men who in all probability took out a pardon for the simple reason that they had been insurgents.

Some members of the upper ranks of the county communities, the gentry, also played a role in the rebellion. What cannot be ascertained are numbers or names. The numbers receiving pardons, which in the case of Kentish knights, esquires, and gentlemen were one, twenty-one, and seventy-six respectively, are no gauge of the number participating.[19] Socially and politically they were closely connected to the forty-shilling freeholder class whose support as electors and jurors could be vital to them in county politics and administration. According to Gregory's chronicle Cade compelled 'alle the gentellys to arysse whythe hem'.[20] But if some members of the gentry took part in the rising through compulsion, others are likely to have been there by their own volition. It is, after all, unlikely that all the many gentlemen who appear on the pardon roll were non-participants. Cade's carver and sword-bearer, for one, was a Sussex gentleman, Robert Poynings, son of Lord Poynings. He may well have joined the rising as the best available vehicle for pursuing a quarrel with his stepbrother, William Crowmer, rather than through any commitment to reform. It was during the rising that his servants made a raid on Crowmer's property in London and restored to Poynings goods he claimed as his own.[21]

John Sinclair, esquire, of Faversham, Kent, and Thomas Burgess, esquire, his near neighbour at Graveney, present an intriguing case of possible insurgents of gentry status. They both had their names placed on the pardon roll of July 1450 as persons seeking exemption from the hand of the law after Cade's rebellion.[22] That in itself, as has been noted, is not a suspicious circumstance since innocent parties could sue for a pardon merely for extra security. What alerts interest is the circumstance that in 1440 this pair had been accused by a Kentish felon, a mole-catcher from Ospringe who had turned 'king's evidence', of having been in 1438–9 the producers of deadly potions made with the stated intention of killing the king, his brother Duke Humphrey,

---

[18] For example, Thomas Undirdowne was a former constable of the town of Dartford. KB9/233, m. 11; *CPR*, 1446–52, 363. And Stephen Crouche was a former constable of the hundred of Twyford. KB9/255/2, m. 8; *CPR*, 1446–52, 343.

[19] Fleming, 'The Character and Private Concerns of the Gentry of Kent 1422–1509', 32.

[20] *Gregory's Chron.*, 190.

[21] R. M. Jeffs, 'The Poynings–Percy Dispute: An Example of the Interplay of Open Strife and Legal Action in the Fifteenth Century', *BIHR* 34 (1961), 148–64.

[22] *CPR*, 1446–52, 364, 366.

and the duke of Norfolk.[23] John Sinclair, according to the felon, was aggrieved by the war with France, by the scarcity and high price of wheat in Kent, and by the practice of purveyance which entitled the king to take grain from the county at will. The felon's tale was not believed and he suffered the penalties for treason for his allegations. However, his story may have carried within its garrulous circumlocutions some elements of fact. The mole-catcher had not misjudged Sinclair's character; independent evidence reveals Sinclair receiving a murderer at his house in Faversham in December 1439.[24] The allegations concerning the plans to poison the king do not need to be taken too seriously, but it is entirely credible that these esquires—and a good many others of their class—did hold the stated grievances and that in 1450 they might join a demonstration which gave vent to such views.

John Gibbes, gentleman, is another interesting figure, although, here again, nothing absolutely conclusive can be said about his involvement in the rising. He was a gentleman from London involved in Kentish society during the 1440s. In the pardon roll of 1450 he designated himself, or was designated, as coming from Great Chart, a village just west of Ashford.[25] His involvement in this locality had been of the most active kind to do with a long-standing dispute over property.[26] In October 1446 he had allegedly led a gang of over a dozen men who had struck east to the coast and made forcible entry into a manor of some 283 acres of land in the parish of Capel-le-Ferne and into another sixty acres in the next parish of Folkestone, land all claimed by one man, Robert Brandrede.[27] They had successfully kept Brandrede out of the property until the following spring. The incident itself is not particularly significant; its interest lies in seeing Gibbes the London gentleman being able to employ and organize men of a lower social station (husbandmen, labourers, a tailor, an apple seller), whom he had recruited not only from the immediate vicinity of Great Chart and Ashford but also from further afield, from places like Stonden, Tenterden, and Leeds, the last some fourteen miles away to the west.

---

[23] R. L. Storey, *The End of the House of Lancaster* (London, 1966), App. 1 (pp. 199–209), prints the long and highly circumstantial account of the king's approver in all its detail. Also implicated in the plot was a Richard Croft, yeoman, living at Graveney with Burgess; a Richard Croft, gentleman, is named as from Faversham in the 1450 pardon roll. *CPR*, 1446–5, 366.   [24] KB9/243, m. 64.
[25] *CPR*, 1446–52, 347, 366.
[26] *CCLR*, 1435–41, 408; *CCLR*, 1441–7, 374–5.   [27] KB9/996, m. 27.

In 1450 he allegedly acted as a kind of recruiting officer for Cade, being sent down into Essex to raise insurgents there. Whether he was active before this in arousing the men of his district of Kent is unknown, although Great Chart, conveniently enough, was itself a hundred meeting-place.[28] What is related is that he was received in Colchester as Cade's messenger and representative and that he instigated in some degree the rising which allegedly took place there on 1 July 1450.[29] There is no known reason why this alleged activity of his during the rebellion should be untrue, but it must be cautioned that all the evidence for it comes from proceedings in February and June 1453 from juries keen to attack York's supporters. The evidence is inconclusive. But later, in November 1471, he would be one of those who received a general pardon for insurrections in Surrey and Kent before the previous July.[30]

But if some members of the gentry were followers of Cade and had exhorted others to join him, there is no suggestion that they were a leading force in the rising. To the contrary, insurgents appear to have regarded the gentry as having sided against their rising. When in October 1450 a demonstration took place at Horsham and another in November at Hastings the would-be insurgents on both occasions (stoneroofers, a mason, a dyer, husbandmen, a tailor, and a thatcher) allegedly sought the heads of certain gentry, and 'especially of those who were against Jack Cade'.[31]

The trades of these erstwhile followers of Cade who rose up in Sussex in the autumn of 1450 are a reminder that the artisan and poorer element among the rebel ranks must not be overlooked. To take the example of Colchester. Also allegedly rising up at Colchester on 1 July 1450 besides Gibbes were two other gentlemen, a William Frere of Little Clacton, a village eleven miles south-east of Colchester, and William Lecche of Colchester, merchant, MP for the town 1449–50, and bailiff of Colchester in 1450.[32] Both men were subsequently pardoned. But indicted alongside them were eighty-nine other men of the town, almost every one of them an artisan. Furthermore, complaint in the rebels' bills on behalf of 'simple and poor people that use not hunting' (that is, were not forty-shilling freeholders who were entitled

---

[28] Great Chart was the hundred meeting-place for the half hundred of Great Chart. J. K. Wallenberg, *The Place-Names of Kent* (Uppsala, 1934), 403.
[29] KB9/26, m. 17; /273, m. 86; /279, m. 92; KB27/778 *rex* side, m. 8.
[30] *CPR*, 1467–77, 302.   [31] KB9/122, mm. 16, 21.
[32] KB9/26, mm. 16, 17; Wedgwood, *Biographies*, 532.

to hunt), showed that the concerns of a group below that of the forty-shilling freeholders were being voiced. Numerically, the poorer artisans and husbandmen may have been the largest social element among the insurgents. Anomalies in the tax collection system in Kent or the rigging of elections would not affect such people, but they could be alarmed by rumours that the king intended to turn Kent into a wild forest in revenge for the duke of Suffolk's death. They wanted a less corrupt county administration, and everyone, without exception, had an urgent concern about defence. The loss of France was a major spur to popular insurrection. It led to a fear of imminent attack upon the vulnerable south-eastern portion of England, and now that England no longer controlled both coasts of the Channel there was also greater fear of foreign piracy. Ill-government could be endured for years, but not when it endangered the defence of a whole region of England. There must have been many men in the position of Thomas Man and John Crowelynke, both of whom are named on the pardon roll, holders of neighbouring crofts, Salmonnescrofte and Sampsonescrofte, down at Seaford in Sussex, who lived in communities where land was held *super litus maris*—bordering upon the seashore itself.[33] Nicholas Gate, a roper from Milton on the northern coast of Kent, is named on the pardon roll. He owned no more than a messuage and a bit of land in his town and a few acres in nearby Borden.[34] If he lacked the wherewithal to have much business in the courts or to excite the greed of county officials he was no doubt as anxious as anyone to keep what property he had out of the hands of the French. Likewise with John Cokke, a shipman from Milton, who is named on the pardon roll and for whom it can also be speculated that he was there as an insurgent. He was no great property-owner, possessing very few acres of land, some portable stalls in Milton market-place (perhaps for the sale of fish), and holding three messuages: his main asset was his boats and their tackle.[35] The matter of the keeping of the seas and of the advance of the French was of the first importance to such a man. From Milton he sailed up Milton Creek and around the Isle of Sheppey into one of the most pirate-infested stretches of shipping around the coast of England, the opening of the Thames into the North Sea making a splendid natural bottleneck for marauders. Perhaps it is significant that

---

[33] DL29/442/7122; *CPR*, 1446–52, 360.
[34] 'Milton Wills', *Arch. Cant.*, 45 (1933), 18.
[35] 'Milton Wills', *Arch. Cant.*, 44 (1932), 98–9.

no fewer than ten other shipmen from Milton are named on the pardon roll besides John Cokke.[36]

The picture which emerges of the insurgents of 1450 is not that of a single economic or political group. The rebel ranks would appear to have been made up of gentry, yeomen, artisans, and miscellaneous joiners-in and hangers-on (the rabble without a cause) from both towns and the countryside who acted together from shared and individual motives. But if the rebel ranks formed no single class, the rising at its core appears to have stemmed from the grievances and been sustained by the anger of an identifiable group, the broad base of the county community within each south-eastern county, many of whom were in the income bracket of the forty-shilling freeholders: those men who formed the solid, lower-middle ranks of their respective county societies, the village and small town notables. They most resented the lack of a strong, solvent, and militarily competent central government and the intrusion of a corrupt, closed circle of household men into the counties where otherwise they themselves stood to flourish.

II

It is very hard to say either just what numbers of people took to the road and joined Cade's army on its route to London, or just how much normal life was affected in the counties of the South-East as a consequence of this exodus. Undoubtedly there were some wives of insurgent yeomen and smallholders, kept busy enough in normal circumstances at their kneading troughs and dressingboards and in their dairies and poultry yards, who felt acutely the inconvenience of being short-handed that June as the meadow grass was ripening for mowing and the recently calved cows were giving their heaviest milk yields.[37]

The few hundred and manorial court records from the South-East remaining for 1450 indicate that the routine of court attendance carried on. So, in north-western Kent a court was held on 29 May at

---

[36] *CPR*, 1446–52, 365, 369. For a discussion of how rich an area of exploitation the Thames estuary was for pirates, see C. F. Richmond, 'Royal Administration and the Keeping of the Seas, 1422–1485', D.Phil. thesis (Oxford, 1962), 131–8.

[37] In the Christ Church estates—and doubtless elsewhere too—regular milking began on the feast of St George (23 Apr.). R. A. L. Smith, *Canterbury Cathedral Priory* (Cambridge, 1969: repr. of 1943 original), 159.

Northfleet despite the fact that settlements to the east of the county were already astir, and that its own inhabitants may well have shortly joined their ranks.[38] On 29 June, by which time rumour had had time to spread that Colchester was stirring in support of Cade, a manorial court was held at Maldon on the Blackwater estuary. The court records kept unswervingly to local troubles: John Fretherich's great sow was wandering about destroying neighbours' gardens; John Gate, junior (who would shortly appear on Cade's pardon roll), had attacked a female servant in the town; the wife of Thomas Estwode (he would also be on the roll) was illegally regrating ale.[39] Likewise on 28 May and 30 June in the middle of Essex at Pleshey the locals carried on holding their views of frankpledge for High Easter, Hatfield Peverel, and Mashbury, worrying about their ale-tasters, fierce dogs, and overgrown hedges.[40] These were villages lying immediately west of the parish of Great Waltham which would be mentioned on the pardon roll. On 7 July as pardons were being issued in Southwark and the rebels were dispersing from London, up at Saffron Walden in northern Essex the view of frankpledge was deliberating over the nuisance caused by the dead pig someone had put in the water at Stonebridge at the end of the town by the windmill.[41] Courts also continued to be held on some of the archbishop of Canterbury's Kentish estates, such as those held on 1 and 22 June at Aldington, south-west of Ashford, and on 2 June at Lyminge, north-west of Folkestone.[42] Whilst down in Sussex on 3 June a manor court was held at Laughton, half a dozen miles east of Lewes.[43] The few surviving accounts of bailiffs and reeves for the summer of 1450 give a similar impression of an untroubled season.[44]

---

[38] Lambeth Palace Library, ED 766; Thomas Flucke and Simon Letot mentioned on this roll are both named on the pardon list. *CPR*, 1446–52, 345.

[39] Essex Record Office, D/B 3/3/30.   [40] DL30/71/877.

[41] Essex Record Office, D/DBy M5.

[42] Lambeth Palace Library, ED 136, 617.   [43] BL Add. Roll 32004.

[44] For example, the beadle and rent collector at the Christ Church manor of Eastry appear to have collected a wide range of rents throughout the year (Lambeth Palace Library, ED 416); similarly at Mayfield, Sussex, the beadle, the farmer of the rectory, and the parker appear to have had no difficulty collecting money rents and renders in kind during 1450 (ibid. 715, 716, 717). Other examples of non-committal accounts for this year are those of the chamberlain at Ringmere, Sussex (ibid. 941); the farmer's account for Bishop's Marsh in Cliffe on the north Kent coast (ibid. 269); the reeve's account for Reculver on the north Kent coast just east of Herne Bay (ibid. 926); the reeve's account at Burwash, north-east of Heathfield in Sussex (East Sussex Record Office, Ashburnham 200A); the beadle's account for the manor of Chiddingly some miles south of Heathfield (BL Add. Roll 31416); the reeve's account for Bibleham in

They, allegedly, composed ballads and rhymes telling how the king by the counsel of the duke of Suffolk, the bishop of Salisbury, the bishop of Chichester, and Lord Saye (this is just a list of those courtiers killed in 1450) had sold the realm of England and France and that soon the king of France would be monarch in England.[59] These compositions were then stuck up on windows and doors throughout Bury St Edmunds for all to read. And, the allegations continued, these men sent these communications more widely out into other counties, especially into Sussex and Kent, in order to raise the people there to rebellion. On 12 April John Cade, allegedly, was created captain at Bury before going to assemble at Blackheath with other rebels. On 26 May letters were sent from Bury to the men of Kent to incite them to rise and letters were also sent to the duke of York in Ireland asking him to depose Henry and to remove his councillors. On 10 June there was allegedly a rising at East Bergholt.[60] Then on 7 July, the day the pardons were issued in London to Cade's followers and others, there was supposedly a rising in support of Cade at Hadleigh, a cloth-manufacturing town with a manor belonging to Christ Church, Canterbury, down in the southern part of the county, not far east of Sudbury.[61] The men concerned, the indictment related, went together down to join Cade at Blackheath.

It was at about this time, they said, during the early part of July, that at Melton, on the river Deben, a mile north-east of Woodbridge, the vicar was attacked and robbed.[62] The 8 July saw another insurrection at Hadleigh in support of Cade.[63] On 10 July an unfortunate William Buxton was imprisoned and tortured by the commons of Kent, Essex, and Suffolk at Stratford in Suffolk and was threatened with being taken off to their master Cade to be killed.[64]

---

[59] KB9/118/1, m. 30; /271, m. 117; KB27/770 *rex* side, m. 3; /776 rex side, mm. 2, 2ᵛ, 27; /797 *rex* side, m. 7.

[60] Ibid. The indictments merely say 'Bergholt' and I have taken this to be the Suffolk Bergholt, East Bergholt on the river Stour nine miles south-west of Ipswich. There is of course also a West Bergholt in north-east Essex on the river Colne three miles north-west of Colchester.

[61] KB9/118, m. 6; M. N. Carlin, 'Christ Church, Canterbury, and its Lands, from the Beginning of the Priorate of Thomas Chillenden to the Dissolution 1391–1540', B.Litt. thesis (Oxford, 1970), 16, 96.

[62] KB9/118, m. 32. The indictment names the village as 'Multon by Dallyng' which I have taken to be Melton, the centre of the dean and chapter of Ely's liberty of St Audrey and thus one of east Suffolk's two administrative capitals; it would attract rebels again in 1549. D. MacCulloch, 'Kett's Rebellion in Context', *Past and Present*, 84 (1979), 41.

[63] KB9/271, m. 67; KB27/770 *rex* side, m. 27.   [64] KB9/118, m. 27.

According to these indictments the troubles in Suffolk carried on well into the autumn and winter of 1450. Assaults and thefts were committed at Hadleigh in September by men who had allegedly risen up behind Cade during July.[65] William Dunton of Hadleigh, merchant alias gentleman, was assaulted and lost a box of charters and seals worth £20.[66] Another man had weapons stolen. Moreover, the rising resulted, it was said, in a protracted breakdown in law and order: after the spring of 1450 William Barre and others from Framlingham, Hadleigh, Ipswich, and Debenham rode about for two years in an armed multitude so that no official of the king could arrest them.[67]

This account of the troubles in Suffolk, derived from the jurors of 1453, should be modified somewhat in the light of other sources, although the discrepancies may arguably have been merely the result of defective memories. It is not impossible, but it seems unlikely, that men would be rising up in Suffolk to join Cade or threatening to take prisoners to him after the issuing of the pardons and the dispersal— with Cade in the van—of the rebels from London. There is not, however, clear external evidence with which flatly to contradict the notion of Bury St Edmunds as the very seat and origin of the rising with its poster campaign, election of Cade, and letter-sending to Sussex and Kent. All that can be said is that the indictment savours very strongly of an attack on York's East Anglian affinity. Even so, if these are fabrications, some of them at least can be shown to be fabrications built with some plausibility upon a background of troubles which certainly did go on in Suffolk that year. The town of Hadleigh, mentioned by the jurors as the scene of risings in support of Cade on 7 and 8 July and of lootings by his followers in September, is conspicuously the one Suffolk town to appear on the pardon roll of July 1450.[68] And with its location in southern Suffolk not far from the Essex border it is by no means improbable that some of its inhabitants may have ridden down to London to support the rising. Fifteen individuals are named on the pardon roll from Hadleigh, the cloth industry being well represented among them: four fullers, three weavers, and a mercer. Whether this suggests some particular

---

[65] KB9/271, m. 67; /272, m. 12; KB27/770 *rex* side, m. 27.
[66] Dunton's description as a merchant alias gentleman comes from another source: E159/225 *Brevia directa baronibus Michaelmas.*
[67] KB27/797 *rex* side, m. 7; KB9/118/1, m. 29.
[68] *CPR*, 1446–52, 343, 356, 359.

disaffection among the cloth workers in Hadleigh or merely reflects the town's involvement in the trade it is hard to say. The 1440s, it must be said, were not the heyday of the Suffolk cloth trade.[69] The prosperity of the industry in East Anglia, reflected in the construction of splendid perpendicular churches such as that at Lavenham with its one hundred and forty-one foot tower, was to come later in the 1480s.[70] In the sixteenth century Hadleigh was notorious as a centre of radical heresy: so it may be that something of this tradition existed already in 1450 to succour insurgency there.[71]

If Hadleigh's presence on the pardon roll suggests that the stories from the jurors in 1453 may be based on some truth, corroboration of the attack upon the vicar of Melton is even firmer. He later petitioned chancery about this outrage, telling how 'in the grete trobull' tyme', he was attacked by night by a large gang of parishioners, 'desciples and of the affynyte of the grete traytor John Cade' who would have had his head off had he not fled.[72] Cheated of their purpose, they ransacked his house and stable and awaited his return so that he dared not go home and keep his cure.

A state of widespread unrest and lawlessness in Suffolk that season was also evidenced in an attack on 20 June—the day after Lord Saye had been put in the Tower—by a gang of Beccles men upon the property and tenants of the abbot of Bury St Edmunds at Beccles. This was up in east Suffolk, as Beccles lies on the river Waveney, eight and a half miles west of Lowestoft, suggesting that the breadth of the county may have been infected with trouble. The majority of the twenty-seven men named in the subsequent indictment for this attack (presented at Henhowe in January 1451) were either designated husbandmen (twelve) or yeomen (five). The remainder were trades-men: a merchant, a spicer, two mercers, a candlemaker, a cordwainer,

---

[69] D. Dymond and R. Virgoe, 'The Reduced Population and Wealth of Early Fifteenth-Century Suffolk', *Proceedings of the Suffolk Institute of Archaeology and History*, 36 (1986), 73–100.

[70] The tower at Lavenham took almost forty years to build. H. C. Malden, 'Lavenham Church Tower', *Proceedings of the Suffolk Institute of Archaeology and History*, 9 (1897), 370–2.

[71] A. G. Dickens, *Lollards and Protestants in the Diocese of York, 1509–1558* (Oxford, 1959), 48.

[72] C1/19/388a; C. L. Kingsford, *Prejudice and Promise in Fifteenth-Century England* (Oxford, 1925; repr. London, 1962), 49. The date of the petition given as Thursday next after the feast of St Peter the Apostle 1450 could well be the night of Thursday 2 July/ morning of 3 July if the feast is taken as Saints Peter and Paul.

a roper, a barker, a hosier, and a butcher.[73] What lay behind the attack is not altogether clear, although an old and powerful house such as Bury St Edmunds was almost permanently locked in struggles with its tenants over privileges and rights.[74] Moreover, this had been a Lollard district, a tradition which could well have kept alive. In April 1430 six suspected heretics from Beccles had appeared before the bishop and been punished.[75] The interest the incident affords here is as a gauge of the unsettled state of the county during Cade's rising, independent of the evidence of 1453. It also, of course, makes more suggestive the allegations of trouble at Bury St Edmunds itself.

Other independent evidence besides the vicar of Melton's petition is to be found in chancery records. There William Bedston from Brampton, Suffolk, complained how 'in the moost trouble[st] [se]ason and tyme of that greet Traitour John Cade late Riser in Kent' a local squire had with great force and violence entered upon the lands which he, William, had lately bought.[76]

The suggestion made by the evidence of 1453 that this unsettled state did not melt away at the end of July when one of Cade's quarters was carted through Suffolk on its way to Norwich appears to have been right. On 1 August a commission of oyer and terminer was issued to go up into Norfolk and Suffolk to deal with all trespasses and insurrections recently committed there.[77] But on 4 August at the village of Alderton, Suffolk, set among the flat fields which lie between the North Sea and the estuary of the Deben, John Squyer, the village parson and, fatally, former chaplain to the duke of Suffolk, was murdered by his own parishioners and by men from the neighbouring villages of Ramsholt and Sutton. A gang of them broke into the rectory, dragged the parson out on to the road and beheaded him with a sword.[78] One of those later indicted for this outrage was a gentleman, Alan Martyn, of nearby Bawdsey. He obtained a pardon in March 1452 on the grounds that this had merely been a malicious

---

[73] KB27/765 *rex* side, m. 6ᵛ.

[74] M. D. Lobel, *The Borough of Bury St Edmund's: A Study in the Government and Development of a Monastic Town* (Oxford, 1935), 123.

[75] Edwin Welch, 'Some Suffolk Lollards', *Proceedings of the Suffolk Institute of Archaeology and History*, 29 (1963), 154–65; Norman Tanner (ed.), *Heresy Trials in the Diocese of Norwich, 1428–31* (Camden Soc., 4th ser., 20, 1977), 84–9, 107–38, 194–5; J. A. F. Thomson, *The Later Lollards, 1414–1520* (Oxford, 1965), 123–4.

[76] C1/16/453.   [77] *CPR*, 1446–52, 388.

[78] C1/19/144; Kingsford, *Prejudice and Promise*, 49; *CPR*, 1446–52, 528; KB27/764 *rex* side, m. 2; /769 *rex* side, m. 17ᵛ; /792 *rex* side, m. 5ᵛ; KB9/118/1, m. 49.

indictment, but since he was in need of another pardon for other unstated trespasses in May 1455 one wonders whether he might not have had something to do with the Alderton murder.[79]

Another of Suffolk's associates to be victimized, albeit much less harshly, was his widow, the duchess of Suffolk, who saw persistent attacks upon her East Anglian estates in this year of her husband's overthrow. One of the manifestations of the rivalry which existed between the dukes of Suffolk and Norfolk had been the occasional poaching of deer from one another's parks by large armed groups of their retainers. In February 1450, for example, the duke of Suffolk's park at Eye had suffered a raid from a party headed by five of Norfolk's esquires from Framlingham, causing the loss of an estimated forty deer.[80] However, after Suffolk's death the daring and audacity of his assailants reached new heights. Poachers raided the duchess's parks repeatedly, in June, July, August, and October 1450; in July and August 1451; and again in August and December 1452.[81]

There can be no doubt that the county of Suffolk was involved in Cade's rising. For some people in the south of the county this may have been as direct an involvement as riding all the way to London to join the insurgents there. But it is likely that, for most, their action took the form of violent attacks within the county against the property of the duke of Suffolk and that of his followers. What must remain uncertain is how much Bury St Edmunds was involved with the inception of the revolt.

IV

Among the counties to experience these satellite troubles during the summer Wiltshire stands out as that which saw the most orchestrated and sustained attacks on people and property.[82] The reason for this is likely to have been, in part, that West Wiltshire and the area around Salisbury together formed one of the most intensive cloth-producing districts in England, and as a consequence was one of the parts of the country to experience most keenly the depression in the industry. It is

---

[79] *CPR*, 1446–52, 528; *CPR*, 1452–61, 239.

[80] KB9/118, m. 22; KB9/270A, m. 29.

[81] KB9/118, mm. 7, 12, 22; KB9/270, m. 2; KB9/270A, m. 29; KB27/778 *rex* side, m. 28.

[82] Benet's chronicle records for 1450 that it was the counties of Kent, Essex, and Wiltshire which rose. *Benet's Chron.*, 202.

striking how many of those indicted for the risings here were men connected with the textile trade. Another factor was that this was the diocese of the bishop of Salisbury, one of the most hated men in Suffolk's group, whose destruction Cheyne's and Jakes's followers had called for in the previous January.[83] In view of what was shortly to happen the atmosphere at this time must have been rife with animosity against such figures. Aiscough must surely have been aware that June as he travelled across the country in flight from London that his life was at risk even away from the capital.

On 20 June a cask and a half of his red wine was taken at Potterne (south of Devizes) by Philip Baynard, a gentleman and sheriff of the county and a group of other men,[84] and on 28 June a valuable horse belonging to the bishop was stolen at Imber.[85] More ominously, an attack was also made on 28 June by a gang from Warminster and Maiden Bradley upon the bishop's baggage train as it preceded him along his route to the safe keeping of his castle at Sherborne. The attackers entered the house of the substantial merchant at Maiden Bradley in whose custody it was being kept that night, broke up the bishop's chariot, and carried off large quantities of valuables, including, according to different indictments, one far more extravagant in its claims than the other, vestments, church books, silver vessels, and even Aiscough's pearl-encrusted mitre and his silver and gold crozier along with an enormous sum of £3,000 in cash.[86] If this figure is a true one then it does suggest that suspicions of peculation among the high offices was entirely justified in the bishop's case. There is some suggestion that the looters stayed around the village the following day, stealing money, books, and other goods from the inhabitants there.[87]

At Maiden Bradley Aiscough's baggage train had been almost at the

---

[83] A more detailed account of the disturbances in Wiltshire during 1450 is to be found in J. N. Hare, 'Lords and Tenants in Wiltshire *c.*1380–*c.*1520 with Special Reference to Regional and Seigneurial Variations', Ph.D. thesis (London, 1976), 297–337; also in his article, 'The Wiltshire Risings of 1450: Political and Economic Discontents in Mid-Fifteenth Century England', *Southern History*, 4 (1982), 13–31.

[84] KB9/134/1, m. 22.   [85] Ibid. m. 37.

[86] KB9/133, mm. 19, 30; /134/1, mm. 9, 15, 20; /134/2, mm. 79, 80. The confusion arising around these various indictments of 1451 and 1452 concerning the date of the looting—as to whether it took place on 28 or 29 June—is discussed in Hare, 'Lords and Tenants in Wiltshire', 297–300.

[87] One of the despoilers of the bishop's goods, a Richard Page of Warminster, gentleman, was charged by two men from Maiden Bradley with stealing their goods and money that Monday, 29 June. KB9/134/2, mm. 79, 80.

Dorset border; the bishop himself was following at a distance of some a dozen miles or so; so that on the day after the attack, 29 June, the feast of Saints Peter and Paul, he was further back on the road at Edington. It was when he was celebrating the feast-day mass there in the house of the Bonhommes that a large armed mob converged on the village, coming in from the surrounding districts, from places such as Trowbridge and Westbury to the west, Market Lavington to the east, and Heytesbury to the south. This gathering of at least a hundred and perhaps several hundred insurgents entered the church of the monastery proclaiming Aiscough to be a public traitor to the king. A clerical recorder of this incident, Thomas Gascoigne, tells, however, that Aiscough's murderers' major grievance was that the bishop was forever with the king and never in his diocese.[88] He was dragged from the altar out to a nearby hill and there barbarously killed with boar spears, cudgels, and staffs in an ugly outbreak of violence reminiscent of the murder of Adam Moleyns, bishop of Chichester, at Portsmouth six months earlier.[89] The mob then turned upon the house of the rector at Edington and plundered horses, harness, and money.[90] The monastery buildings themselves were attacked and damaged to some serious extent. Two full years later in June 1452 the rector and brethren of the monastery would be able to petition successfully to be excused collecting tenths because 'they have sustained of late intolerable damages through the sons of perdition who ... breaking down the houses and building of the monastery, took and carried away the goods and jewels of the petitioners'.[91] It is possible that the rector in 1452 was somewhat cynically turning the events of 1450 to his advantage, but there is every reason to believe that the initial attack was very savage and damaging to the monastery.

Whilst the mob was murdering and stealing at Edington there were troubles away to the south-east of the county in Salisbury itself. This was perhaps to be expected. The inhabitants of Salisbury had struggled against the dominance of their bishop since a settlement

---

[88] Thomas Gascoigne, *Loci e Libro Veritatum*, ed. J. E. T. Rogers (Oxford, 1881), 158–9.

[89] KB9/133, mm. 7, 8, 9, 10, 14, 20, 40; /134/1, mm. 6, 7, 26; /105/1, m. 4. Two different numbers of insurgents are offered by subsequent indictments, 40 and 600; but since 74 are named in the indictments, the true figure must stand at well over 40 and perhaps rather fewer than 600. Hare, 'Lords and Tenants in Wiltshire', 301.

[90] KB9/133, m. 6; /134/1, mm. 2, 4, 14, 32, 33.

[91] *CPR*, 1446–52, 560.

early in the fourteenth century by which the bishops had attained lordship of the soil in the city and full jurisdiction over the citizens through their court.[92] Moreover, Salisbury was a city with conspicuous Lollard connections. It was here that London Lollards had sent their bills and posters for distribution in March 1431, and here that a rising had taken place in the May of that year, allegedly with the intention, amongst other things, to attack the cathedral.[93] The sharp example made of the ringleaders at that time, led as they were out of the city from Fisherton to the gallows at Bemerton, a village to the west of Salisbury, there to be hanged, drawn, and quartered, would not have been forgotten. The cathedral now housed the tomb of Walter, Lord Hungerford, the man who had headed the team of justices responsible for the sentences passed on the Lollards of 1431.[94] He had died in August 1449 aged seventy-one, a veteran campaigner and trusted servant of Henry V and of his son whom he served as treasurer 1426–32.[95] How the old soldier was regarded in Salisbury is unknown; his close ties with the cathedral (he had belonged since 1413 to its distinguished lay fraternity, and his executors included a canon, Walter Bayly)[96] cannot have increased his popularity. His grandson, Robert, Lord Moleyns, was clearly very unpopular. In June 1449 he had been attacked by citizens whilst he was at The George Inn and had had to be rescued by Walter Bayly and another canon, Nicholas Upton, and led to the safety of the cathedral close.[97] In 1450 William Wodeward, a brewer, acted as captain to a crowd of insurgents from the city, many of them artisans and small tradesmen—butchers, carpenters, coopers, and weavers—but which also included two men described in one indictment as esquires, in another as gentlemen.[98] Wodeward was organized enough to have his own clerk and letter carrier. The subsequent indictments estimated that over three hundred men rose up in Salisbury that Monday and further alleged that these rioters were confident that there were ten thousand men of their own mind willing

[92] E. F. Jacob, *The Fifteenth Century 1399–1485* (Oxford, 1961), 496.
[93] KB9/225, m. 21; /227/2, mm. 1B, 2, 23.
[94] N. Pevsner, *The Buildings of England: Wiltshire* (London, 1975), 417.
[95] For details of Walter, Lord Hungerford's distinguished career in royal service, see Griffiths, *Henry VI*, 33–46; for his fortunes from war, see K. B. McFarlane, *The Nobility of Later Medieval England* (Oxford, 1973), 128.
[96] C. Wordsworth (ed.), *Ceremonies and Processions of the Cathedral of Salisbury* (Cambridge, 1901), 145–50.
[97] Salisbury Dean and Chapter Muniments, Register of John Burgh, fo. 24. I am grateful to Dr A. D. Brown for supplying me with this and the other references cited from the bishop's register.   [98] KB9/133, mm. 2, 3.

to join their cause. It appears to have been primarily an anti-clerical demonstration; the rebels were alleged to have wanted to destroy all ecclesiastical houses in the county, and to have exacted sums of money from canons of the cathedral and sought the death of the dean of St Mary's, Gilbert Kymer. The two esquires in the Salisbury mob went out south of the city to Harnham hill the following day to incite men there to rise up with them against the late bishop.[99] With the long hours of sunlight which June affords, a group, now also including some locals from Westharnham, were able to take themselves off that day from Harnham to Woodford north of the city where Aiscough owned a manor and there plundered lead from the manor house roof, swans and their young from the manor pond, and a flock of three hundred sheep worth forty marks from the manor farm.[100]

These looters must have been aware that Aiscough had been killed the previous day, but apparently the news had not yet reached some corners of the county, since that day, 30 June, a clerk up in Meysey Hampton in Gloucestershire, just over the far northern border of Wiltshire, allegedly conspired for Aiscough's death along with a group of others.[101]

Throughout that week Monday's butchering continued to release into the open pent-up feelings of hatred and anger in Wiltshire—nor, as has already been seen in the case of Salisbury, was this simply against Aiscough alone. On Wednesday, 1 July in Salisbury there was an attack on the houses of three canons of St Mary's, one of whom was Nicholas Upton who had led Lord Moleyns to safety from his persecutors the previous year.[102] On Thursday there was an affray of some kind at Tilshead on Salisbury Plain between Edington and Salisbury by a couple of labourers, one of whom had apparently travelled there from Harnham via Woodford.[103] On the Saturday (as Cade's followers were looting and executing in London) there were renewed disturbances in Salisbury by some of Monday's rioters. The bishop's palace was attacked and broken into and from it taken the late bishop's charters, registers, court rolls, and all the written material that could be found that was connected either with him, with Gilbert Kymer the dean, or with the cathedral. This was all carried off to a

---

[99] Ibid. m. 24.
[100] Ibid. m. 11; KB9/134/2, m. 117.
[101] KB27/700 *rex* side, m. 29; KB9/271, m. 53.
[102] KB9/133, m. 27; Salisbury Dean and Chapter Muniments, Register of John Burgh, fo. 24.   [103] KB9/133, m. 17.

field outside the city and cut up and burnt, no doubt with considerable relish.[104]

The following Monday, 6 July, as Cade was negotiating a settlement in Southwark, the demonstrations against Aiscough began to tail off. That day more of his manors, on this occasion at Potterne and Ramsbury, were attacked and their muniments stolen,[105] but the next outbreak of trouble was not until 12 July at Devizes when an armed gang allegedly rode about inciting others to rise against the ecclesiastical orders and temporal lords of the county; one of the gang, a husbandman from Draycote, even carried an axe ready for the beheading of appropriate victims.[106] On 20 July a similar sort of disorder occurred at Wilton, just west of Salisbury.[107] The movement towards more general lawlessness was further exhibited in a riotous assembly to ambush and kill Philip Baynard, the sheriff of Wiltshire, on 29 July, and by an ambush on 31 July on an individual at Biddestone by men exciting others to rise and riot.[108]

Just over the border in Dorset at Aiscough's manor of Sherborne the news of the bishop's death was the signal for much looting and rioting by his tenants. Here insurrection carried on for months to follow, transferring itself to an old quarrel with the monks of the abbey there.[109] The episode reportedly ended in an atmosphere of contrition with the collection of a fine from every adult of the town, the people believing that otherwise the king would reap retribution from the whole shire.[110]

Disorders in Hampshire broke out just a few days later than those in Wiltshire, beginning on Saturday, 4 July with an anti-clerical rising at Crawley by a gang of men, apparently largely from Newbury in Berkshire, who continued their disturbance by striking southwards even further from their home town and making a mob visitation upon the abbey of Hyde near Winchester in the south-western corner of the county. They threatened the abbot with mutilation and with the destruction of his house and extracted from him the very considerable sum of £100.[111] The following day saw an even more violent

---

[104] KB9/133, m. 32.   [105] Ibid. m. 36.   [106] Ibid. m. 15.
[107] Ibid. m. 34.
[108] Ibid. mm. 12, 23. Baynard had had his own differences with the rector and brothers at Edington that previous autumn in his capacity as tax collector, which had led him to distrain temporarily on 300 of their sheep. E159/226 *Communia* Easter Term.
[109] *EHL*, 346–9.   [110] *Gregory's Chron.*, 194–5.
[111] KB9/109, m. 12 (badly preserved, so see also KB27/771 *rex* side, mm. 21, 23). The abbot had sustained malicious damage to his property earlier when in 1440/1 a

demonstration on the Isle of Wight. There a certain Robert Spycer, a spicer from Newport, set himself up as captain of an angry mob who turned upon Robert Russell, a close counsellor of the late Adam Moleyns, bishop of Chichester, and beheaded him.[112] Perhaps it was the news of the murder of Aiscough that previous Monday which sparked off this new act of hatred against Moleyns and his kind, demonstrating very clearly that bitterness against the king's ministers was as strong as ever in the region.

In this disturbed atmosphere old animosities flared up into open violence, such as the anti-alien rising which took place that July at Romsey where the local textile industry was controlled by Genoese merchants. These Italian merchants had established a trade importing unfinished cloth, both English and Netherlandish, through Southampton and sending it out to Hampshire villages where labour was particularly cheap to be fulled, dyed, and mended. They then exported the finished cloth to the Mediterranean.[113] It was an enterprise on a considerable scale: in 1441, for example, over one thousand broadcloths were carried up to Romsey and then back again to Southampton. Romsey, seven miles north-west of Southampton, was the centre for this finishing industry and its men evidently held a grudge against their perhaps exploitative foreign employers. So in 1450 they decided to take advantage of the atmosphere of lawlessness and violence to march upon Southampton and wreak revenge on their Italian masters. The steward of Southampton's book recorded that a group of them 'camme to Towne for to have robbyd the lumbardes'.[114] However, the mayor and citizens of Southampton protected their

tailor from Pewsey in Wiltshire had fired some of the abbot's buildings in Pewsey. *Calendarium Inquisitionum ad quod damnum*. Henry VI Anno. 19. The document itself, OBS1/364, cannot be traced at the Public Record Office.

[112] KB9/109, mm. 9, 20 (again, badly preserved, so see KB27/763 *rex* side, m. 7'). It is possible that the John Boney, John Mewe, Richard Coupelond, and William Skynner named among the 18 names still legible on these indictments were involved in some way with the murder of Adam Moleyns in Jan. 1450, since they are explicitly excluded from the pardons later given out to the inhabitants of the Isle of Wight in 1451, a pardon denied only to those who were pirates, slayers, or privy to the death of Adam Moleyns or who had been indicted for the crime. *CPR*, 1446–52, 420–1, 470–1.

[113] E. B. Fryde, 'The English Cloth Industry and the Trade with the Mediterranean, *c*.1370–*c*.1480' (ch. 15 in *Studies in Medieval Trade and Finance* (London, 1983)), 353; O. Coleman (ed.), *The Brokage Book of Southampton, 1443–4* (Southampton Record Society Series, 4, 1960), pp. xxv–xxvi.

[114] A. A. Ruddock, *Italian Merchants and Shipping in Southampton, 1270–1600* (Southampton, 1951), 166–7.

Italian colony, defending the city with patrols along the streets and walls for three days and with townsmen guarding the Galley Quay. Finally, the sheriff and thirteen other men from Southampton escorted the ringleaders to Winchester gaol.

On 21 July at Wells in Somerset Bishop Beckington, who had had a lot to do with French negotiations during the 1440s, met with local disturbances on such a scale that he called in Lord Bonville to help him control the situation. At one point clerks guarded the cathedral day and night for four days, and then Welshmen were hired for the cathedral's defence. The rumour some time that summer that a large French fleet had come into Southampton must have added considerably to the trouble at Wells and throughout southern England.[115]

Other riots and disturbances took place at about this time elsewhere in the country, although many are obscure and lacking in any clear chronology. It may have been at about the same time as the sheriff of Wiltshire was attacked that July that an attack was made upon the under-sheriff of Worcestershire at Tewkesbury.[116] At this time too other absentee court bishops were victimized as they fled the dangers of court to their neglected bishoprics. At Winchester Bishop Waynflete's palace was sacked; in the Midlands Bishop William Booth of Lichfield was besieged in his palace; in East Anglia Bishop Lyhert of Norwich was threatened by an angry mob; and in Gloucester Abbot Boulers's manor of Wyreyard was sacked and plundered.[117] Both Lyhert, who had been promoted to his bishopric at Suffolk's wish, and Boulers had gone on embassies to negotiate with the French and were members of that court group associated with Suffolk's regime. This was the season when all his associates were suffering. His steward, Sir John Hampden, was killed in Flint castle and his secretary was arrested.[118]

In Wiltshire the trouble that had looked as if it were quietening down at the end of July revived in August. On 1 August Robert Godfray, the labourer from Westharnham who had gone with others and stolen goods from Bishop Aiscough's manor at Woodford in July, took himself off once more, this time to Little Woodford and again carried off lead and other valuables from the bishop's property.[119]

---

[115] HMC, *Report on the Manuscripts of the Dean and Chapter of Wells*, ii. (1914), 77–8.   [116] *EHL*, 366.

[117] Griffiths, *Henry VI*, 645.   [118] *EHL*, 366.

[119] KB9/133, m. 15. The Woodfords, now comprising three villages: Upper, Middle, and Lower Woodford, set beside meanders of the Avon, were in the fifteenth century two manors of Great and Little Woodford.

This kind of activity may then have quietened down for a while, but on 20 August there was renewed disturbance with a riot to despoil the parish church at Bradenstoke.[120] Then on 28 August trouble flared up again at Edington, probably in quite a dramatic fashion judging from the unusually large number of twenty-two individuals indicted for the offence. What exactly the purpose was of the rising is not clear—the indictment speaks of congregating to kill the true lieges of the king and the procuring and exciting of many true lieges to rise, phrases which amount more or less to a set form of words. It is, however, interesting to see that this demonstration, exactly two months after the first attack on Aiscough's chariot and baggage, drew on the same supporters as had run riot there then in Maiden Bradley and Edington. According to the record of the indictments, sixteen of the twenty-two men who rose up at Edington on 28 August had previously congregated there two months before and either taken part in the looting of the monastery and murder of the bishop or plundered his luggage at Maiden Bradley. None of them, it should be further noted, were Edington men, but tailors, weavers, husbandmen, and barbers from such places as Westbury, Heytesbury, Potterne, Imber, and Maiden Bradley.[121] Evidently these risings, far from being local and uncoordinated, must have been carefully organized affairs bringing in people from a wide area and capable of being repeated at another date. This kind of organization may have been part of the function of the men from Salisbury riding about the county that summer inciting rebellion.[122]

On 19 August James Gresham had written to John Paston that it was reported that there were nine or ten thousand men who had risen in rebellion in Wiltshire, but he thought this unlikely for there had been little more talk of it.[123] The number is rather improbable, but the evidence does suggest that during the August of 1450 the focus of insurrection perhaps moved from the South-East to southern England. What is more, there is even some suggestion that some of Cade's followers may have made their way there. In a later year a London dyer was to tell the tale of how well into that August whilst he was down in Dorset at Wimborne he had encountered a merchant riding along the road who had greeted him with the enquiry, 'What news of Normandy?' (doubtless a common enough question during that summer). The dyer had replied that the whole country had been lost.

---

[120] KB9/133, m. 35.
[121] Ibid. m. 37; KB27/770 *rex* side, m. 20ᵛ.
[122] KB9/133, m. 2.
[123] *PL*, ii. 162.

'And so will England be', the stranger had rejoined. However, he knew of one who could govern better than the present king, and he had gone on to persuade the dyer to ride along with him and join a fellowship of Cade's followers who met up that day at Cranborne, some ten miles away to the north near the Hampshire border. There the dyer had sworn loyalty to their plans and opinions. What gives credence to this story is that the merchant riding to Cranborne that day was a former soldier from Normandy, Thomas Odiham, who came from Hadleigh, the west Suffolk cloth town which may well have supported Cade's rising the previous month.[124]

Cade's rebellion was undoubtedly not restricted to the South-East alone, the area to which the chroniclers have largely confined our attention. Courtiers—the 'false traitors' of the rebels' petitions—and their associates were attacked throughout southern England. By early July the authorities may have managed to quell the rebel force which had been ejected from the capital, but they were unable to counter the offshoots of the rising which sprang up all around the country throughout the remainder of the summer.

[124] KB27/759 *rex* side, m. 6ᵛ; *CPR*, 1446–52, 343, 356, 359; KB9/271, m. 67; KB9/118/1, m. 6.

6

POPULAR REVOLT DURING
THE 1450s

ON 28 July Henry returned to the capital from which he had fled, although not with the intention of staying long. He offered at St Paul's, went from there out to Westminster and intended to travel up river to Eton for the feast of the Assumption. He was unable to do so, however, owing to the numbers of redundant soldiers home from Normandy who now disrupted the city and its surrounds with their disorderly presence.[1] The large numbers of unemployed soldiers in the south of England that summer, many of them evidently congregating upon London, were an important constituent of the protest and discontent of 1450. Here were a body of men rendered aimless and disaffected by what they saw as a gross mismanagement of affairs in France.[2] They were, moreover, a blight which brought the loss of France home to the inhabitants of the south of England in a very immediate fashion.

One source suggests that the continuing disasters in France were popularly regarded as a vindication of the rebels' complaints. A poem, probably of the later part of 1450, harped on the theme of the loss of France, blaming it upon the likes of Daniel and Trevilian for their exclusion from influence of the good soldiers among the king's traditional noble councillors:

> Therfore [what] the commyns saith is both trew an kynde
> Bothe in Southesex and in Kent.[3]

The presence of the redundant soldiers caused fears among those in authority that new outbreaks of insurrection might take place. It is likely that it was these fears which influenced the concession then made: on 1 August, as the duke of Somerset in retreat from Normandy passed through London with his defeated troops, the king ordained a

---

[1] *Benet's Chron.*, 202.
[2] On 25 Aug. 1450 soldiers who were still being a nuisance to the household were given fifteen days' maintenance. B. P. Wolffe, *Henry VI* (London, 1981), 239 n. 2.
[3] *Political Poems*, ii. 221–3.

commission of oyer and terminer to go into Kent to make inquiry into all miscarriages of justice, extortions, trespasses, and oppressions. Unlike the commission of 1 July, set up during the rebellion to investigate all treasons, Lollardies, and insurrections in London, this Kentish commission was not intended as a punitive measure, solely to bring order to a disaffected area. It was a genuinely conciliatory gesture by Henry to the rebels which sought to investigate the corrupt local government of which they complained. It represented the government's one positive concession to the rebels' demands, a concession elicted by fear of further unrest in a region receiving Normandy's defeated troops.[4] The commission was headed by the archbishops of York and Canterbury and the bishop of Winchester (negotiators with Cade over his pardon), and Humphrey, duke of Buckingham, none of whom were royal household figures or supporters of the duke of Suffolk. Indeed, in September the archbishop of Canterbury would give additional recognition to the commons' outcry against the reputation of Suffolk's supporters by a commission he established to audit the accounts of the administration of the goods of the late Duke Humphrey—who had died intestate. The administration of these goods had been entrusted to Lord Saye, Sir Thomas Stanley, John Somerset, and Richard Chester: complaint had reached the archbishop that they had embezzled some of these goods and wasted others.[5]

The Kentish commission sat at Rochester 20–2 August, at Maidstone 16–19 September, at Canterbury 22–4 September, and at Dartford on 22 October.[6] Thirty-two men named on the July pardon roll were among the jurors who made presentments before this commission.[7] As it emerged the jurors did not treat simply of the major

[4] *CPR*, 1446–52, 388. Included in this commission was William Wangford a Kentish justice. He may be the same William Wangford who had been expelled from Stone castle and manor in 1447 by John Trevilian. Virgoe, 'Ancient Indictments', 221–2.

[5] *The Register of Thomas Bekynton, Bishop of Bath and Wells 1443–1465*, Somerset Record Society, 49 (1934), 204–6.

[6] Virgoe, 'Ancient Indictments', 215–16.

[7] Ibid. 220–43. This file (KB9/46) covers the inquests held in 1450 in Kent by the commission of 1 Aug. 1450. None of the jurors for the 6 hundreds of Wingham, Calehill and Chart, Westgate, Larkfield, Maidstone, or Tonbridge can be found named on the pardon roll. However, at least one person from each of the 3 juries for the hundred of Hoo, Axton, and the body of Kent (which gathered at Dartford in Oct.) can be identified on the roll. The number rises to 3 in the case of the single jury for the hundreds of Codsheath, Brasted, and Wrotham; 4 for Shamwell hundred; 5 in the case of the city of Rochester; 6 for the joint hundreds of Chatham and Gillingham; and a remarkable 11 for the hundred of Teynham: a total of 32 men. *CPR*, 1446–52, 338–74.

culprits alone, but dealt with the alleged offences of some seventy-two men and women, ranging from knights and county officials to humble clerks and husbandmen. Robert Est, 'the great extortioner', as one of the rebels' petitions described him,[8] had the distinction of being charged by various juries on eleven different counts. Seven indictments were made against Lord Dudley, and four against both Thomas Daniel and Thomas Stanley. It is quite possible that almost thirty other supporters of the duke of Suffolk's regime may have been indicted during the late summer or autumn.[9] The impression that the surviving indictments give is of the releasing of long-pent-up grudges and injuries nursed over several years concerned with a range of offences from the extortionate practices of Kent's own sheriffs and under-sheriffs down to unpunished crimes by ordinary men of the county. Some of those indicted were not found guilty by the court, some were fined, and for others such as Dudley, Daniel, and Stanley the verdicts are unknown. How much of a triumph for their cause Cade's followers felt these hearings to be it is hard to guess, the evidence of subsequent events would suggest that they were not satisfied by them.

The commission, indeed, carried on its activities against a background of riots and assemblies, for, as was noted in the previous chapter, the ending of Cade's revolt left the South-East in a continuing state of turmoil. In future Cade's name and his title of 'Captain of Kent' were to be catchwords amongst insurgents. Not only was his cause not dead but some would even assert that Cade himself was still alive. Most of the risings and demonstrations that took place in the South-East during the following two years and beyond were to be expressions of frustration specifically concerned with aspects of Cade's rebellion. Disaffection was most marked in the industrial villages of the Weald and along the Medway valley in Kent. Men were angry at how few of their grievances had been met and at how little the parliamentary Commons of 1450 had been allowed to achieve in the way of the resumption of Crown lands. Moreover, they were to feel cheated and bitter over the matter of the pardons and the king's harsh dealings with insurgents. The continuation of a state of turmoil into the late summer and autumn of 1450 may also be ascribed in part to the fresh impetus given to popular reforming fervour by the return, unbidden, to England of the duke of York, Henry's lieutenant in

---

[8] See Ch. 2, sect. III, above, and also for Daniel and Say.
[9] Virgoe, 'Ancient Indictments', 216 n. 2.

Ireland.[10] It was probably in late August that rumour of his impending departure reached England. Sir William Oldhall, York's chamberlain, had gone over to Ireland during the summer; his was doubtless one of the reports received by the duke that season to make him amply aware of the tide of popular opinion (and even expectation) running in his favour in southern England. The duke's participation in the events of 1450 at last took on clear definition.

At the very end of August 1450, as York began to stir from Ireland and the king's commission began its first hearings in Rochester, troubles continued in Wiltshire, Dorset, and Suffolk. In the county where the commission sat, William Parmynter, a smith from Faversham, came forward calling himself the second captain of Kent. He was fomenting trouble in north-central Kent early in August,[11] but his uprising took place on the last day of the month. It covered a broad band of country running roughly east–west across the north and the middle of Kent from Teynham, Faversham, Canterbury, and Ospringe westwards along to Marden, Sevenoaks, Otford, Hawkhurst, and Appledore.[12] Support for his rising was later to extend across the Weald to Mountfield in Sussex and down through Hailsham, Willingdon, and Jevington to the coast at Eastbourne where there was a rising on 16 September.[13]

That Parmynter commanded a sizeable following is suggested by the number of localities from the two counties involved in the rising, showing clearly just how widespread disaffection continued to be. The names are known of only sixteen of Parmynter's alleged Kentish followers: four husbandmen, three labourers, four yeomen, two tailors, a weaver, a roofer, and a baker.[14] Many of these appear in the records as recipients of pardons in the spring of 1451. In Sussex the dozen men accused (although not all found guilty) of rising as supporters of Parmynter were yeomen, labourers, cobblers, a smith, and a butcher.[15] Of these the butcher alone was found guilty of treasonably saying that he would like to shoot down the king like a buck.[16] The Sussex men

---

[10] R. A. Griffiths, *The Reign of King Henry VI: The Exercise of Royal Authority, 1422–1461* (London, 1981), 684–92; id., 'Duke Richard of York's Intentions in 1450 and the Origins of the Wars of the Roses', *Journal of Medieval History*, 1 (1975), 187–209; P. A. Johnson, *Duke Richard of York 1411–1460* (Oxford, 1988), 78–83; Wolffe, *Henry VI*, 240–3.   [11] KB27/790 *rex* side, m. 4ᵛ; *CPR*, 1446–52, 469.

[12] KB27/790 *rex* side, mm. 4ᵛ, 44, 47ᵛ; KB27/770 *rex* side, m. 38; KB27/759 *rex* side, m. 2; Virgoe, 'Ancient Indictments', 253–4; KB9/270A, m. 56; C237/42, mm. 4, 6, 7, 14; *CPR*, 1446–52, 423, 424, 453, 461–1, 469, 497.

[13] KB9/122, m. 40; KB27/766 *rex* side, m. 28.   [14] As n. 12, above.

[15] KB9/122, mm. 27, 40; KB27/766 *rex* side, m. 28.   [16] KB9/122, m. 40.

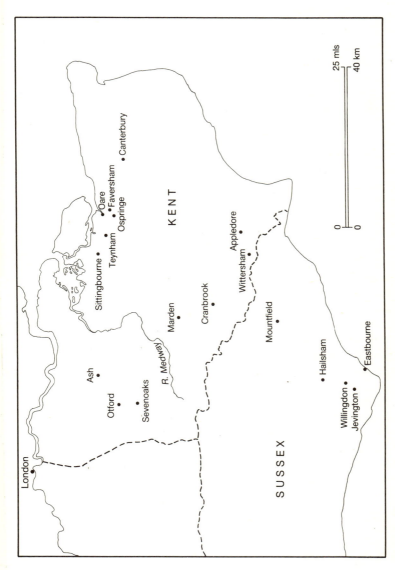

The Places in Kent and Sussex Involved in Parmynter's Rising August–September 1450

were said to fear that the king wanted to destroy them and their county with force, and they had quite specific grievances concerning the price of renting land.[17] Only one of them is named in the pardon list of July 1450, a John Sherman of Hailsham, cobbler, but there is good reason to suppose that they all had risen under Cade. As for the Kentish followers, none of their sixteen names are to be found on the pardon list, but that they too had supported Cade is very likely. Their leader Parmynter's title of the second captain of Kent, the close timing of the two risings, and their description as Cade's 'late accomplices' make a connection probable.[18]

Later, in 1451, when the matter was before the courts, some said that 200 men had risen up behind Parmynter, others guessed at 400, and, they added, Parmynter and his followers were trusting to the backing of 4,000 armed men sharing their views. None of these figures are very helpful. The rebels were accused of levying war against the king and of wishing to destroy and despoil certain magnates and clergy, purposing to hold possessions in common. The rising provoked these rather formulaic accusations normally cast against Lollards and seditious behaviour in general because it had been an opportunity to continue in Kent the destruction and despoiling associated with Cade's rising. Men with grievances lobbied this new captain and his followers, petitioning for the plundering or even murder of certain hated figures. A John Burgh, for instance, was in gaol in Leeds castle by November 1450 for having allegedly told Parmynter and his men that two procurators of the vicar of Charing were fit to die because they 'went with the gentilmen to execute the kynges commyssion'. He suggested the taking of both their goods and their lives. He had hoped too that the fellowship might have searched the bottom of the coffers of a certain John Knyght. Furthermore, he regretted how many of his goods the vicar of Charing had taken away to safety, for Burgh would have then fared so much the better in his own takings.[19] This is an extraordinary insight into the atmosphere of retaliation and violence out of which Parmynter's rising had grown.

Whereabouts Parmynter was captured is unknown. He and some half a dozen of his main henchmen were rounded up by a squire of the duke of Somerset with a posse of twenty-four men on horseback who held them for several weeks before taking half their number off to the safe custody of Windsor castle, the remaining half journeying on to

[17] KB9/122, m. 27.   [18] KB27/759 *rex* side, m. 2.   [19] C244/64/242.

Winchester castle.[20] Parmynter, inevitably, was eventually sentenced to death.[21]

At least one of Parmynter's followers evaded being brought to court by fleeing to that refuge from the arm of the law, the sanctuary of St Martin's in London. However, this individual, William Cayme of Sittingbourne, who had been among the rebels supporting Parmynter at Faversham on 31 August and who had also incited people at Canterbury that day, found upon his arrival at St Martin's that the dean took a dim view of sheltering traitors. He found himself placed in the sanctuary prison. None the less in February 1451 the dean would give stout refusal to a royal request that he should surrender Cayme up to trial in Rochester. At which Henry, conferring with his councillors, decided not to break the sanctuary's immunities but recommended that Cayme should be kept close from perpetrating other crimes against his person. Soon after, in May 1451, Cayme received the king's pardon.[22]

On 12 September 1450, twelve days after Parmynter's rising, there was trouble again in Sevenoaks with gatherings and speeches against the king.[23] At Sevenoaks and in the Weald generally impatience with the government was especially persistent. On 26 September Thomas Michell, a baker from Sevenoaks, gathered there with a score of others 'to make war and levied such war against the king until 27th January then following'.[24] Thomas, indeed, had some cause for grievance, since Lord Dudley and his troops had robbed him of twenty marks during their raid into Kent in June that year.[25] At Sevenoaks and Cranbrook Parmynter's adherents were still congregating and plotting into late December.[26]

Parmynter was not the only captain going about Kent that autumn. A John Smyth also rose up calling himself the captain of Kent and allegedly made a great gathering of people—although whereabouts in the county and at what date exactly is unknown. As we have just seen there was a demand for leaders to organize gangs of violent looters against those whom they felt had betrayed Cade's cause or against whom there were old grievances. John Smyth was captured some time

[20] E404/67/180.   [21] KB29/82, m. 15.
[22] A. J. Kempe, *Historical Notices of the Collegiate Church of St Martin-Le-Grand* (London, 1825), 136–7; *CPR*, 1446–52, 424.
[23] KB27/790 *rex* side, m. 45.   [24] *CPR*, 1446–52, 460–1.
[25] KB9/266, m. 84; KB27/765 *rex* side, m. 26; Virgoe, 'Ancient Indictments', 232.
[26] *CPR*, 1446–52, 453.

before early October 1450 by the duke of Somerset who was going about Kent subduing and punishing would-be insurgents.[27]

Throughout Kent political agitation was deteriorating into mere lawlessness. In October 1450 at Penshurst a group of some hundred men from the Sussex and Kentish Weald carried out a massive poaching raid on the park of Humphrey, duke of Buckingham.[28] They followed the poachers' practice of painting their faces and of wearing long beards for the purpose of anonymity.[29] It was perhaps somewhat tongue-in-cheek that they hid their identity behind the description 'servants of the queen of the fairies' in a clear echo of Thomas Cheyne, the hermit Bluebeard, who had risen in Kent during the previous January.

In Sussex rioting and lawlessness had resumed immediately after Cade's rebels had dispersed from London with their pardons from 7 July onwards. At Sedlescombe in eastern Sussex, not far from the Kentish border, there was a riot at a lathe court on 14 July led by a Simon Sture, a yeoman and former soldier from nearby Winchelsea, who claimed to be a kinsman of Cade; he appears to have spent much of September and October taking part in similar agitation and in robbing local Sussex clergy.[30] Just over a week later on 24 July in the same locality two gentlemen from Ashburnham, John and Richard Assheburneham, with sixteen and more husbandmen and artisans to help them, forced their way into Richard Fiennes's manor at Ewhurst and held it for eight days. The action was lent a certain bravado by the fact that almost a third of this invading group had had their names inscribed on the royal pardon roll only seventeen days beforehand.[31] Fiennes, as a nephew of Lord Saye and Sele and as a member of a family of prominent court servants, the most powerful family in the South-East, was an obvious target for any kind of attack at this time. The Assheburnehams had long been bitterly contesting the right of the Fiennes to the manor of Ewhurst in court; no doubt this seemed as good a time as any to settle the matter out of court.[32]

During August disturbances in Sussex took on a purposeful aspect. At Chichester in the west of the county on 6 August a group of men

[27] *PPC*, vi. 101.
[28] Virgoe, 'Ancient Indictments', 254–5; KB27/790 *rex* side, m. 44ᵛ.
[29] For example, the English *Faulx-Visaiges* of Normandy in the 1440s, mentioned in J. Stevenson (ed.), *Narratives of the Expulsion of the English from Normandy, 1449–1450* (RS, 1863), 255–6.   [30] KB9/122, m. 62; KB27/770 *rex* side, m. 30ᵛ.
[31] KB9/265, m. 147; *CPR*, 1446–52, 353, 359.
[32] East Sussex Record Office, Battle Abbey Estate, MS 2711.

from villages north of the Downs, from Midhurst, Pulborough, Steyning, and Sutton, began to organize an insurrection by exhorting all the true men of the county to gather there at Chichester on the forthcoming 27 August. Written messages were sent about Sussex to this effect.[33] There is no exact information as to what this rising was about except for the usual opaque allegations about rising against the king to kill him and his lords in battle with the intention of ruling the realm and holding all things in common, but it does give an interesting insight into how risings were orchestrated. William Howell, a gentleman from Sutton, and others masterminding the event, sent peremptory orders to local constables by letter: 'We will and charge yow that ye apere byfore us at Chichestre upon thoresday next after Seynt Bartolomewes day and brynge with yow all defencyble men withynne yowre office upon payne of deth.'[34] On the eve of St Bartholomew's some insurgents made preliminary gatherings at local gathering-points, such as Bramber, Sutton, Steyning, and Fittleworth, before taking the road to Chichester, for some of them a twenty-mile journey, where the rising took place the following day, 27 August.[35] The leading agitants received a positive response to their call from a wide area of western Sussex; men converged on Chichester from points as far apart as Selsey in the extreme south and Horsham away up in the north-centre of the county.[36] There were all sorts of men too: drapers, barbers, glovers, grooms, husbandmen, clergy, and even a sorcerer, a Henry Whyteberd from Upwaltham, three and a half miles south-west of Petworth.[37] Such a pattern of events is likely to have been typical of many risings of this period. The key lay in having an individual or a group of men to give decided leadership.

For such a reason Cade's name had become a shibboleth among the discontented in eastern Sussex. The continuation of unrest among Cade's former supporters was very marked here. In September they had risen behind William Parmynter, the second captain of Kent, and on 5 October one of Cade's followers from Hastings and some fellow

[33] KB9/122, m. 7; KB27/765 *rex* side, m. 21; KB27/766 *rex* side, m. 33; KB27/770 *rex* side, m. 48.

[34] KB9/122, m. 55; KB27/766 *rex* side, m. 33; KB27/770 *rex* side, mm. 33, 48.

[35] KB9/122, mm. 48, 51; KB27/766 *rex* side, m. 33; KB27/770 *rex* side, mm. 9ᵛ, 48; KB27/775 *rex* side, m. 3; *CPR*, 1446–52, 472.

[36] KB9/122, mm. 7, 24, 48; KB27/765 *rex* side, m. 21.

[37] The sorcerer and a husbandman from Upwaltham, one of the ringleaders from Sutton, and the rector from Selsey were subsequently pardoned. KB27/765 *rex* side, m. 21ʳ⁻ᵛ; KB27/776 *rex* side, m. 3.

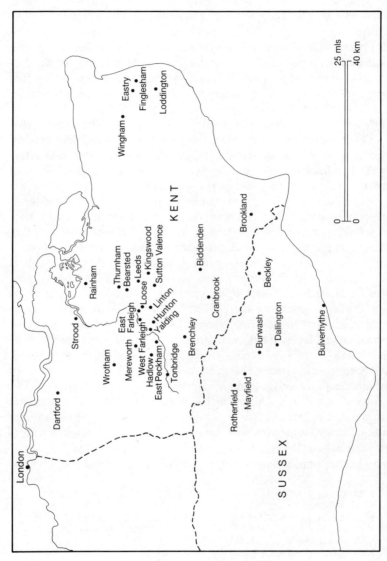

The Places in Kent and Sussex Involved in Hasilden's Rising April 1451

townsmen, also likely to have been Cade's followers, gathered at Hastings agreeing amongst themselves that Henry was not of a sufficiently powerful mind to be king. They wanted a king who knew better how to govern.[38] Again, it was probably another of Cade's men who led a demonstration at the sheriff's court at Deerfold, in the parish of Battle, on 14 October.[39] Whilst on 23 October rebels rose up at Horsham (including one of the town's notorious thieves who had almost certainly already joined in the rising on St Bartholomew's day two months earlier).[40] They wanted to despoil Sussex gentry and to have the heads, so it was alleged, of some of the gentlemen of the county, especially of those who had been against Cade.[41] This was also the alleged aim and intention of a group of rebels who rose up at Hastings on 20 November. They included in their number at least two former supporters of Cade and it is likely that all of them had been fellow insurgents during June and July.[42]

There were too plenty of petty local leaders ready to take up the title of 'captain' and to settle local grievances or inflame old quarrels in this atmosphere of seething unrest. On 25 November 1450 a 'Captain of Burwash' led some sort of a riot in demonstration against the abbot of Robertsbridge's fair whilst it was being held. This may well have been an old argument over the abbot's privileges surfacing again.[43]

An interesting aspect of the troubles in the county was the way in which they extended into the hundred courts in some places. At the meeting of the hundred of Shiplake on 6 October the tithing men from Waldron, Chiddingly, East Hoathly, Ripe, and Laughton, villages and hamlets just west of Hailsham, all asked for a postponement of the payment of their usual common fine until the next meeting of the

---

[38] A John Clypsam, carpenter, of Hastings is named both in the pardon list of Cade's followers (*CPR*, 1446–52, 361), and in the indictment for plotting against the king on 5 Oct. (KB9/122, m. 15).

[39] A Richard Wellys, carpenter, of Warbleton is named in the pardon list (*CPR*, 1446–52, 359), and a Richard Wellys of the parish of Warbleton, millward, is named in an indictment for the demonstration on 14 Oct. (KB9/122, m. 61).

[40] Indictments for the events of 26 and 27 Aug. name a John Herkyn of Horsham, husbandman (KB9/122, m. 48 and KB27/766 *rex* side, m. 38), and indictments for the events of 23 Oct. name a John Herkyn of Horsham, dyer (KB9/122, m. 16 and KB27/766 *rex* side, m. 38); a John Herkyn of Horsham, dyer, is also described as a notorious thief and accused of various thefts, housebreaking, and assault over a period 1439–45 (KB9/248, m. 46). [41] KB9/122, m. 16; KB27/766 *rex* side, m. 38.

[42] KB9/122, m. 21; KB27/781 *rex* side, m. 33ᵛ, both of which concern the rebels at Hastings on 20 Nov., name a William Mason, mason, and an Osbert Watte, husbandman, of that town; both of them are to be found on the pardon list (*CPR*, 1446–52, 361). [43] KB9/122, m. 26.

hundred court. The steward granted his permission to this request (one would like to know with how much grace). But, to all appearances at least, this unconventional action passed off without acrimony and the fines were duly paid at the next hundred court held the following April.[44] In contrast, in the rolls of the neighbouring hundred court of Battle the same disobedience (which had already been demonstrated at the Easter lawday) was felt to merit some explanation. The tithing men who came to the court on 9 October 1450 paid no common fines *'propter inobedienciam populi rebellantis contra tales consuetudines usitatos'*. They also refused to pay the chevage owed by servile tenants living outside the abbot's manors. In the manorial court of Battle the abbot's beadle was unable either on 9 October or at the two courts held there that November to collect fines or debts on account of the insurrection and disobedience of the people, and he was to continue to have trouble extracting them well into 1451.[45]

To look at Essex during this period of July to December 1450 is to see a similar, but not entirely parallel, pattern of plottings, uprisings, and lawlessness of a kind which makes rather amusing the detached and cursory notice jotted in the margin of the Oath Book of Colchester under 1449–50: 'In this same year John Cade made an insurrection in Kent.'[46] Here too during July after the revolt men continued to meet to exchange treasonous opinions about the king and his lords, as happened at Great Tey, not far west of Colchester, on 24 July.[47] Yet whilst the commissioners and juries who investigated the events in Kent and Sussex of this period were to use the term 'Lollard' very loosely to mean anyone who dissented in a way unacceptable to the Crown, and therefore applied it to former supporters of Cade, here in Essex there appears to have been an actual Lollard movement based upon religious unorthodoxy and characterized by a strong anti-clericalism.

September saw an outbreak of this religious insurrection focused around a yeoman and weaver from Bocking, Robert Helder. On 5 September he was preaching at Bocking against the necessity either of infant baptism or of confession to a priest, which were, he said, merely devices to heighten the priests' power and prestige, and he

[44] BL Add. Roll 32473.

[45] East Sussex Record Office XA3/2, 287; E. Searle, *Lordship and Community: Battle Abbey and its Banlieu, 1066–1538* (Toronto, 1974), 398–9.

[46] W. Gurney Benham (ed.), *The Oath Book or Red Parchment Book of Colchester* (Colchester, 1907), 118.

[47] KB9/268, m. 19; KB27/769 *rex* side, m. 28.

argued for a fair division of all goods.[48] Helder was evidently working to inflame already existing local antipathies towards the church and its ministers since four days later at Sible Hedingham he and a large gang of men from Bocking and Sible Hedingham took part in a vicious anti-clerical attack. They broke into the house of John Smyth, rector of the church at Sible Hedingham, killed and beheaded him and looted his belongings, carrying off his horse, saddlery, and household effects, much in the manner of the attack on the duke of Suffolk's chaplain at Alderton, Suffolk, the previous month.[49] In the light of this incident it is rather surprising that Helder was able to obtain a pardon within a couple of years.[50]

On 8 September the earl of Oxford and Viscount Bourchier and a posse of Essex knights and esquires were commissioned to go into Essex to gather up a force of whatever estate, rank, and condition to go with them against these insurgents both in Essex and its neighbouring counties to arrest and imprison them.[51]

In the mean time, alongside the bitter anti-clerical activity, former supporters of Cade's rebellion were still invoking their leader's name. On 10 September at Colchester, not far away to the east of Sible Hedingham, a baker of the town and a miller from West Bergholt with some fifty or so others gathered and declared that Cade was alive yet and that they continued to support his ideas.[52] Some of their number led by a Colchester brick-maker, Richard Taillor, ran riot and robbed goods, including a large sum of a hundred shillings in cash, from the parson of St Leonard's, Colchester. Taillor was imprisoned by the town bailiffs. However, in a town with a populace as insubordinate as Colchester's was at this time, it is not surprising to hear that some of his fellow insurgents in Cade's cause (who had like Taillor gone on the long trek down to Mile End in July) broke into the gaol a few days later and released him.[53]

On 11 and 12 September insurgents, said to number between six hundred to seven hundred men drawn from the surrounding district, rose up at Horndon in southern Essex claiming that Cade was still alive and that they shared in his opinions.[54] Then on 14 September Cade's supporters in Colchester and West Bergholt staged yet another

---

[48] KB9/268, m. 41.
[49] Ibid. mm. 40a, 41; KB27/770 *rex* side, m. 34; KB9/26/1, m. 35.
[50] C67/40, m. 34.   [51] *CPR, 1446–52*, 431.
[52] KB27/765 *rex* side, m. 1.
[53] KB9/268, m. 41a; /26, mm. 16, 17; *CPR, 1446–52*, 415, 503; KB27/772 *rex* side, m. 6.   [54] KB9/268, mm. 32, 34; KB27/773 *rex* side, m. 5.

rising this time on Bergholt Heath.[55] The following day a large gang of them accomplished the break-in at Colchester gaol. The month drew to a close with an insurrection at Ardleigh, just north-east of Colchester, on 21 September.[56]

As for Norfolk and Suffolk, there too disturbances took place in the aftermath of Cade's rising, the murder on 4 August of Suffolk's chaplain at Alderton being the single most significant incident. The extent of this disturbance is evidenced by the amount of law enforcement that these two counties were thought to need during the late summer and autumn. On 1 August, the same day on which the commission of oyer and terminer was set up to go into Kent, a similar commission was appointed to ride up into Norfolk and Suffolk. It was led by the bishop of Ely, the duke of Norfolk, and the earl of Oxford. They were accompanied by Sir John Fastolf, Sir Andrew Ogard, and Sir John Hevenyngham.[57] Also included were men who had sat on the London commission set up on 1 July: Thomas Scales, John Prisot, William Yelverton, and John Markham. There was a good deal of thankfulness up in Norfolk when the word got round that such a commission had been appointed, for the county was restive that August with a renewed desire to see the punishment of de la Pole adherents. A threat was in the air that the county would rise up if some amends were not made.[58] Thomas Daniel of Castle Rising in Norfolk, summoned to appear before the king that Michaelmas term (October to early November), defaulted. With reason, he did not trust himself to the roads at that time 'owing to the evil disposition of the king's lieges then rebelling within the realm'.[59] At this same time James Gresham was writing to John Paston about how vital it was that a man of great birth and livelihood should serve as sheriff for Norfolk and Suffolk, someone sufficient in substance to hold down counties which now 'stonde right wildely' following the overthrow of the duke of Suffolk.[60] Those with grievances against the old order were not risking taking them to court until they are assured of a trustworthy sheriff and under-sheriff to guarantee fair legal process.[61]

[55] KB9/26, mm. 12, 15.   [56] KB9/268, m. 41a.   [57] CPR, 1446–52, 388.
[58] PL, ii. 168.   [59] CPR, 1446–52, 413, 468.   [60] PL, ii. 182.
[61] Ibid. 190–1. For a discussion of the important role played in the administration of justice in the counties by the sheriff, see R. Virgoe, 'The Crown, Magnates and Local Government in Fifteenth-Century East Anglia', in J. R. L. Highfield and R. Jeffs (eds.), *The Crown and Local Communities in England and France in the Fifteenth Century* (Gloucester, 1981), 72–87.

On 1 November a commission of oyer and terminer was set up to go to Norwich in particular.[62] There was therefore a good deal of judicial work going on in East Anglia that winter: hearings took place at Swaffham on 17 September and at Norwich on 22 September, 16 November, and 15 December when the sitting lasted seven days; the August commission continued its hearings through the winter into the spring of 1451 at Lynn, Norwich, and, in May, at Walsingham.[63]

London and Middlesex were also in an unsettled state. On 7 September a gang of some twenty-five men broke into the house at Cranford of John Trevilian, 'the Cornish chough' of ill-repute, taking goods valued at £40.[64] And indeed, news of the capital's troubled atmosphere had reached the Mediterranean. The Venetian senate expressed its concern that October for the safety of their visiting galleys since the city of London and the whole island were understood to be in great combustion.[65]

As for the king during the later part of 1450, he was at Westminster from 31 July to 8 October. He then spent the remainder of the month itinerating from Essex to western Surrey, from thence to Hampshire and back to his palace at Sheen in Surrey, so skirting the more troublesome areas of the south.[66] From 5 November, with the new parliament about to open, he returned to Westminster where he stayed for the rest of the year. Well might the parliament summoned that September to assemble in November have among its agenda not only the problems of the defence of the realm, the keeping of the sea, and the support of Gascony, but also the question of dealing with the continuing riots and insurrections at home.

The elections that October for the forthcoming parliament appear in some places to have been conducted in a manner which anticipated the charged atmosphere of the impending session. When, for example, the electors for Gloucester made their selection on 28 October they did not choose their long-serving JP and MP, Thomas Derehurst, gentleman and lawyer. This was despite the fact that he had represented Gloucestershire in the previous parliament of 1449–50,

---

[62] *CPR*, 1446–52, 432.

[63] *PL*, ii. 145. This gives the Norwich hearing as the Tuesday after St Mathias's day, in the 29th year of Henry VI (2 Mar. 1451). In context this is an obvious misreading for 'St Mattheus' whose feast falls on 21 Sept. There is also mention elsewhere of the duke of Norfolk being at Norwich on 15 Sept. ready to sit upon the oyer and terminer commission. Ibid. 171.   [64] KB9/265, m. 56.

[65] R. Brown (ed.), *Calendar of State Papers, Venice*, i. (1864), 74.

[66] Wolffe, *Henry VI*, 368.

and that prior to that he had represented the county in 1445–6 and the borough of Gloucester in 1433, 1437, 1447, and 1449.[67] On 12 October, sixteen days before the election, he had been involved in a demonstration in Gloucester which had 'raised the public voice against the king'.[68] Here, in a town which had seen violent looting and rioting against Abbot Boulers, where the bailiff and burgesses had been recipients of one of Cade's quarters in July, and which had submitted to a commission of oyer and terminer set up on 28 September, it would appear that men were too chastened that October to elect an openly disaffected MP—albeit a man of standing and their usual choice.[69]

II

The gatherings of Cade's die-hards in Kent, Sussex, and Essex during August and September 1450 with their hectoring leaders and unruly supporters drawn from nearby localities offer a contrast to the movement of men about eastern England during the second week of November. Then whole platoons of some communities were mobilized at the recruitment of their overlord, the duke of York. At Grantham, for example, some fifty-two men congregated. They may have comprised a significant segment of their community's artisans: tanners, butchers, millers, cooks, weavers, glovers, and the like.[70] York, returned from his post in Ireland early in September, was seeking to bolster his position in the new parliament which had commenced at Westminster on 6 November. During the following week he raised retinues from towns and villages from a wide stretch of country: in Cambridgeshire from Caxton and Wendy to Newmarket and Isleham; in Lincolnshire from Grantham and Stamford; in Northamptonshire from Fotheringhay; and in Essex from Thaxted from where a contingent marched down the county through Chelmsford.[71] The orchestrated movement of retinues such as this, a

---

[67] *CPR*, 1436–41, 583; *CPR*, 1441–6, 466, 471; *CPR*, 1446–52, 139, 285, 297, 589; Wedgwood, *Biographies*, 270–1; Wedgwood, *Register*, 106, 136, 164; *VCH* Gloucester, iv. (1988), 37.

[68] KB27/761 *rex* side, mm. 15ᵛ, 16ᵛ. In May 1451 he obtained a royal pardon for all trespasses, offences, etc. committed before the Mar. of that year. *CPR*, 1446–52, 429.

[69] *PPC*, 107–9; *CPR*, 1446–52, 432–3.

[70] KB9/65A, m. 19.

[71] KB9/7/1, m. 10; /65, mm. 19, 36, 38, 41, 42; /278, m. 51; /94/1, m. 5; /26/1, m. 28; KB27/777 *rex* side, m. 7ʳ.

significant phenomenon of the 1450s, throws into clear focus the fact that not all gatherings of the inhabitants of townships were 'popular uprisings'.

York, who had not been involved during the years immediately preceeding 1450 in the diplomatic and military failures in France, and who was clearly not an associate of Suffolk, was one of the few magnates to command the respect of the common people. Just as the duke of Somerset was coming to be regarded in a similar light to the late duke of Suffolk,[72] so the mantle of 'Good Duke Humphrey', a true-born aristocrat not permitted to carry his proper weight in the royal council, was falling upon York. Exactly how far York was directly implicated in Cade's rising is one of the most intriguing questions raised by the story of 1450. There is no direct evidence from the participants themselves beyond their call that Henry should take about him the 'high and mighty Prince the Duke of York, late exiled from the king's presence by the motion and stirring of the traiterous Duke of Suffolk and his affinity', but it was a plea they made also with regard to the dukes of Exeter, Buckingham, and Norfolk.[73] Yet the authorities were highly suspicious of some connection between the revolt of 1450 and the duke. During the rising the king and his ministers believed Cade to be called Mortimer and even after they had been disabused of this notion they still regarded the leader's assumption of such a name as most significant. This accounts for the government's nervousness and agitation upon York's arrival in England in September 1450. It explains too why Reginald Boulers, the former abbot of Gloucester, now bishop-elect of Hereford, John, Lord Dudley, Sir Thomas Tuddenham, and John Heydon, all of them courtiers execrated by Cade's followers, fled to the duke for safety, a safety they were willing to purchase.[74] In 1456 Henry VI would write to the king of Scotland that ever since the time Jack Cade or Mortimer raised insurrection everything had been in turmoil willed by the duke of York of Mortimer descent.[75] Tudor historians made this contemporary suspicion into a matter of fact. It was easily done. By 1580 Stow would introduce the subject of the revolt,

---

[72] A local thief who was among York's retinue at Grantham demonstrated his loyalty by stealing valuables from the duke of Somerset at Grantham later that Nov. KB9/65A, m. 26.

[73] Stow, *Annales* (1631), 389b–390ᵃ.

[74] Griffiths, *Henry VI*, 686–7; *Benet's Chron.*, 202.

[75] Rymer, *Foedera*, xi. 383.

In the moneth of May the commons of Kent in great numbers assembled, having to their Captaine Jacke Cade, who named himselfe Mortimer, cosin to the Duke of Yorke, or as he was named of some John Amendall.

It was not a far step to Stow's seventeenth-century edition which ran,

The death of the Duke of Suffolke brought not the Realme in quiet, for those that favoured the Duke of Yorke, and wished the crowne upon his head, procured a commotion in Kent.[76]

Earlier than Stow, William Darell, chaplain to Queen Elizabeth, in his history of Dover castle, stated baldly that Cade's rebellion had been stirred up by the duke of York and his adherents, and Edward Hall told his readers with cunning reasoning that the rising had begun in Kent just in order that suspicion might be deflected from the duke.[77]

Evidence from the events of the rising itself, for example, that in July 1450 men from York's town of Newbury rose up and went into Hampshire, whilst suggestive, is inconclusive.[78] No more decisive as evidence was the increasing association with York's name among insurgents who rose up after 1450,[79] particularly in south-western Kent, since—and this is what gives the matter its great ambivalence—on his return to England in the autumn of 1450 York took on the role of petitioner and reformer formerly assumed by Cade. It was York now who, probably in the second half of September 1450, presented the king with two bills of complaint. One was a protestation of his own innocence of allegations of treason, the other was a list of those things he wanted attended to in parliament. Setting himself forth as the upholder of justice, he complained of the failure to bring due justice to those persons who had been indicted by the recent commissions of oyer and terminer in August.[80]

The nearest suggestion of a popular initiative to back the duke was the activity of a group of men from Navestock, north-west of Brentwood in Essex, who rose about the county at the end of

---

[76] Stow, *Chronicles* (1580), 652; id., *Annales* (1631), 388[a].

[77] W. Darell, *The History of Dover Castle* (trans. A. Campbell, London, 1786), 55; Hall, *Chronicle*, p. lxxvii.

[78] See Ch. 5, sect. IV, above.

[79] Some of those who rose as York's adherents after 1450 are known to have been insurgents in 1450. For example, men accused of attacking the vicar of Melton, Suffolk, in July 1450 would also be accused of rising in support of York in Feb. 1452. KB9/118, mm. 32, 33; C67/40, m. 1; C1/19/388A.

[80] Griffiths, 'Duke Richard of York's Intentions in 1450', 187–209.

November proclaiming that shortly they should have a new king.[81] No one but York could really be meant by this. The name of one of this group appears on the pardon list of 7 July, so it is possible that they were earlier followers of Cade who now saw their hope for reform to lie with the duke of York.

By returning to East Anglia and Northamptonshire that autumn before the new parliament opened in early November, York had placed himself in a region whose population was not only favourable to him as their landlord in many instances, but also deeply hostile to the associates of the late duke of Suffolk there. The duke of Norfolk was married to York's niece and as York's ally had met him in October at Bury St Edmunds to agree as to who should stand as knights of the shire for Norfolk in the forthcoming parliament. It was York's hope to have men of his mind returned not only for Norfolk but also for Suffolk, Northamptonshire, and Oxfordshire. In this they were only partially successful.[82] However, it was clear that Suffolk's affinity were, for the time being at least, in political retreat. A clerk employed by Justice Yelverton—himself no member of the Suffolk group—suggested to his correspondent at this time that the town of Swaffham should use York's visit there as a public demonstration against the likes of Tuddenham and Heydon. They should present York with a bill concerning these oppressors and there should be shouting in the streets by all the inhabitants asking that York do 'sharp execucyon' upon them. The same procedure should be followed in Norwich.[83]

So with East Anglia released into a state of public outcry against its oppressors through York's return, the duke went down to the parliament now under way accompanied by a strong retinue raised from several counties. He arrived at the capital on 23 November knowing that on 9 November the Commons had elected his chamberlain, Sir William Oldhall, as speaker, offering a clear sign that they were in a mood for change and that they were looking to York to achieve it. London was in an ill-governed state, still unsettled from July's revolt. Burdened both with the presence of redundant soldiery out of France and with magnate retinues up from the provinces, it was in no position to resume its normal running.

It was probably during November that the Commons had introduced a bill demanding the dismissal for life of certain named individuals

---

[81] KB9/26/1, m. 14; Francis at Bury, yeoman, of Navestock, who was named on this indictment had earlier had his name written on the pardon roll of 7 July. *CPR*, 1446–52, 373.   [82] Griffiths, *Henry VI*, 689.   [83] Ibid. 690.

from the king's entourage. This list, which ran to some twenty-nine names, included the widowed duchess of Suffolk, Edmund duke of Somerset, William Booth, bishop of Coventry and Lichfield, Reginald Boulers, abbot of St Peter's, Gloucester, Edward Grimston, Thomas Daniel, John Trevilian, John Say, and Stephen Slegge.[84] The bill sought to have these people removed from the king for the term of their lives and they were not to come within twelve miles of Henry ever again. It is perhaps a sign of how volatile he felt the situation to be that Henry was even willing to contemplate some compromise on this matter. He agreed that these persons should go from his presence for the space of a year, except any who were lords and except also 'certein persones which shall be right fewe in nombre the which have be accustumed contynuelly to waite uppon his persone'.[85] In this way Henry took much of the bite from the bill. Anger provoked by the king's refusal to take action against Somerset and his associates grew to such a degree that on 30 November it burst out in Westminster with stormy scenes in parliament.[86] The Commons and an invading mob of lords' retainers cried out for justice to be done upon the false traitors, with 'showtes orribles' calling 'Justice! Justice!'[87]

Somerset, seen in his role as lieutenant-general as responsible for the débâcle in France, now became a major victim of looters and rioters. On 1 December up in Suffolk his property at Sudbury was ransacked[88] whilst in London a mob attacked Blackfriars with the intention of killing him there. He had to be taken away by boat to the safety of the Tower by the earl of Devon whilst the mayor gathered a force to put down the riot.[89] The chronicler Benet believed York to have been responsible for ensuring Somerset's rescue in this way, however, away from such a pro-Yorkist source, a strong suspicion remains that York himself may have instigated the attack upon this, his declared adversary. Nine days later his tenants would ransack Somerset's chief residence at Corfe castle in Dorset.[90] Yet if York

---

[84] *RP*, v. 216–17.   [85] Ibid.   [86] *Benet's Chron.*, 203.

[87] KB27/777 *rex* side, m. 7ᵛ; this account, which comes in the form of an indictment against William Oldhall in 1455, dates the incident to 1 Dec. 1450 in what I take to be an error of memory. Chronicle sources agree upon 30 Nov. 1450: *Bale's Chron.*, 137; *Benet's Chron.*, 203. The indictment offers the allegation that Oldhall procured men from Kent for this demonstration in Westminster Hall.

[88] KB9/118/1, m. 16; KB27/796 *rex* side, m. 10ᵛ; KB27/798 *rex* side, m. 8; it was probably at about this time that goods of the duke of Somerset were despoiled near Wisbech. M. K. Jones, 'Somerset, York and the Wars of the Roses', *EHR* 104 (1989), 288.   [89] *Bale's Chron.*, 137.

[90] *Benet's Chron.*, 203; Jones, 'Somerset, York and the Wars of the Roses', 288.

wished to cast himself in the role of champion of justice he could not permit such scenes of wild lawlessness in the city. On 2 December the property of Hoo and Tuddenham fell victim to the crowd's retributive violence, prompting York to make an example of one of the looters by sending him off for execution at the king's instruction.[91] On 3 December the king, the duke of York, and all the lords then in London with their retinues rode through the streets in a great show of strength in order to pacify the city. The London chronicler Gregory noted mournfully that this 'was a gay and gloryus syght if hit hadde ben in Fraunce, but not in Ingelonde'.[92] It smacked too much of the action of an occupying force menacing enemy natives.

After 5 December London may have quietened. It was perhaps at this point that Henry had to deal with another Commons petition for resumption, similar to that of the previous May. Indeed, it was the petition which had already been accepted at Leicester in the spring of 1450, but now strengthened by various careful revisions. For example, it was suggested that a committee should be appointed to supervise all the king's future grants. This idea was rejected, but Henry would eventually accept the petition, and by the time parliament dissolved at the end of May 1451 he would have added only forty-three provisos of exemption, far fewer than had been the case the previous year. The act, then, was of positive effect. Here the Commons had gained something of a triumph.[93]

III

By December 1450 Henry had evidently judged that the time for inquiries into grievances was over. On 14 December—perhaps to counter the popular image growing of the duke—he had appointed York to head a commission of oyer and terminer to do justice on those rebels and traitors who had risen in Kent and Sussex since 8 July 1450.[94] There is no evidence, however, that York ever sat on this commission.

[91] P. A. Johnson, *Duke Richard of York 1411–1460* (Oxford, 1988), 90–1.

[92] *Gregory's Chron.*, 196.

[93] Wolffe, 'Acts of Resumption in the Lancastrian Parliaments, 1399–1456', *EHR* 73 (1958), 604–5. In suggesting the second or third week of Dec. 1450 as the date of this undated act I follow Johnson, *Duke Richard*, 93.

[94] *CPR*, 1446–52, 435.

Such was the atmosphere in Kent at the end of January 1451 that a gentleman from Staplehurst, Stephen Christmas (who had, it is interesting to note, served York in Ireland), went with others about villages of central Kent, Tenterden, Staplehurst, Leeds, and Harrietsham, publishing the news that Henry intended to ride upon Kent with a great posse of Lancashire and Cheshire men to lay waste the county.[95] On 28 January, as such rumours circulated, the king embarked on the first judicial progress of his reign in the company of some of his most distinguished subjects, the dukes of Somerset and Exeter heading an entourage of several thousand men. The intention was to show the men of Kent just how the king dealt with traitors and rebels. The terms of reference of this commission, appointed on 27 January, had been to deal with all those offences committed in Kent since the pardon of 7 July 1450 which were not being attended to by the commissioners assigned on 1 August.[96] This of course meant the troubles associated with Parmynter's risings on 31 August and all the other disturbances in the Weald and elsewhere during the later part of 1450. Essentially, though, what the commission was about was a punitive show of strength only thinly veiled by the trappings of legal procedure. These commissioners in practice did not make too nice a distinction between those who had risen after 8 July and those, supposedly now immune, who had risen before. In judicial sessions visited upon Canterbury, Rochester, and Faversham that February the commission hanged some thirty Kentishmen whom it found guilty of having risen with Cade or of having declared their disdain for the king and their preference for the duke of York.[97] As villagers of northern Kent saw the shocking sight of carts going laden from the gallows along the wintry roads to exhibit their cargoes on London Bridge they dubbed the royal progress 'the harvest of heads'.

At the end of February as Henry made his way back to London through northern Kent a host of unpunished misdoers—3,000 it was said—awaited him on Blackheath to plead for his mercy.[98] Some of these had been Parmynter's men.[99] Henry must have felt a keen satisfaction at this public humiliation of former rebels as he rode past men prostrating themselves before him naked to the waist and with cords tied around their necks. Later, in April, some pardons were

[95] KB9/267, m. 93; *CPR*, 1446–52, 264.
[96] *CPR*, 1446–52, 453–4.
[97] *EHL*, 372; *Benet's Chron.*, 204; *Gregory's Chron.*, 196–7.
[98] *Benet's Chron.*, 204.   [99] *CPR*, 1446–52, 453–4.

issued to these men, an April complacently described in one royal patent letter as a 'time of indulgences and remissions'.[100]

Tenterden was one of the villages where there had been disturbances in January due to the rumours about the king's alleged intention to lay the county waste with Lancashire and Cheshire men.[101] On 8 February Thomas Gribell, John Frank, John atte Wode, and William Roger, all yeomen and husbandmen from Tenterden, were judged on charges of high treason and hanged before the commission at Canterbury. They left behind them in the familiar landscape of the eastern Weald carefully accumulated farmsteads, livestock, and fields of arable and pasture land all to be dismembered by opportunist neighbours and the royal escheator. Thomas Gribell was a yeoman of some standing: with a messuage and hundred acres of land worth 53*s.* 4*d.* a year stocked with livestock and goods worth £21 25*s.* 6*d.*, he must have been one of the more prosperous farmers in his community.[102] The other three men were rather more modest-scale farmers with thirty, twenty-two, and sixteen acres respectively, but all were men with roots and responsibilities who in normal circumstances would have spent 8 February foddering their cattle, horses, and pigs, and keeping an eye on lambing ewes. No one from Tenterden had their name placed on the pardon roll of 7 July 1450 and the exact details of the charges of which these men were found guilty is unknown, but they were among that 'harvest' who were made a ferocious example of as traitors to the Crown.

These show trials had precisely the kind of terrorizing effect they were intended to produce. On 9 February, the day after the Canterbury hangings, men were agitating at Maidstone and Birling, a village just to its north-west, trying to stir up the populace to ride to Canterbury to force the king to grant them letters of pardon, and to tell him that there were 5,000 men armed and at the ready in Maidstone if he refused their request.[103]

IV

The judicial progress of February 1451 was a frightening and chastening experience of royal vengeance for Kent. Yet in a spirit of

[100] Ibid. 453–4, 460–1.   [101] KB9/267, m. 93.
[102] E357/42 Kent and Middlesex: Lands, tenements, goods, and chattels of traitors, outlaws, felons, and fugitives.   [103] *CPR*, 1446–52, 505.

reckless defiance on 24 March at Solestreet, midway between Canterbury and Ashford, men allegedly met together and agreed, with the sound of men on the defensive, that Cade was still their captain and leader, that he was still alive, that he was of the blood of Mortimer, and that the kingdom belonged by right to him and not to Henry.[104]

Despite such shows of bravado the atmosphere that spring was one of great mistrust and apprehension. After their months of ascendancy Cade's followers were now living under the fear of potentially county-wide witch-hunts and hangings. Walter Langley, JP, was one of the more unsavoury figures among the gentry of east Kent.[105] With his locality subdued and prone to wild rumours of retribution he saw this as an opportune moment at which to resume the action in the courts against John Chamberleyn, gent., of Nonington and an esquire of the same village which the troubles of the rebellion had caused him to abandon. In April 1451 at Nonington, just south-west of Eastry and close by Langley's seat at Knowlton, Chamberleyn rode about the district announcing to his fellow parishioners as they worked in the fields that Langley intended to indict him and 4,000 men of eastern Kent. If Langley had his way, he told them, the king would get them all up to London and hang the lot of them, giving dramatic emphasis to this piece of news by turning to his horrified listeners as they stood at their ploughs and declaring, 'Thee he will hang! And thee he will hang!'[106]

In such an atmosphere it is not perhaps surprising that later that same April there were disturbances in Kent and Sussex as widespread and intense as any under Parmynter's captaincy, some occurring in the very hundred of Eastry where John Chamberleyn had been spreading alarm. There was, supposedly, a prelude to this disturbance on 17 April when one William Dalby, a gentleman of Brookhampton

---

[104] Virgoe, 'Ancient Indictments', 244–5.

[105] As a JP Langley had sat as sessions of the peace during the 1440s alongside such figures as William Isle and Richard Bam, for example. KB9/255/1, m. 31. His untrustworthiness was discovered by men such as Robert Aleyn of Herne who enfeoffed Langley in his tenement and fourteen acres for its safe keeping whilst he was away serving the king in Calais for four years, only to find on his return home that Langley would not re-enfeoff him in his property, and offered him violence. C1/19/322; Virgoe, 'Ancient Indictments', 243. In 1448 Sandwich had seen fit to expel Langley from the liberties of the town. KRO Sa/AC 1, fo. 74ᵛ.

[106] C1/18/126–129C. These documents can be dated to 1451 from internal evidence: they are written between 1450 and 1453 when Kemp was chancellor and during a year in which Passion Sunday fell in Apr. The only year of the four to fufil both requirements is 1451.

(Warks.) and London, and others said to be of Cade's following, allegedly met in the forest of Worth in northern Sussex, near the Surrey border just east of Crawley. There, it was later claimed, they declared that they would shortly be delivered from Henry's rule by a certain 'marvellous and terrible man of high birth and of the ancient royal race' carrying on his arms a red lion and a white lion with an army of 200,000 men gathering from various parts of England.[107] His subsequent indictment also hinted that Dalby was in contact by letter with an unnamed duke of the realm.[108] Leaving aside the fact that Cade's expressed intentions had never included Henry's deposition, this whole incident in the forest of Worth with its uncharacteristically fanciful and cryptic language sounds suspiciously like a fabrication with which to implicate York.

It seems far more probable that it was on the following Wednesday and Thursday, 21 and 22 April, that the troubles in Kent and Sussex really recommenced that spring. In essence it was a Wealden rising; the insurgents were, almost certainly, earlier followers of Cade.[109] They had reason to be dissatisfied with what had been achieved by Cade's revolt, but their discontent may well have been as much economic as political in origin, for these were weaving villages hit by the slump in trade.

On 21 April Kentishmen, some of them from villages and towns of central Kent such as Yalding and East Peckham, gathered at Eastry and Brenchley in the far east and south-west of the county respectively, allegedly planning to do away with the king and the lords spiritual and temporal of the realm. Perhaps they were encouraged by the knowledge that all but one of the lords on the 'hit-list' drawn up at Eastry in January 1450 were now dead. They further intended, it was alleged, to set up a dozen peers from among themselves to rule the country.[110] Those gathered at Brenchley also lay in wait, it was said, to attack one of the constables of the hundred of Brenchley.[111] On the Thursday, as the trouble persisted at Eastry and Brenchley, the risings

[107] *VCH* Sussex, i. 513; KB9/122, m. 23.

[108] This would have been the duke of York. Dalby declared that the battle between the 'marvellous man' and Henry would take place on Hounslow Heath; and there was a demonstration of York's supporters there in Feb. 1452. KB27/777 *rex* side, m. 7.

[109] For example, Henry Bedell of Thurnham, William Bacheler of Detling, and John Martyn of Dallington, indicted for rising at Rotherfield on this occasion, had their names inscribed on the pardon roll of 7 July 1450. *CPR*, 1446–52, 352.

[110] Virgoe, 'Ancient Indictments', 245–6, 247, 252. The request for twelve peers is one which recurs in a rising of 1456; it is an idea drawn from popular metrical verse (see n. 170, below).   [111] Ibid. 250.

and gatherings extended northwards through the Kentish Weald and westwards into the Sussex Weald as Kentishmen, notably Stephen Strode of Biddenden and John Herry and John Hale, both of Wingham, crossed the border carrying their reforming enthusiasm.[112] In Kent weavers, husbandmen, and labourers from villages on the northern edge of the Weald met that day at Tonbridge.[113] Meanwhile in Sussex at Rotherfield and Mayfield the inhabitants were gathering, joined by men who had made the hour or so long journey (if by foot) from Dallington and by others who had travelled in for longer from Beckley, and they allegedly declared that they wanted the heads of certain Sussex gentlemen, especially of those who were against Jack Cade.[114] The Kentishmen also heckled and roused the men of Burwash that day who gathered in numbers and debated the idea of overthrowing the king and his lords and of installing twelve men from among themselves in their place.[115] Apart from the Kentish leaders who had moved into the Sussex Weald that Thursday the main ringleader to these demonstrations was a Henry Hasilden, a shingler from Rotherfield. The troubles at Rotherfield continued into the following day[116] and even into the following week at Linton, King's Wood, and Cox Heath, villages just south of Maidstone, where men from the surrounding district met to give their assent to Hasilden's proposals.[117]

Men such as Hasilden who could engender a desire for radical methods of reform in this way over a wide area of country (some eighty miles in breadth) were obviously to be given short shrift at law. At an inquest held at Lewes in the first half of May Hasilden was hanged along with a fellow Rotherfield man and the itinerant Kentish agitators, John Herry and John Hale from Wingham.[118] Stephen Strode gained a reprieve by turning king's approver and appealing a whole group of his fellow insurgents.[119]

That May as the sheriff rounded up thirty-six rebels in Sussex,[120] Kent continued in the state of restless distrust of the king and his councillors into which the county had been thrown by February's executions. On the northern coastal marshes of Kent at Cliffe, at

---

[112] KB27/762 *rex* side, m. 25; KB27/760 *rex* side, m. 1.
[113] Virgoe, 'Ancient Indictments', 251.   [114] KB9/122, mm. 46, 52.
[115] KB27/769 *rex* side, m. 43; KB27/760 *rex* side, m. 1.
[116] KB9/122, m. 44.   [117] Virgoe, 'Ancient Indictments', 244, 249.
[118] KB27/760 *rex* side, m. 1. The sale of Hasilden's forfeited goods and chattels fetched a modest 26s. 8d. E136/212/12.   [119] KB29/82, m. 17.
[120] E404/68/137.

Strood, and in the parish of Frindsbury rumours were circulated by local husbandmen and a miller that Henry intended to go over to France to bring the king of France back with him to destroy the people of Kent.[121] Similar tension was shown in the eastern part of the county later in the month by the activities of a Sandwich weaver who rode about through the villages and towns of Sturry, Wingham, Canterbury, and Sarre rousing the populace to rise up against the king.[122]

On 20 May the king responded to this continuing unrest by issuing commissions of oyer and terminer to go into Suffolk, Hampshire, Wiltshire, Surrey, Sussex, and Kent.[123] In Surrey and Sussex the commissioners were to deal with all treasons and insurrections and the like since the issuing of the pardons, that is, since 8 July 1450; in Kent they were to deal with the troubles arising since the establishment of the previous commission on 27 January 1451.

During June 1451 justices, still acting under the January commission and dealing with Parmynter's supporters of 1450, were in session at Tonbridge from 26 June to 1 July.[124] They also dealt with the more recent troubles associated with Henry Hasilden. On 24 June they hanged a Henry Bedell from Thurnham for his part in the risings at Eastry and Brenchley on 21 and 22 April.[125] In something of a contrast, other supporters of Hasilden, such as Richard Payn of East Peckham, managed to obtain a pardon.[126] At Thurnham Henry Bedell's neighbours were to see his sixty-acre farm made a gift of by the king: a John Roger was the favoured squire on this occasion.[127] Henry may have been made an example of among Hasilden's supporters as a particularly turbulent agitant. The charges against him also included the committing of assault and robbery that April, but, more importantly, as the only man among the forty-eight or so indicted as followers of Hasilden to have his name written on the pardon roll of 7 July 1450 he was possibly known as a supporter of Cade.[128]

The session at Tonbridge was the beginning of another judicial progress through the South-East as the king took his justice in person to a particularly recalcitrant area of his kingdom. In July he and the commission headed by the duke of Somerset moved westwards from Tonbridge into Sussex to make inquest into all troubles there since

[121] Virgoe, 'Ancient Indictments', 246.   [122] Ibid. 248–9.
[123] *CPR*, 1446–52, 477.   [124] Virgoe, 'Ancient Indictments', 216.
[125] Ibid. 247; E357/42 Kent and Middlesex: Lands, tenements, goods, and chattels of traitors, outlaws, felons, and fugitives.   [126] KB27/788 *rex* side, m. 27ᵛ.
[127] E357/42 Kent (this is the source that reports him as having 60 acres of land); E379/174 Kent (reads 40 acres).   [128] *CPR*, 1446–52, 374.

8 July 1450, sitting first at Lewes and then at Chichester. Here in Sussex too the king exacted an exhibition of subjection from those seeking pardons. Such men were made to prostrate themselves to the ground, stripped to the waist before him in the streets of Chichester. One man who paid this price in personal dignity for a pardon was John Westbourne, a yeoman from Hollington,[129] north-west of Hastings, who exemplifies well the mixed roles found among many of the insurgents in the South-East at this time. He had risen up at the lathe court at Sedlescombe on 14 July 1450 associating with a man who on other occasions that year had allegedly called himself a kinsman of Cade; but in other years Westbourne had sat himself as a juror at inquests upon miscreants.[130]

Also humbling himself before the king that July at Chichester was William Page, a gentleman from Warminster in Wiltshire, who had taken part in the pillaging of the valuables of William Aiscough, the bishop of Salisbury, at Maiden Bradley in June 1450.[131] The king was out to punish not just Surrey and Sussex but also Hampshire and Wiltshire. By 14 July the commission had progressed to Winchester where it sat for four days. There indictments were at last brought against certain individuals charged with the murder of Adam Moleyns, bishop of Chichester, a year and a half previously. One such accused was a sailor from Worthing, another was a soldier, Cuthbert Colvile, who had been retained by the king in November 1449 for half a year's military service abroad.[132] That Friday, 16 July, as the commission continued its hearings at Winchester men were gathering at Thorpe by Norwich allegedly saying that they wished to do as John Cade, once captain of Kent, had done before; they made out a list of local and national 'traitors' whom they should kill, including Thomas Hoo, Lord Hastings, the former chancellor of Normandy.[133]

The year 1451 may well have seen a change in mood among the common people of the South-East: the risings that had taken place since Cade's revolt had all proved ineffectual despite their wide geographical base, and the king's offensive against the counties during the spring and summer of that year left a bitter memory. The records of 1451 tell us largely of the troubles under Hasilden in eastern and central Kent and eastern Sussex, but disruptions may have occurred to the routine of life all over the South-East in the year which followed

---

[129] *CPR*, 508.   [130] KB9/122, m. 62; /255/1, m. 6.
[131] *CPR*, 1446–52, 508; KB9/133, m. 19; /134/1, m. 15; /134/2, mm. 79, 80; /133, m. 30.   [132] KB9/109, mm. 16, 25; E403/777, m. 4.   [133] KB9/85/1, m. 6.

the summer of 1450. This is hinted at by the case of Street in southern Kent, a few miles inland from Hythe overlooking Romney marsh, where the common fine usually paid in the manorial court went unrendered that year, '*causa insurrectionis populi sive comitatus kanc*'.[134]

Whatever their opinions of Henry had been, and there are numerous indications that the king was unpopular before 1450, especially following the death of Gloucester in 1447,[135] Cade and his supporters had been careful not to implicate him in their complaints along with his evil councillors. By 1451, however, Henry was seen as an unpredictable enemy who had brought the South-East metaphorically and literally to its knees. For the time being the region was subdued. Men might gather that autumn in a Kentish village and say that Henry was not fit to be king, but they did not pursue the matter further.[136]

V

The duke of York who had come to the parliament of November 1450 in such assertive fashion had seen, even over the period of that same parliament, dissolved May 1451, household figures regain authority, the introduction of a bill of attainder against the traitor Jack Cade (of Mortimer fame), and a punitive judicial progress through Kent against erstwhile petitioners for reform. Little had been achieved by way of reform. Edmund Beaufort, the duke of Somerset, so hated for his part in the loss of Normandy that he had been the target of mob violence in December 1450, had even so in April 1451 been appointed captain of Calais, a clear sign of his secure position in the king's favour. Moreover, the MP for Bristol, Thomas Young, York's lawyer-councillor, had been dispatched to the Tower for his motion that the duke of York should be accorded formal recognition as Henry's heir presumptive.[137] With a descent from two of the sons of Edward III, York was a very reasonable candidate for heir to the throne: moreover, it was a matter which the childless Henry needed to resolve. To be

---

[134] Library of the Dean and Chapter, Canterbury, Sacrist Roll 38. During 1451–2 another large ecclesiastical landholder, the prior of Westminster abbey, was troubled by insurgents at his manor at Belsize, Middlesex. Westminster Abbey Muniments 33289, fo. 59ᵛ. I am grateful to Miss B. F. Harvey for drawing this incident to my attention.

[135] See Ch. 2, sect. V, above.   [136] KB9/271, m. 9.

[137] Griffiths, *Henry VI*, 691–2.

spurned in this manner was a humiliation for York. The Commons had backed the proposal, but the lords were having none of it. The duke may have enjoyed support from a section of the Commons in that parliament and from the disaffected of the realm outside it, but he was becoming increasingly isolated from the confidence of his fellow magnates and of his king.

By 1452 York was set upon a scheme to amend the error of the king's ways not by reform in parliament but by force. In two letters sent from Ludlow in January and February he first made public his allegiance to the king and then, secondly, went on to deplore the diminution not only of the country's commerce, but also its honour and its security from enemy invasion which had attended the loss of Normandy and other lands in France. The blame for this loss he laid squarely at Somerset's feet: this all happened whilst he had been commander in Normandy.[138] He further alleged that Somerset planned his, York's, undoing and disinheritance.

As York's agents began that February to raise men from his own lands in support of the duke, letters couched in these apologetics appear to have been sent out about the towns of southern England—in effect an appeal to the South to rise in civil rebellion. Some of these towns, however, upon the receipt of the duke's letters sent them on to the king to alert him to what was happening. The towns to which Henry then replied, commanding them to give the duke's letters no credence and to ensure that no gatherings took place such as the letters sought, were Oxford, Sudbury, Colchester, Winchelsea, and, significantly, three major towns of the recently insubordinate county of Kent: Maidstone, Canterbury, and Sandwich.[139] Even in the face of this apparent docility Henry was mistrustful. On the same day as he issued these instructions, 17 February, he ordained commissions to go into Kent, Norfolk, and Suffolk to punish and arrest conspirators.[140]

Accompanied by a force mustered from his tenantry in the west country, Lincolnshire, Northamptonshire, Cambridgeshire, and Essex, York made for London only to find the gates of the city locked against him. This had been done upon the king's instructions by the mayor, aldermen, and Common Council whose policy was to maintain the city's neutrality and the status quo: it was a policy they would pursue

[138] Griffiths, *Henry VI*, 694; Johnson, *Duke Richard*, 108.
[139] *PPC*, vi. 90–2; R. L. Storey, *The End of the House of Lancaster* (London, 1966), 98, 249.   [140] *CPR*, 1446–52, 577.

right up until June 1460.[141] Their action obliged York to cross the river into Surrey at Kingston and enter northern Kent where he had property near Dartford. Mindful of the previous summer's great uprising, Kent was a county he must have counted upon to rise up in his support. It scarcely moved. Sir William Pecche of Lullingstone, immediately to the south of Dartford, who had sat for Kent in the 1450–1 parliament, brought some men to join York, but there was no groundswell of popular support.[142] This striking lack of response gives clear measure of the success of the commissions against insurgents and rebels which had worked through the county in 1451. Kent had learnt a bitter lesson in royal vindictiveness.

On 1 March the king progressed to Blackheath with a great force, its numbers swelled by county levies from the shires of the South-East, including Sussex, Surrey, and, it is likely, Kent.[143] York was with his army just away to the east at Brent heath, his military presence extending also on to the Thames where seven ships lay in the estuary laden with supplies and arms. Yet the matter was defused without recourse to arms. York, faced by the overwhelming force of a royal army and without any support from his fellow nobles (except for the earl of Devon) or from the commons of the South-East, was cornered into humiliating apology. The Dartford incident had been for him a piece of gross political miscalculation from which he retreated to his castle of Ludlow, absenting himself from the politics of the realm for the following two years.

VI

In the spring of 1452, probably in April, an incident took place which throws light on the atmosphere which prevailed in East Anglia at this time of precarious order. Roger Church, the bailiff of Blofield hundred in Norfolk, met with a gathering of some fifteen men in a wood at Postwick, four miles east of Norwich, with a view to stirring up insurrection. Church told his fellowship that he had remembered a good name for their captain, it should be John Amendalle.[144] This was, of course, a name by which Cade had been known. If this sounds like

---

[141] C. M. Barron, 'London and the Crown 1451–61', in *The Crown and Local Communities in England and France in the Fifteenth Century*, ed. J. R. L. Highfield and R. Jeffs (Gloucester, 1981), 94–100.

[142] KB9/955/2, m. 3; KB27/784 *rex* side, m. 5.

[143] Johnson, *Duke Richard*, 110–11.

[144] C1/19/487; *PL*, i. 113–15; ii. 263–4, 266, 267, 270–2, 274, 312.

the beginnings of a rising by Cade's followers in Norfolk, that was precisely its intention. The gathering at Postwick was a piece of fraud which was acted out in order that one set of Norfolk men might place another into trouble. Roger Church, who flaunted the law under Thomas Daniel's protection and who was an associate of men such as Charles Nowell and Robert Dallyng, became chief actor in this charade at the instigation of Robert Ledeham who had assured him of a pardon through the influence of Daniel. And so Church had himself arrested by some of his own associates as a riser and promoter of sedition just so that he might appear before the duke of Norfolk to be judged by law. Once in this position he could offer to turn king's evidence on his accomplices and name a list of innocent men from his neighbourhood—husbandmen, farmers, and gentlemen—whom he alleged were involved in this 'rising'. It was a cunning piece of calculation, although it apparently did not succeed. It is a nice example of the way in which Cade's name might be invoked by individuals interested only in their own private purposes.

The next major popular disturbance which did occur in the region which had supported Cade came in Kent in May 1452—too late to assist York's attempted coup of March. The captain of this delayed and unproductive Kentish rising was one John Wilkyns, a pedlar from Stratford-upon-Avon. In 1446 Wilkyns had reached such a state of indebtedness to certain citizens and mercers of London, Robert Hallum, Roger Middlemore, and Edward Grimston, that he had been obliged to give up to them all his goods and chattels.[145] This grievance against particular individuals may well have inspired a hatred for the entire corrupt and prospering group to which they belonged and have fired Wilkyns's concern to see that the issues of 1450 were not forgotten. As with the indictments concerning Parmynter's supporters in 1450, here too a connection with Cade was made explicit. Another recurring element was the localities involved. As with the risings led by Henry Hasilden in April 1451, the areas of Kent participating in the disturbances were the Weald and the villages of central Kent just to the north of the Weald: Cranbrook, Goudhurst, Marden, East Peckham, and Yalding. Assembling in these villages from Saturday, 6 May until Monday, 8 May were men from the north of the county, from Gravesend, Cliffe, Cooling, and Rochester as well as the inhabitants of nearer communities such as Wrotham, Mereworth,

[145] *CCLR*, 1447–54, 103–4.

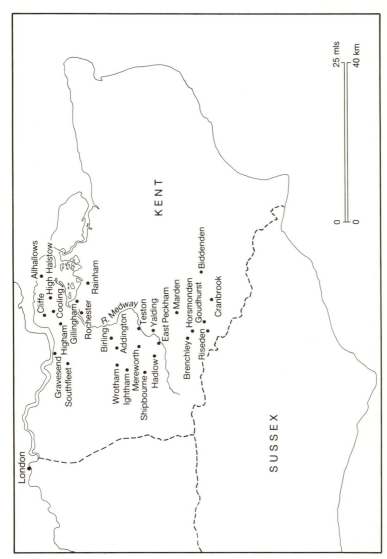

The Places in Kent and Sussex Involved in Wilkyns's Rising May 1452

Hadlow, Horsmonden, Ightham, and Shipbourne.[146] The names are known of over 130 of the men who were charged with rising up behind Wilkyns during these three days, so that the alleged number of 300 insurgents meeting in the villages at this time may well be somewhere near the truth.[147]

The wide geographical span of the rising may well have been achieved by the movement of Wealden men about north-western Kent rousing other men to rise. When on the Sunday royal officials in Aylesford, just north of Maidstone, were seeking Wilkyns they encountered a group of his supporters there from Goudhurst, Horsmonden, and Biddenden, all Wealden villages away to the south. These men refused to co-operate in their search and asserted moreover that Wilkyns came as a friend of the king and not as a traitor.[148]

The insurgents' alleged demands were for an assortment of political and religious reforms. They wanted the petitions sought in the last parliament by them and all Kent put into effect 'even in the unwilling teeth of the king'; they wanted to do away with the power of the bishops; they desired that priests should possess nothing more than a chair and a candlestick for reading; and they, like certain men of Essex late in 1450, asserted that Cade was 'alive and their chief captain in carrying out their decisions'.[149] It was suggested that York's son, the earl of March, was going to arrive in Kent with a great posse of Welshmen to help them obtain these petitions, and that Lord Cobham and his brother would aid them too.[150] These insurgents were being charged as supporters of York above all else.

Yet that these men were former supporters of Cade is suggested not only by their claim that Cade was still alive, but also by the fact that among these insurgents charged with rising behind Wilkyns, thirteen of them had had their names placed on the pardon roll of 7 July 1450. Here then Cade's cause may be seen merging into the Yorkist cause. That these insurgents had not risen to support York that March is an indication of the fear and loathing inspired in this chastised county by the king whose swift deployment of a commission to Kent in February

---

[146] Virgoe, 'Ancient Indictments', 257–65, duplicated in KB9/955, m. 8; /275, m. 7; /273, m. 11; /271, m. 60.

[147] Numbers cannot be too precise, as some names appear in several indictments carrying slight variations of place or employment that suggest they might well be the same person. The total figure includes ten who rose at Aylesford on the Sunday. KB9/955/2, m. 14; KB9/268, m. 132.   [148] KB9/955/2, m. 14; /268, m. 132.

[149] Virgoe, 'Ancient Indictments', 258.   [150] Ibid. 259.

1452 and whose presence there the next month at the head of a great army had effectively quashed any insurgency. It is noteworthy that the insurgents rising with Wilkyns abandoned the convention, upheld by Cade's rebels, that although he might be misled by evil counsellors the king himself was just. These rebels would go against the royal will if need be.

The rising came to nothing, but in conjunction with the events at Dartford it was serious enough to merit a swift and strong response. On 11 May, only three days after Wilkyns's men were gathered in Marden, Cranbrook, East Peckham, and Yalding, a commission of oyer and terminer headed by the earl of Shrewsbury, John Talbot, veteran campaigner of the war, was set up to go into Kent to investigate all treasons committed in the county since 7 July 1450, that is to say, since the issuing of pardons to Cade's followers.[151] The following day the justices began their sitting at Dartford and continued their investigations there until 16 May.

A reward of £20 was offered to anyone capturing Wilkyns so that he might be brought to law, a sufficient inducement to make a Thomas Burton, esquire, take himself off on horseback with a company of twenty-four others to seek him out amongst the wooded slopes and isolated farmsteads of the Weald.[152] There by the use of spies and guides Burton took Wilkyns in late May or in the first days of June, and so Wilkyns was conveyed to the Tower of London. On 28 June he was taken by boat downstream to Dartford where he was dragged on a hurdle to the gallows and there hanged, drawn, and quartered.[153] Twenty-eight others are said to have been hanged.[154] Besides these, a couple of his followers paid fines, a few were found not guilty of the charges against them, and a sizeable proportion of them obtained pardons that June. For half a dozen of them this was their second royal pardon in almost exactly two years.[155]

VII

By and large the airing of grievances and the staging of demonstrations were spring and early summer rather than late summer activities.

[151] *CPR*, 1446–52, 577.   [152] E404/68/133.
[153] *CPR*, 1452–61, 93–102.   [154] Virgoe, 'Ancient Indictments', 219.
[155] Thirty-eight men were pardoned on 17, 18, and 21 June 1452. *CPR*, 1446–52, 553–4. The London vintner who joined the rising also obtained a pardon subsequently. KB27/788, *rex* side, m. 29.

During the busy harvest season all else had to wait. So the continuation of agitation sparked by the confrontation of the spring of 1452 into the following July and August in East Anglia and Kent gave measure to men's outrage and their sense of a loss of order. Although York's abortive rising of March 1452 had been staged in Kent the duke's army of followers themselves had come from outside the county. February had seen the raising of his followers at Grantham, Stamford, Huntingdon, Cambridge, and Chelmsford.[156] During the summer of 1452 East Anglia continued to seethe with political rivalries. On 6 July, shortly after the Kentish rebels had been dealt with by the authorities, there was a rising in north Suffolk at Syleham, a village where the late duke of Suffolk had a manor and which lay not far from his seat at Wingfield.[157] The men who rose 'against the king' at Syleham, inhabitants of nearby villages on either side of the Suffolk–Norfolk border, were the same individuals who were accused of attacking the property of the duke of Somerset at Sudbury in December 1450. That is, with the exception of the Suffolk gentleman, Hugo Assheton of Botesdale, and three men from Framlingham who apparently were not involved in the second demonstration.[158] The incident at Syleham demonstrated that York had his supporters in East Anglia who were not going to be intimidated by the downswing of his fortunes and who were determined to oppose their rivals amongst the very much alive followers of the late duke of Suffolk.

Kent, too, was in a state of turbulence not to be easily calmed. The men of the county felt that the king had broken faith with them: their grievances had not been remedied. The county was still in the hands of corrupt royal officials. At Harrietsham east of Maidstone, a demonstration took place which reflected this sense of disillusionment and betrayal among Cade's followers in Kent. On 21 August 1452 men of the district met there, including Henry Hamon, a sawyer from Headcorn, William atte Chamber, a fuller from Harrietsham (both of whom had taken out pardons after Cade's rebellion and were likely to have been former supporters of Cade), and Robert Naissh, a labourer from Frinsted who had supported Wilkyns in the spring of 1452. They wanted to see the fulfilment of the petitions put forward by the

---

[156] KB9/65, mm. 20, 21, 29, 33, 39; /42, m. 16; /7/1, m. 4; /26/1, mm. 24, 30.

[157] For a list of the duke of Suffolk's manors in East Anglia, see L. E. James, 'The Career and Political Influence of William de la Pole, First Duke of Suffolk 1437–1450', B.Litt. thesis (Oxford, 1979), fig. 1 (p. 236).

[158] KB9/118/1, mm. 16, 17; KB27/796 *rex* side, m. 10'; /798 *rex* side, m. 8.

commons of Kent and they proposed that Henry Hamon should carry sealed letters written in invisible ink (to be read by holding them against the fire) from them to the duke of York or the earl of Devon. Besides this they made out a list of those men holding public office in the county whom they thought were working against the good of the people: Alexander Iden, the man who had caught Cade in 1450 and who had replaced the murdered Crowmer as sheriff of Kent; John Roger; John Fogge; Thomas Horne; William Hadde; John Cobbe; John Brede; and Thomas Pittelesden, 'officers of the king in Kent labouring against the county'.[159] The rebels' intention, allegedly, was to kill these named individuals and to place bills on their corpses explaining that they had been so killed because this was how it was done in the time of Jack Straw—evidence that the precedent of the 1381 rising was still in everyone's mind. These Harrietsham insurgents were angry because they felt that the Kentish petitioners at the time of Cade's revolt had been deceived by the bishops (these would be the archbishops of Canterbury and York and the bishop of Winchester who had negotiated the pardon with them) and by the king who had put certain persons to death against the promise given in his pardons to them.

Two months later at Chelsfield in north-western Kent, south-east of Bromley, a former parson of the parish church there and some others were dreaming of a second Cade's revolt. They allegedly sent an embassy to a certain John Sharp to ask if he would be their governor to raise war against the king and to behead certain magnates such as the archbishop of Canterbury, believing that they could call on the support of some four or five thousand men.[160] This John Sharp had been one of the men (at least two of whom were hanged) who had risen up in the ward of Baynard's Castle, the duke of York's London residence, on 6 March 1452 with the intention, it was said, that men from the March of Wales and from Kent should join to dethrone the king, rising again on 20 April at Ludlow.[161] He was quite obviously an adherent of the duke of York. The indictments for these two spring risings had been presented during August and Sharp may still have been in the Marshalsea prison or just released from it when he received this embassy.

The Chelsfield plans of October 1452 were apparently nothing

[159] KB9/955/2, m. 2.
[160] KB9/273, m. 134. 'Jack Sharp' had been the nickname assumed by the Lollard leader William Mandeville, hanged in 1431.   [161] KB9/270, m. 34.

more than indiscreet plotting, but in a matter of months the same Chelsfield priest, one Robert Colynson, had managed to create quite a stir in the king's council by rather more subtle means than those proposed in October. He publicized in various parish churches that he had been confessor to the Kentish leader, John Wilkyns, hearing his confession that June in Dartford as he lay tied to a hurdle on his way to be hanged, and that Wilkyns had disclosed to him at that time information seriously implicating Ralph, Lord Cromwell, as a traitor.[162] In reply to this slander Cromwell was to produce witnesses to say that Wilkyns had spoken to no confessor on his journey out from Dartford parish church to the gallows. He had made his confession to a priest on the boat coming down to Dartford from the Tower. Cromwell asserted that the claims being made were 'fals, untrewe and oonly proceded of malice and of fals groundes and ymaginacions'. He made out a strong case, not only pointing out his own long history of loyal service to the Crown, but also revealing Colynson's disreputable past, his expulsion from Cambridge for an unpriestly life and seditious sermons, his association with Sharp, and his womanizing, fraud, and evil living throughout many different parts of the country. Cromwell was cleared of any taint of guilt, but the fact that he had had to make a very long and elaborate defence before the king and his council in reply to the charges of a notorious trouble-maker is an extraordinary incident, lighting up the kind of enmities at work among the king's council, now becoming more and more in evidence.

Early in 1453 Robert Poynings, the Sussex gentleman who had been Cade's carver and sword-bearer, began kindling support for a new demonstration in the South-East. On 2 January he made a gathering in Southwark of 'much sympell and noghtie pepill'. These people are likely to have been previous supporters of Cade since some of them had been outlawed for treason.[163] The canvassing of Cade's insurgents continued on 28 January at Westerham in Kent, west of Sevenoaks, where Poynings met with Thomas Bigg, a yeoman from Lambeth who had been one of Cade's petty captains, and some thirty other individuals.[164] The letter writing which had characterized Cade's campaigning for support was evident on this occasion, for a few weeks later, in February 1453, Poynings sent out letters to two men in

---

[162] *CPR*, 1452–61, 93–102. William Tailboys is thought to have been behind this accusation against Lord Cromwell. Virgoe, 'William Tailboys and Lord Cromwell: Crime and Politics in Lancastrian England', *BJRL* 55 (1973), 465, 467–71.

[163] KB27/789 *rex* side, mm. 4^{r-v}; *RP*, v. 396.   [164] Ibid.

Sussex, men who had been indicted of high treason by the commission taken to Chichester. One of them was Robert Poyntell, a husbandman from Sutton, Sussex, who had been one of the ringleaders of the rising at Chichester in August 1450.[165] These two men responded by answering Poynings's summons to Southwark, meeting him there on 28 February, where, and this is interesting to note, they received money from Poynings. Poynings thanked them for their goodwill and asked that they might continue in it and be ready to come to him at such time as he should alert them. Not only, then, did the rebels of 1450 remember each other but they were in contact and even allegiance with one another.

Another of Cade's former under-captains harking back to the causes of 1450 during 1453 was Michael Skellys, the Scarborough leech. He had now taken up residence in Southwark in the Marshalsea prison. In October 1453 Skellys was charged with expressing his regret during August that the captain of Kent had not reigned and of having declared that under Cade's reign it would have been a merry realm, for the king was but a sheep who had lost all that his father had won: he should have died at birth. Moreover, the leech was charged with conspiring with a fellow prisoner to rectify this unfortunate state of affairs by killing Henry through magic and necromancy. These two conspirators also allegedly sought the heads of John Kemp—the archbishop of Canterbury and chancellor—of the duke of Somerset, and of the duke of Buckingham in payment for the taking of Cade's head.[166]

In March 1454 the canvassing and contacting achieved by Robert Poynings during the early part of 1453 blossomed into action of sorts. On 14 March Robert congregated at Westminster with some of his associates including Thomas Bigg who had been raising support the day before in Southwark. They agreed to ride into the counties of Middlesex, Kent, and Sussex to rouse others to join them.[167] The following day Poynings was in the district of Dartford in northern Kent at North Cray and Crayford; from there his cavalcade travelled down to Ightham and then across to Friningham, north-east of Maidstone.[168] Nothing appears to have come of this rallying beyond the theft at Friningham of some money and silver spoons, and in the spring of

---

[165] KB27/789 *rex* side, mm. 4[r-v]; *RP*, v. 396; KB9/122, m. 7; KB27/765 *rex* side, m. 21[v].   [166] KB9/273, m. 103.
[167] Ibid. mm. 21, 100, 101.
[168] KB27/772 *rex* side, m. 31; /789 *rex* side, m. 4[v]; KB9/273, m. 30.

1458 Poynings would be pardoned all his misdemeanours of 1453–4.[169] His agitation in north-western Kent in March 1454 was the last notable attempt to rouse popular dissent that the South-East would see for some time. On 27 March the duke of York was appointed protector and defender of England in response to the crisis of the king's mental collapse: his government faced no popular protest. Uprising was initiated by great nobles of the realm in May 1454 when Lord Egremont joined by the duke of Exeter mustered forces in the north against the Nevilles, but this was not popular protest.

The king made a recovery some time in December 1454 only to see his feuding nobility turn to bloodshed and battle as York and his associates contrived against the renewed favours enjoyed by the dukes of Somerset and Exeter. At the encounter at St Albans in May 1455 the duke of Somerset and the earl of Northumberland were both killed, and the king himself sustained a slight wound. York, now in possession of the king, headed the country's administration once more. In November 1455 he was appointed as protector for a second time. It was only after York's resignation as protector in February 1456 that the voice of popular discontent was heard again.

VIII

This next outbreak of trouble was yet again a south-eastern rising carrying reverberations of Cade's rebellion. It was led by John Percy, a tailor from Erith in north-western Kent, who called himself John Mortimer in direct imitation of Cade. It took place in the Weald over five days, Monday to Friday, during the last week of April 1456 at the villages of Hawkhurst, Rolvenden, and Lamberhurst. This was no small disturbance. For what went on that week a man was hanged and over a hundred villagers from the Weald were fined, the great majority of these being from Hawkhurst and Rolvenden. Their alleged aims were to make some very drastic reforms among the county clergy, killing the pluralists and mutilating the rest. They intended further-more to kill the lords and gentlemen of Kent and of all the realm, and to elect twelve peers from among their own number to govern and rule the county and to implement all the articles put forward by Jack Cade. Finally they asserted that Cade, alias Mortimer, was still alive and that

---

[169] KB27/789 *rex* side, m. 4ᵛ.

their leader John Percy, alias John Mortimer, was John Mortimer, alias Cade.[170]

Although three of the Hawkhurst insurgents went about the county inciting others to rise, this would seem to have been a strongly localized disturbance.[171] It included a few men from Robertsbridge, Wadhurst, Linton, East Peckham, Goudhurst, and Pluckley, but the great majority came from the villages of Hawkhurst and Rolvenden themselves—although less so from Lamberhurst, the third village in which the risings took place. This apparent solidarity among the men of the two communities may belie the facts. Percy would seem to have been an insistent captain: forty-seven of the 126 men later indicted for supporting him were reckoned by the presenting jury to have done so under Percy's threat, compulsion, and force and not of their own free will.[172] In the Lollard rising of 1414 Oldcastle's agents had persuaded members of the sect to rise up with offers of money; Percy apparently employed not persuasion but coercion.[173] William Sandherst of Lamberhurst, a former constable of the hundred of Brenchley, was bold enough to resist this general press-ganging and so the mob (including in its own number men supposedly there under duress) turned upon his house and sought William out, so it was alleged, to kill him.[174] If the allegation is correct that a large proportion of men did rise only under threat and force—and the possibility that this was merely a device to evade punishment is weakened by the fact that these men were fined just as others were—then a new and subtler light is cast upon the popularity of ostensibly 'popular' insurrections. The crucial nature of the leadership of such demonstrations which was observed before is here given an interesting twist.

Occurring in the last week of April, this Wealden rising came just a

---

[170] KB9/49, mm. 4, 5, 6, 10, 11, 13, 14, 15, 16; /288, mm. 58, 59; /289, m. 88; KB27/787 *rex* side, m. 6; /788 *rex* side, m. 19. It is interesting to see popular verse acting here as an inspiration for political action. The 'dusypers' or 'douzeperes' were Charlemagne's twelve paladins: spelt in a great variety of ways, they are to be found frequently in Middle English texts, many of them metrical romances, which deal with the 'Matter of France', that is, romances telling stories of Charlemagne and those which take the name of single knights such as *Sir Ferumbras* or *Sir Otuel*. I am grateful to Miss S. J. M. Hitch for this information.   [171] KB9/288, mm. 58, 59.

[172] KB9/49, mm. 4, 11. The total given here of 126 has been calculated by conflating all variant readings of any given name, for example, John Basden of Hawkhurst, tailor, is taken to be the same person as John Basden of Hawkhurst, yeoman—so the number represents only the absolute minimum of persons. The actual total might be larger.

[173] McFarlane, *John Wycliffe and the Beginnings of English Nonconformity* (London, 1952), 151, 157.   [174] KB9/49, m. 13; /289, m. 88.

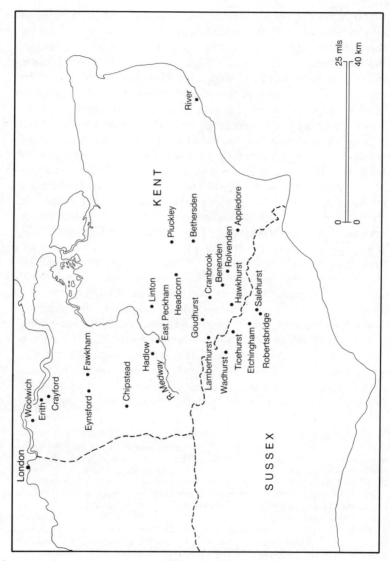

The Places in Kent and Sussex Involved in Percy's Rising April 1456

week before the outbreak of anti-alien rioting in London.[175] The two incidents do seem to be separate despite what appears to have been a common connection with the cloth export business. The riots in London were largely of mercers' men angry at what they saw as the unequal trading with the Lombards and other Italians of good English cloth for bits of trinkets and trash. In the Weald, as has been seen, Percy's followers were asking for wild and unlikely reforms as well as for the settlement of Cade's petition, although the men who were agitating in this way did, in considerable proportion, come from the cloth business. Over 29 per cent of those indicted for supporting Percy were active as tailors, weavers, fullers, or clothiers. So when, during May, the sub-escheator of Kent went to Hawkhurst extorting fines from Percy's followers, or, failing that, goods and chattels (quite illegally, since no charges had yet been made) what he came away with was quantities of woollen and linen cloth.[176]

John Percy's ineffectual Wealden rising of April 1456 to the familiar rallying cry of Cade was the last of the series of ripples sent across the surface of south-eastern society by the great rockfall of 1450. Disaffection, naturally, persisted. In February 1459, for example, a yeoman of Westminster gathered in Brixton hundred with like-minded persons and allegedly conspired against the king.[177] However, after 1456 for the remainder of the 1450s the gathering and movement of large bodies of men was to be confined to the activities of noble retinues pursuing private warfare: effective, independent, popular protest had for the time being come to an end.

IX

The risings which took place in Kent in the months and years immediately after Cade's rebellion, from Parmynter's in August 1450 to Percy's in the last week of April 1456, were all connected by a common outcry that Cade's sought-after reforms should be implemented. The insurgents were variously described as Cade's 'former accomplices', they were alleged to have declared on more than one

---

[175] R. Flenley, 'London and Foreign Merchants in the Reign of Henry VI', *EHR* 25 (1910), 650–2.   [176] KB9/49, mm. 7, 12.
[177] KB9/292, m. 14; the place at which they gathered was 'Horsedowne', for which see J. E. B. Gover, A. Mawer, and F. M. Stenton, with A. Bonner, *The Place-Names of Surrey*, English Place-Name Society, xi. (Cambridge, 1934), 32.

occasion that Cade was still alive and to have called for the implementation of the articles which he had presented to the king. There was a geographical coherence about the area in which the several risings occurred: along the north coasts of Kent from Faversham up to Woolwich, up the Medway valley, and, overwhelmingly, in the Weald and its immediate periphery. A certain interlinking of persons between the different Wealden risings further suggests some adherence to a common cause. Robert Nowell, a labourer from Cranbrook, for example, was indicted twice, for supporting Hasilden in April 1451 and Percy in 1456.[178] Robert Naissh, a labourer from Frinsted, who supported Wilkyns in May 1452 was among those who protested at Harrietsham in the August of that year that the king and his bishops had gone back on their agreement of 1450.[179]

Despite their averred allegiance to Cade, the risings which followed hard upon the events of 1450 should not be seen as a mere extension of the rebellion of that year. They were distinct, despite common sympathies. The bulk of the insurgents of 1451–6 were of a lower standing than many of those of 1450 and their discontent was as likely to have been social and economic as political. A survey of their occupations and home villages makes this clear. What is known of the livelihoods of those who supported Parmynter has already been mentioned—an assortment of trades. In the fuller lists for the other risings the preponderance of labourers and artisans is striking: carpenters, a quernbeater, thatchers, smiths, wheelwrights, fletchers, bakers, and workers in the cloth industry, who in the case of Percy's rising made up over a quarter of all those indicted. These risings were in part a reaction to the trade slump suffered by the cloth-manufacturing villages of the Weald and the Medway valley from which most of these troubles arose, an area, moreover, of strong local Lollard traditions, described above in Chapter 2. Judging by the villages involved, Tenterden and Cranbrook in particular, it would seem very probable that some Lollard element was to be found in most of the Wealden risings of the 1450s, an association which would perhaps account for the vehemently anti-clerical strain present in most of the post-Cade risings. Its tradition of religious unorthodoxy and fluctuating economic fortunes made the Weald the most precipitant

[178] Virgoe, 'Ancient Indictments', 251; KB9/49, mm. 14, 15.
[179] KB9/955/2, mm. 2, 14.

region of a more than usually rousable county. Lesser gentry and yeomen—the leaven of Cade's rebellion—were much less in evidence in these risings. They formed just under 5 per cent of those indicted for following Hasilden in 1451, 8 per cent of those indicted as followers of Wilkyns in 1452, and just over 2 per cent in the case of Percy's revolt in 1456. Strikingly, of the esquire, three gentlemen, and seven yeomen among those indicted as Wilkyns's supporters, all the gentlemen came from London and one of the yeomen from Wiltshire—and were the only risers to come from outside the county apart from a London vintner and Wilkyns himself, the Warwickshire pedlar. This relative absence of gentlemen and yeomen is all one with the picture they offered of themselves in their 1450 manifesto as reasonable men and petitioners. Unlike the artisans of the Weald and the lower Medway valley, the solid yeomanry of Kent were not given to unfocused and uncoordinated local uprisings that preached lurid violence and unworkable solutions.

7

THE OUTCOME OF CADE'S
REBELLION

JUDGED in terms of the objectives set out by Cade's followers themselves, the rebellion of 1450 achieved scarcely anything whatsoever. Indirectly its outcome was far from negligible. The very failure of the government to respond to the popular outcry of that year and its vindictive crushing of the movement ensured that the South-East would give concerted support to the Yorkist earls who in 1460 once more raised the banner of reform, and went on to achieve not mere reform but an overthrow of the king.

In only two areas of grievance can any positive outcome be measured. A commission of inquiry was granted Kent in 1450 to investigate the abuses the county had complained of, and some amendment came in the matter of the king's finances. (This was something parliament had been addressing before it was dismissed in the spring of 1450.) The Act of Resumption of 1451, although weakened by exceptions for Henry's favourites, did go some way towards answering the insurgents' cry that the king should live of his own. In all other respects the rebels' bills of petition remained unanswered or were remedied only after decades. It would not be until some fifty years later that the inconvenience of long cross-county journeying to the sessions of the peace was removed from the inhabitants of the South-East. In 1496 it was directed that standard weights and measures should be deposited in certain cities and towns. For Kent the towns of Maidstone and Rochester were the places selected. This appears to be the first time that Maidstone was chosen to supersede Rochester or Canterbury.[1] Then, in the same reign at the beginning of the sixteenth century, it was provided that the shire court for Sussex should be held alternately at Chichester and Lewes, rather than only at Chichester.[2] Such a change came to Kent some time after

---

[1] R. Furley, *A History of the Weald of Kent*, ii. pt. i. (London, 1874), 419.
[2] Ibid. 420.

this, so that by the time of William Lambarde, who published his *Perambulation of Kent* in 1576, the division of the Quarter Sessions between Canterbury and Maidstone was a well-established practice.[3]

There was a complete failure to answer the cry that inquest be made upon those who had caused the loss of France so that they might be dealt with at law as traitors. Charges were prepared against the duke of Somerset but he was never formally brought to answer for his military disgrace in Normandy.[4] The French continued to be a threat to the southern and eastern coasts of England which suffered occasional raids. Harwich, for example, was harried several times during the first half of the 1450s[5] whilst in 1457 the French made a daring attack upon Sandwich. Nor was the matter of the free election of the knights of the shire in Kent resolved. In 1455 we find Henry VI writing to the sheriff of Kent, Sir John Cheyne, ordering free elections because it had been drawn to the king's attention that there was 'busy labour' by certain persons in relation to the election of the knights for Kent.[6] Cheyne's past credentials were not good. He had sat as knight of the shire for Kent in 1449, a time when the influence of the infamous Lord Saye had been at its height in the county. 1450 did see a change of faces among the county commissioners and JPs for Kent: in the December of that year eight of those appointed to the previous commission of 1447 were absent, five permanently.[7] But the new men to join the quorum found little favour among the ordinary people of the county. Figures such as Robert Horne, John Fogge, and John Warner were viewed as no better than the likes of Richard Bam, Edward Guldeford, or John Bamburgh whom they replaced.

The last of the requests made by the captain of the great assembly in Kent on one of the three bills had been for something to be done about 'the great extortioners', Slegge, Crowmer, Isle, and Est. Crowmer of course was murdered during the troubles in London, along with his father-in-law, Lord Saye. Among the three surviving, Stephen Slegge, despite being one of Lord Saye's closest associates and a law-breaker

---

[3] F. Hull, *Guide to the Kent County Archives Office* (Maidstone, 1958), 1.

[4] M. H. Keen, 'The End of the Hundred Years War: Lancastrian France and Lancastrian England', in M. Jones and M. Vale (eds.), *England and her Neighbours 1066–1453: Essays in Honour of Pierre Chaplais* (London, 1989), 297–8.

[5] Essex Record Office (Colchester), D/B 4/38/8; *CPR*, 1446–52, 528–9.

[6] *PPC*, vi. 246–7.

[7] *CPR*, 1446–52, 590.

of the first order, apparently went quite unpunished. With regard to the charges made against him in Kent at the end of 1450 in the immediate aftermath of the revolt, he was either declared not guilty or the indictments of him insufficient.[8] At another inquest held at Canterbury in April 1452 he was charged with violent break-ins and thefts from the property of Lord Abergavenny in 1449. Although this resulted in Slegge going up to Westminster, rendering himself prisoner of the Marshalsea and then being granted bail, he was in the end found not guilty.[9] He survived until 1460, so outliving his old associates James Fiennes and William Crowmer by ten years.[10]

William Isle's career subsequent to the rebellion was rather more chequered than Slegge's. He made an apparent recovery, but then fell foul of the new Yorkist regime. His public denouncement by Cade's followers in 1450 may possibly have led to the hiatus of three years from December 1450 to July 1453 in his county career as a JP. In 1453 he was again being employed as a justice, however, and then went on to act annually throughout the remainder of the 1450s either as JP or on commissions of array.[11] But with the coming of Edward IV to the throne his fortunes changed dramatically. In December 1461 a commission was appointed to inquire into the extortions and oppressions committed in Kent by Isle and five others from his home district of Sundridge, just west of Sevenoaks near the Surrey border.[12] Another such commission followed in July 1463, extending its ambit to misdeeds committed in Kent, Surrey, and Middlesex.[13] Even before this second commission had been appointed, Isle's fall from protection and favour was being exploited by men of the district. Their actions, which had the vehemence of long-held grievances which at last see their chance, pre-empted any legal proceedings which might have been brought against this 'great extortioner'. That June of 1463 Isle's manor of Sundridge had been broken into and ten cattle stolen;[14] in August it was twenty-two oxen; in September it was twenty.[15] These

    [8] Virgoe, 'Ancient Indictments', 225, 233–4, 239.
    [9] KB9/267, m. 71; KB27/765 *rex* side, m. 23ᵛ. I say 'thefts' in 1449 since although the indictment actually states one break-in to be in Oct. 1449 and the other to be in Sept. 1448, the latter follows the former so closely in all its details that I assume the clerk dealing with a date very early on in the regnal year (4 Sept.) has inadvertently put '27 Henry VI' for '28 Henry VI', and intends both months for the same calendar year of 1449.   [10] *CFR*, 1452–61, 282.
    [11] *CPR*, 1452–61, 168, 311, 401, 406, 408, 558, 561, 563, 668.
    [12] *CPR*, 1461–7, 133.   [13] Ibid. 301.   [14] KB9/50, m. 20.
    [15] Ibid. mm. 21, 22.

men—labourers, husbandmen, yeomen, tanners, and a couple of gentlemen, from Sundridge and neighbouring Birling, Brasted, Chevening, Chelsfield, and Hever—were not to be cheated of the satisfaction of settling their own score with Isle. On 23 September they ganged up together in the parish of Chelsfield, to the north of Sundridge and for two days actively resisted the progress of William Pecche, kt., and others sent to take and arrest trouble-makers in the district.[16] Their score was finally settled a couple of months later during the night of 14 December. As Isle lay sleeping in the vicarage at Freningham (where he was perhaps taking refuge) his persecutors broke in and killed him in brutal fashion. It was something of a notorious incident. Four months later, in April 1464, Clement Paston knew his correspondent would be interested to hear that 'the Kyng hathe ben in Kent and ther ben endityd many for Isleis dethe'. Over a score of men were indicted for the crime.[17]

Robert Est, the gentlemen infamous for his custody of Maidstone gaol, and the third of the surviving 'great extortioners', apparently came to no great harm for all his unpopularity during 1450. As noted above in Chapter 5, the uprising of his county left him unchastened and in September 1450 he was carrying on in his accustomed manner, denying knowledge of the existence of his own prisoners and extorting money from them for this dissemblance.[18] He pleaded not guilty to the numerous specific charges made against him in the autumn of 1450 and is not recorded as paying any fines for them, whilst under the general charge of being a common extortioner and oppressor he was let off *sine die* by the court.[19] He appears to have resumed the life of a county official, being appointed in July 1453 on to a commission to arrest shipping and sailors.[20] Likewise, his employment as a receiver to the archbishop of Canterbury was taken up once again 1454–6.[21] It is even possible that by the end of the century his own townsmen in Maidstone may have remembered him mainly as the co-founder of their gild of Corpus Christi.[22]

As for those courtiers lampooned in popular verse and denounced in parliament in 1450, of whom Say, Trevilian, and Daniel were perhaps the most hated, the great majority of them survived and thrived during

[16] Ibid. m. 26. [17] *PL*, iv. 101; KB9/50, mm. 27, 34, 35, 36, 38, 53, 54.
[18] Virgoe, 'Ancient Indictments', 231. [19] Ibid. 224.
[20] *CPR*, 1452–61, 123.
[21] F. R. H. Du Boulay, *The Lordship of Canterbury* (London, 1966), 272–3, 400.
[22] *CPR*, 1441–6, 361.

the 1450s and then went on to serve Edward IV. John Say, indeed, was to become a Knight of the Bath under the new king. Say, who had been so active as a JP, commissioner, and MP in Hertfordshire and East Anglia during the 1440s, and who had been serving as sheriff for Norfolk and Suffolk during 1450—a strong indicator that he was likely to be a member of Suffolk's coterie—suffered little through the Act of Resumption passed at Leicester in the June of that year. He surrendered no more than an annuity of £9 2s. 6s. and lost the keepership of the privy palace of Westminster but was able to retain grants worth £65 8s. 4s.[23] As has been seen, he was amongst those who (in their absence) were indicted of treasons by Cade's followers at the Guildhall in London that same June, and was named among the undesirables around the king on the Commons' bill of the parliament of 1450–1. But he survived: in reply to parliament Henry made exception of those who were accustomed to wait upon him and so shielded his household men in this way. A commission of spring 1451 acquitted Say of the treason charges. With the murder of William Tresham in September 1450 Say had taken up Tresham's office of chancellor of the Duchy of Lancaster and was to continue in it until 1471.[24] In September 1452 the keepership of the privy palace at Westminster was restored to him. In 1453–4 he was knight of the shire for Hertfordshire and went on to enjoy an active parliamentary career, sitting for Hertfordshire (except upon one occasion) during 1455–6, 1463–5, 1467, 1472–5, and 1478. He may also have been elected to the parliaments of 1460 and 1461 but the Hertfordshire returns are not extant.

His formula for survival would seem to have been to have established a close position of trust as a royal servant (for in April 1454, soon after the beginning of York's protectorate, he became a member of the royal council) and to have had connections with the Bourchiers, connections which helped bridge his Lancastrian past over into a career as a servant of Edward IV. It is thought that he owed his elevation to the office of under-treasurer of the exchequer in 1455–6 to this Bourchier tie, an office he would hold again in 1461–4 and 1475–8.[25] Indeed, as was just indicated, his was rather more than mere survival. An acknowledgement of the regard Edward IV had for him came in 1465 when on the eve of her coronation he preceded Edward's queen through the city as a newly created Knight of the Bath. There is

[23] J. S. Roskell, *Parliament and Politics in Late Medieval England*, ii. (London, 1981), 158.   [24] Ibid. 159.   [25] Ibid. 153, 161.

some clue as to what Say thought about all this. After his death his effigy would depict him wearing his Yorkist collar of suns and roses and his will would have prayers requested for the prosperous estate of Edward IV, but also too for the soul of Henry VI 'in whos service I was brought up and preferred'.[26]

John Trevilian, the 'Cornish chough', was one man who did feel some of the effect of the largely ineffective Act of Resumption in 1450. All he salvaged from his collection of royal grants and favours was his office of usher of the chamber with its salary of £25 a year from Helston, the issues of Cornwall, and from Restormel park and Fowey fishery.[27] Like Say, his removal from the king's presence was petitioned for during the parliament of the winter of 1450–1, and in April 1451 parliament had ordered his indictment by a commission. But this kind of persecution did not come from those with real power and patronage. So by March 1452 the king, his crisis of 1449–50 over, could regrant Trevilian, his yeoman of the Crown, 6*d*. a day out of Cornwall to be backdated to 1447. Back came, too, in March 1453 his old office of keeper of the armoury in the Tower, a month after he had received a special pardon from Henry VI. He resumed an active role in Cornish affairs during the 1450s, serving as JP and on commissions there. Attainted by Edward IV's parliament he was none the less pardoned in June 1462, and despite a new commission being issued for his arrest in May 1463 he was pardoned once more in 1468, and indeed would be again after the Readeption.[28] Although he did not prosper under Edward IV in quite as conspicuous a way as Sir John Say, his success was to have sustained his career through the vagaries of the 1460s and to have survived into his own seventies.

Thomas Daniel, king's remembrancer and squire of the body, likewise lived to old age. All the commotion of 1450–1—the Act of Resumption, the popular uprising, the poems, the petitions of mutinous troops, the denunciation of parliament—apparently left him unscathed. Despite the commission set up in October 1451 to indict him for treason and felony he got away with a pardon.[29] He retained his constableship of Castle Rising and he continued to exercise a malevolent influence upon life in East Anglia. In the early 1450s, just as if it were still the 1440s, Sir John Fastolf could make no headway

---

[26] Ibid. 170.
[27] Wedgwood, *Biographies*, 873. J. P. Collier (ed.), *Trevilian Papers*, pt. 1 (Camden Soc., OS 67, 1857), 43–5, 46–7.   [28] Wedgwood, *Biographies*, 874.
[29] Ibid. 254–5.

when he attempted to sue Daniel for slanderous language in response to Daniel's claim to be heir to Fastolf's lands in Suffolk and Norfolk. Serving the Lancastrian regime through the 1450s, Daniel's transition, however, into the reign of Edward may have been less easy than Say's. He fought at Towton in March 1461 and suffered attainder. He may have had to keep fairly mobile and by the later part of 1464 he had made his way westwards to the Lancastrian outpost of Harlech castle. However, if East Anglia thought it had finally rid itself of Daniel its relief was short-lived, for following the castle's surrender in 1468 Daniel was in 1469 to return on to Norfolk commissions and to resume his place on the bench.[30] Whatever his role in the Readeption, he received a general pardon in 1472 and in the parliament which followed his attainder was reversed. In 1475 at the age of sixty he was again made yeoman of the Crown with 6*d.* a day for his fee. It is likely that he lived until 1482.

It must have seemed to the campaigners and insurgents of 1450 that there was no getting done with the men of Suffolk's old affinity. John Ulveston was granted a pardon in 1455 and that same year John Heydon reappeared on the bench (an indictment for treason in March 1451 notwithstanding). Even faced with another indictment in 1461, along with Thomas Tuddenham, Heydon managed to slip away again with a general pardon in 1462.[31]

Only Thomas Tuddenham perhaps, of all the major culprits of the Suffolk regime, came to what might popularly have been regarded as a proper end, although it took a decade in the coming. In July 1451 he had been pardoned all offences except for a sum of £200 which he owed the king and in 1453 was elected as MP for Norfolk.[32] His major opponent in East Anglia, the duke of Norfolk, however, intervened to see that he was not returned again in 1455, writing to the under-sheriff that the shire should have a free election so that neither Tuddenham nor any of the duke of Suffolk's former affinity should be elected. But in 1458 Tuddenham was made keeper of the king's wardrobe and treasurer of the household. It was only with the advent of Edward IV that his career came to an end. His arrest was ordered in April 1461. False rumours went about that he had a pardon; Heydon apparently did, but not Tuddenham, and in February 1462 he, along with Tyrell and John Montgomery, were beheaded on Tower Hill.[33]

[30] Wedgwood, *Biographies*, 895.   [31] Ibid. 452–3.
[32] Ibid. 880–1.   [33] Ibid. 880–1.

II

Yet if the neglected grievances and harsh suppression of Cade's followers in 1451 had rendered the South-East in large part quiescent during the 1450s—apart from some persistent protest from industrial villages in the Weald and up the Medway valley—they equally explain the course of events there in 1460. It was this very memory of broken faith and unamended wrongs which caused the region to give warm reception to the Yorkist earls, March, Warwick, and Salisbury, who landed at Sandwich in June 1460. In the previous year at Coventry these disaffected magnates, allies of the government's leading critic, the duke of York, had together with York been attainted by parliament: declared rebels and their lives, lands, and goods forfeit to the Crown. To offer aid or backing to these men was therefore an act of defiance against the king. As with the rebellion of 1450, so in 1459–60 propaganda was deployed to raise support in Kent. A manifesto went about the county announcing that the earls' aims as Henry's loyal subjects was to rid the king of the traitors about him and to reform the evils of corrupt government.[34] Their objectives held a strong echo of those of 1450. Such was the reputed strength of feeling in Kent in support of the earls that Lord Rivers was dispatched to Sandwich to keep the town.[35] At Canterbury a great ballad was posted on the city gates welcoming the impending invasion.[36] Nor had rumour exaggerated the extent of the popular disaffection in Kent, for upon their disembarkation at Sandwich on 26 June Warwick, March, and Salisbury were met by Archbishop Bourchier 'and a grete multitude of peple wythe hym'.[37] And at Canterbury (which had not lent its support to Cade's rebels) there was a dramatic turnabout of events. John Fogge, John Scott, and Robert Horne, the men appointed to defend the city against the rebels, joined the earls' cause.[38] From Canterbury the rebel host was given an unimpeded passage through the county, gathering more support as it went. From Kent it travelled over the river and into a disaffected capital. It was the prelude to the joining in battle of Yorkist and Lancastrian forces at Northampton in July.

The chronicle sources make it very clear that the Yorkist forces were drawn in important part from the counties which had produced the

---

[34] *Davies Chron.*, 86–90.   [35] Ibid. 84.   [36] Ibid. 91 ff.
[37] Ibid. 94.   [38] C. D. Ross, *Edward IV* (London, 1974), 26.

petitioners-turned-rebels of 1450. Supporting the earls were much 'pepull of Kent, Southesex, and Esex'.[39] This regional polarization was reflected in the unlikely rumour which went about that July shortly before the battle of Northampton that proclamation had been made in Lancashire that if victory were gained over the earls then every man could take what he liked in Kent, Essex, and Middlesex.[40] At the battle, according to one chronicler, it was specifically Kentishmen who slew the duke of Buckingham, the earl of Shrewsbury, and the Lords Beaumont and Egremont beside the king's tent.[41] Deserted by Lord Grey of Ruthin, Henry himself was taken prisoner by the rebels. It is likely that Grey's treachery spelt the king's defeat, but had Henry not forfeited the trust and loyalty of the people of the South-East it is altogether possible that the earls would have met with no such groundswell of support and that he would have maintained his liberty. Southern England[42] and the South-East in particular had turned its face against the king. Its disenchantment with Lancastrian rule was complete. The Yorkist lords wanted reform, and it was this, Gregory's chronicle explains, that caused them to be loved of the commons of Kent and of London.[43] In March 1461 Kentish and Essex men were there alongside the Western men and Welshmen in London to acclaim the earl of March King Edward IV.[44]

Despite their significant role in helping Edward IV on to the throne, it would be misleading to characterize the rebels of the South-East as Yorkist. They were not partisan in that manner. They would support whoever appeared to be the best guarantor of good government. The commons of Kent in particular were a remarkably independent political force. Neither tenants nor retainers of the great magnate houses, they were activated by loyalty only to their own best interests (their personal security and the security of their property) and to what they perceived as the good of the common weal. They demonstrated this in 1450 and 1460, and would do so again in 1471. In May 1471 the Bastard Fauconberg was able to rouse gentlemen and yeomen throughout Kent to support the allies of the now Lancastrian earl of Warwick who had joined forces with Henry and his queen to oust

---

[39] *Short English Chron.*, 74.   [40] *Davies Chron.*, 84.   [41] Ibid. 97.

[42] There is evidence that Edward IV's accession was welcomed in Somerset, Dorset, and Hampshire—all places which had seen demonstrations of discontent with Lancastrian government. R. L. Storey, *The End of the House of Lancaster* (London, 1966), 196–7.   [43] *Gregory's Chron.*, 206–7.

[44] *Short English Chron.*, 77.

Edward from the throne.[45] Some of the eighty or so men who were subsequently pardoned for their part in this failed rising in Kent may have taken out pardons merely as representatives of their communities and not as rebels, none the less it is noteworthy that fifteen of them had also taken out pardons following Cade's rebellion more than twenty years before.[46] Again for the gentlemen, yeomen, and townsmen of Kent the desire had been for good government.

III

Cade's rebellion throws into sharp relief the society it criticized: its debt-burdened monarch, its corrupt and greedy courtiers, its dishonest and cynical local representatives, and its disgraced troops. It is not a handsome picture. But the fact of the rebellion assures us that to a sizeable bulk of the inhabitants of south-eastern England this situation was not merely unattractive but altogether intolerable. It would be a gross anachronism to suggest that by the mid-fifteenth century there existed an expectation of fair and impartial government at either central or county level, but there was evidently a level of unfairness and partiality which was acceptable and one which was not. Inability or incompetence in the matter of defence was one of the major issues to tip the balance towards what was seen as an unacceptable level of misgovernment.

The rebellion of 1450 also illustrates vividly that there was a social group below that of the aristocracy and the gentry who could figure in an important way in political life. They were the group who in conjunction with the gentry made up the county community: men who were not the knights of the shire but who voted for them, who did not own villages, but who carried weight in their communities as village notables. This same class were to be important as instigators of revolt in the sixteenth century when on more than one occasion it seemed 'that those below the level of the gentry initiated and controlled disorder as skilfully as they ran their farms and workshops and led their parish guilds'.[47] These men and women, often obscured in historical accounts of the fifteenth century by the better-known doings of their social superiors, speak out through the grievances of 1450.

[45] C. F. Richmond, 'Fauconberg's Kentish Rising of May 1471', *EHR* 85 (1970), 673–92.   [46] *CPR*, 1467–77, 300–2.

[47] S. J. Gunn, 'Peers, Commons and Gentry in the Lincolnshire Revolt of 1536', *Past and Present*, 123 (1989), 79.

APPENDIX A
THE BILLS OF COMPLAINT OF 1450

THERE can be no certainty about the dating or the sequence of the three different lists of grievances which were written during the course of Cade's rising: only one of them carries a date of composition. Each of the three bills survives in at least one fifteenth-century copy and in at least one sixteenth-century copy. At present knowledge the total number of copies of all three versions is eight. The content and tone of the bills do, however, suggest a probable, if unproven, order of production during the events of the rising. It is in that order (discussed above in Chapter 4) that they are printed here.

i

(*a*) The fifteenth-century copy of what may have been the first bill of complaint to be drawn up by the insurgents is a previously unpublished manuscript: BL Cott. IV 50. It is written on a single sheet of paper in an even, legible hand which is finer and more professional than the fifteenth-century copy of the second bill (ii (*b*) below). It carries almost identical wording as the sixteenth-century copy listed below as i (*b*). However, it is probably not the document from which i (*b*) was made: just occasionally a word or phrase is absent from one or the other and the articles appear in a different order in the two copies.

(*b*) In the sixteenth century John Stow (?1525–1605) included a copy of this version in his *Chronicles of England* (1580), 654–6. (The manuscript from which he printed is among his own historical collections: BL Harleian 545, fos. 136ᵛ–137ᵛ.)[1]

BL Cott. Roll IV 50[2]

The compleyntys & causes of the assemble on blake hethe Fyrst hit is opynly noysyd that Kent shuld be dystroyd with a ryall power & made a wylde fforest for the dethe of the duke of Suffolk of wyche the commones there was nevyr dede doer

---

[1] This version, taken from a later edition of Stow, *Annales or a Generall Chronicle of England*, ed. E. Howes (London, 1631), is printed in R. B. Dobson (ed.), *The Peasants' Revolt of 1381* (London, 1970), 338–41. A slightly shortened edition of Stow's version is printed in S. B. Chrimes and A. L. Brown (eds.), *Select Documents of English Constitutional History, 1307–1485* (London, 1961), 290–1.
[2] Without modernizing the spelling or supplying punctuation, I have, for the sake of clarity, extended words which in the MS are contracted; in addition, I have supplied 'th' where the MS has the letter thorn.

Item that the kyng is steryd & mevyd to lyve only on his comyms & other men to have the revenues of the crown whyche harth causyd porete in his excellence & grete paiements of the peple nou late to the kyng grauntyd in his parlements

Item that the lordys of his ryall blode beyng put from his dayly presence & other mene persones of lower nature exaltyd & made cheyff of privy counsell the whiche stoppyth materys of wronge done in his realme from his excellent audiens & may not be redressyd as lawe wull but yf brybys & gyftys be messager to the handys of the seide counsell

Item the peple of his realme be not payd of dettys owyng for the stuff & purvyance takyn to the use of the kyng to the undoyng of the seyde peple

Item his menyall men of housold & other personys askyn dayly godys & londys of peple enpechyd or endytyd of treson the wyche the kyng grauntyd a non or [before] thei so endangeryd be convycte the wyche causith the resseyvours thereof to enforge labours applied to the dethe of peple be sotell menes of coveityse of the seyde graunte

Item the peple so enpechid & attachid thawgh hit be undrwe [*i.e. untrue*] may not be committyd to the lawe for here delyveraunce but holde styll in person to here utteryst undoyng for coveytyse of good

Item hit is notyd be the comyne voyse that the kyngis landys in Fraunce beyn alyenyd & put a wey from the croune & his lordys & peple there dystroyed be untrewe menys of treson of wyche nou hit is desyryd enquyryes to be made thorows all the realme hou & be whom and yf suche traitours may be founde gylty than to have execution of lawe with oute eny pardon in example

Item thou diverse of the peple have never so gret ryght to here lond yet be untrew clayms enfeffements be made to diverse astats & gentils in maintenance so that the trewe ounere of hit dare [not][3] purseu his ryght

Item the collectours of the xv peny in kent beyng gretly vexid & hurt in paying gret somes of money in the Eschekyr to sewe out a wryt callyd *quorum nomina* for the allowance of Barons of the [Cinque] portes whiche nou is desyryd that here aftyr in re[lief][4] of the seid Collectours the barons aforeseyd may seve hit out for here ease at here ovyn coste

Item the Sherevys & undirsherevys lete to ferme here offices & baylywykys takyng gret sevrete therefore the wyche causith extorcons to be done to the peple

Item simple peple that usith not huntyng be gretly oppressyd be endytements faynede & done be the sayde undyrsherewys & baylyes & other of here assent to cause here fees encrese for payement of the seyd ferme

Item they retourne in names of enquestys be wrytyng in to diverse courtes of the kynges not Somenyd ne warnyd where thorou the peple lese dayly gret sommes of money or the value to here undoyng

Item they make leve [*i.e. levy*] of amerciements callyd the grene wexe in more sommes of money than can be founde dewe of record in the kyngis bokys

Item the peple may not have here fre eleccion in chesyng knyghtys of the Shyre but lettres be sent from diverse astates to the gret reulers there the whyche embrase here tenantes & other peple to chese other personys than hem lykyth

Item thereas knyghtys of the Shyre shold chese the kyngis collectours indeferently with oute eny brybys takyng nou late thei have notyd certayn persones in feynyng to be collectours where upon some have made fyne with hem to be dyschargyd & so the collectours offices is bought & solde extorcionysly as hem lust

Item the ministres of the Courte of dovyr in Kent vexe & areste the peple there thorou all the Shyre oute of castelwarde passyng here boundys usede of olde tyme & take gret fees of the peple at here lust extorcionysly to gret hurt of hem

Item the peple be sore vexid in costys & labours callyd to the cessions of pees [*i.e.*

---

[3] There is a tear in the MS here.

[4] Paper worn away. Stow's copy reads 'in the lieue of the Collectors'.

sessions of the peace] apperyng from the ferthest parts of the West in to the East the wyche causyth v day jornay to some peple wherefore they desyre that apparance to be devydyd in two partyes of wyche on part to apere in oon place & another part in a nother place of the Shyre in relevyng of the vexacion of the peple

ii

(*a*) MS Lambeth 306 is a sixteenth-century copy, made by John Stow, of a manifesto dated 4 June 1450 in which the bills listed here as nos. ii and iii are written as a single bill.[5] However, it is clear that this manifesto must have been transformed shortly afterwards into two separate bills: a longer document reciting grievances against 'false traitors' and asserting the loyalty of the insurgents, and a shorter document made up of demands. It is this longer first portion which is discussed here as the second of the bills of complaint.

(*b*) The fifteenth-century copy of the bill is Magdalen College, Oxford, MS 306. It could be the copy which was brought from Blackheath by John Payn for Sir John Fastolf.[6]

(*c*) BL Harleian MS 543 is a sixteenth-century copy of the bill written in the hand of John Stow. It is he who adds as marginalia here the information that these articles were also employed by the commons of Kent at the time of the arrival of the Yorkist earls in Kent in 1460, shortly before the battle of Northampton. Stow is the only source for this claim. On the other copy he made—MS Lambeth 306 (ii (*a*) above)—the date has been erased from 1460 to 1450 and Stow's marginal note that another copy, i.e. this, Harleian 543, 'hathe 1460 at ye comynge of ye Erles', etc. has been struck out.[7] Presumably Stow saw that the Harleian version was only a part of the much fuller text of the Lambeth document and that it was this pruned Harleian version which had been used (if indeed it had) in 1460, not the long Lambeth edition.

(*d*) There is a late sixteenth-century copy of the bill, Bodleian MS Eng. Hist. C 272, which follows very closely, although not identically, upon the wording of the Magdalen document.[8]

Magdalen College, Oxford, MS Misc. 306

These ben the poyntes, mischeves and causes of the gederynge and assemblynge of us zyoure trew legemene of Kent, the weche we trist to God for to remedye with helpe of

---

[5] MS Lambeth 306 is printed in *Short English Chron.*, 94–9. The MS is also printed, paraphrased into modern English, in B. Wilkinson, *Constitutional History of England in the Fifteenth Century, 1399–1485* (London, 1964), 82–6.

[6] The Magdalen MS is printed in HMC, 8th Report (1881), 266–7, which supplies the text printed here.

[7] BL Harleian MS 543, fos. 165^r–166^v, is printed inaccurately and with important omissions in *The Chronicles of the White Rose of York*, ed. J. A. Giles (London, 1845), pp. lxxiv–lxxvi.

[8] I am grateful to Dr R. W. Hoyle for drawing this MS to my attention.

hym oure Kynge oure Soveraigne lorde and alle the comyns of Inglond and to dye therefore.

I. Furst, we consyderynge that the Kynge oure Soveraygne lord by the satiables covetises melicious pompuses in false and noughte brougthe up dayly and nyghtely abowte his hyghnesse, the same dayly and nyzthly is enformed that good is evulle and evulle is good azenst Scripture seyithe, *Ve vobis qui facitis de bono malum.*

II. Item, they sey that oure Soveraigne lorde is above his lawe and that the lawe is made to his plesure, and that he may make breke hit as ofte as hym lyst withouten any distucsione: the contrarie is trew and elles he schuld not have beene swerune in his Coronacione to kepe hit, the weche we conceyve for the higheste poynt of tresone that anny subgecte may do azenst his prynse for to make hym reygne in perjurie.

III. Item, they seye the Kynge schuld lyve upon his Comyns, and that her bodyes and goodes ern his; the contrarie is trew, ffor than nedid hym nevur to set parlement and to aske good of hem.

IV. Item, they enforme the kynge that the Comyns wolde ffurst destroye the Kynges ffreends and aftur hymeselfe, and thenne brynge in the Duke of Yorke to be Kynge, so that by there false menes and lesynges they make hym to hate and dystroye his verrey ffreendus and to cherysche his ffalse traytours that callen hem selfe his ffreendes. And zif ther were no more resoune to know a freend by he may be know by his covetyse.

V. Item, they seyne hit were a grete reprofe to the Kynge to resume that he hath zevune of his lyvelode, so that they neythur wulle suffur hym to have his owne nor to kepe londes or tenementes fforfetid nor non odur goodes but that they aske hit from hym, or elles they take money of odre to gete hyt hem.

VI. Item, yt is to remembre that thees false traytours wulle suffer no mane to coome to the Kynges presense for noe cause withoutune brybe whereas ther owte no brybe to bee but that every mane myghte have his dewe comynge in dewe tyme to hyme to aske justyse or grace as the cause requirethe.

VII. Item, hit is an evy thynge that the good Duke of Gloucestir enpechid of tresone by on ffalse traytour alone was so sone merderud, and nevur myzt come to onswere. And the ffalse traytour Pole enpechid by all the comynealte of Ynglond, wyche nombur passyd a quest of xx^{iiii} mill. [*i.e. 24,000*], myghte not be suffred to dye as lawe wolde, but rather these sayde traytours of Poles assent that was alse ffalse as ffortegere, wolde that the Kynge oure Soveraygne lorde wolde batayle inn his owne realme to the destructione of all his pepulle and of hymself therto.

VIII. Item, they sey when the Kynge wulle, schalle be traytours, and when he wulle none schalle be none; and that aperuthe wele hiddurto. Ffor ziff enny of the traytours aboute malygnne azenst eny mane hyghe or low they wulle ffynde ffalse menes that they may dye as a traytoure, to have londes and goodes, but they wulle not in suche case to suffur the Kynge to have hem to paye eyther his dettes or for his vitayles therwhit, nor to be the rycher of on penny.

IX. Item, the law serveth of ryghte and noughte elles in this dayes for to do wronge whyche for no thynge almest is spedde but ffalse maters by coloure of the lawe for mede, drede, or favoure, and no remedye is hadde in the Court of Consyens nor otherwyse.

X. Item, we sey that our Soveraygne lorde may wele undurstand that he hath hadde ffalse counsayle, ffor his lordez ern lost, his marchundize is lost, his comyns destroyed, the see is lost, ffraunse his lost, hymself so pore that he may not [pay] for his mete nor drynk; he oweth more than evur dyd kynge in Inglond, and zit dayly his traytours that beene abowte hyme waytethe whereevur thynge schudde coome to hyme by his law, and they aske hit from hyme.

XI. Item, they aske gentille mennys landys and godis in Kent, and calle us risers and treyturs and the kynges enymys, but we schalle be ffounde his trew lege mene and his best freendus with the helpe of Jesu, to whome we crye dayly and nyztly, with mony thousand moe, that God of his ryztwysnesse schall take vengaunse on the ffalse treytours of his ryalle realme that have brouzt vs in this myschieff and myserie.

XII. Item, we wulle that alle men know that we wulle neythur robbe nor stele, but these fawtes amendid we schall go hoom, wherfore we exorte all the Kynges trew loge mene to helpe vs, ffor so whatever he be that wulle not thees fawtes were amendyd, he is ffalser then Jew or Sarsone, and we schall with a good wulle lyve and dye vpone hyme as vpone eyther Jew or Sarsone; whoso is azenst this, we wulle merke hyme, ffor he is not the Kynges trew lege mane.

XIII. Item, we wulle it be knowne that we blame not alle the lordes nor alle that biene aboute the Kynges persone, nor alle gentilmene, nor alle men of lawe, nor alle byschoppes, nor alle preestes, but such as maye be ffounde gilty by a just and a trew enquere by the lawe, whereto we mow and desyre that somme trew juge with serteyne trew lordez and knyztes may be sent into Kent for to enquere of alle suche traytours and brybours, and that justyse may be done vpon hem who so evur they be; and that our Soveraigne lorde derecte his lettres patentes to alle his pepulle there openly to be redde and cried that hit is our Soveraigne lorde his wille and he desyrethe alle his pepulle trewly to enquere of every mannys governaunse and of the defantes that reigne, not lettynge for love, for drede, ne for hate, and that justyse be done forthe with; and ther vpone the Kynge to kepe in his owne handis theyre landes and goodes and not zeve hem to any mane but for to kepe hem for his owne richesse, or elles to make his enarmye into ffraunce, or elles to pay therwhit his dettes. By oure wryttinges ze may conseyve we be the Kynges ffrends or his enemyes. Those forseyd myschieffes thus dewly remedyed, and that from hens foorthe no mane vpone peyne of dethe beynge aboute the Kynges persone take enny brybe for any bille of supplicacione or repetacione or cause spedynge or lettynge, oure Soveraigne lorde schall regne with great worschip, love of God and his pepulle, that he schall be able with God his helpe to conquere where he wille; and as for vs we schall be redy to defende oure contrey from all nacions and to go with oure Soveraigne lord where he wulle comaunde vs.

XIIII. Item, he that is gylty wulle wrye azenst thus but schall brynge hem downe, and theye schulle be aschamed to speke azenst resone; they wylle peraventure say to the Kynge that and they be takune from hyme that theye wulle then put downe the Kynge, for the theves wolde lyve lenger; and we were disposyd azenst oure Soveraigne lorde, as Gode forbede, what myzt his traytours helpe hyme?

God be oure gyde, and then schull we spede,
Who so evur say nay, ffalse for ther money reulethe.
Trewth for his tales spellethe.
God seende vs a ffayre day! Awey, traytours, awey!

iii

(*a*) The fifteenth-century copy of this petition is MS BL Cott. II 23.[9]

(*b*) Stow in his *Chronicles of England* (1580), 656–8, has a copy of this list of demands which carries a number of slightly variant readings, but these differences are not significant.[10] (The manuscript from which he printed is found among his collection of historical documents: BL Harleian 545, fos. 137v–138r.)

[9] The MS is printed in *EHL*, 360–2, which supplies the text printed here.
[10] Stow's copy is printed in Dobson, *The Peasants' Revolt of 1381*, 341–2.

BL Cott. II 23

These ben the desires of the trewe comyns of your soueraign lord the Kyng.

First the Chapteyn of the same Comyns deserith the welfare of oure soueraign lord the Kyng, and of all his trewe lordes spirituall and temporall, desiryng of our soueraigne lord and all his trewe counseill to take ageyn all his demaygnes, and he shall then raign lyke a Kyng Riall as he is born our trewe cristen Kyng anoynted. And who saith the contrary we woll all lyue and dye in that quarell.

Also desiryng his trewe Comyns that he woll voyde all the false progeny and afynyte of the Duke of Southefolke, the whiche ben opynly knowyn traitours, and they to be ponysshed affter custome and lawe of the lond. And to take abowte hym a nobill persone, the trewe blode of the Reame, that is to sey the hye and myghty prince the Duke of Yorke, late exiled from our soueraigne lordes presens of the false traitour Duke of Southfolke and his affinite, and take to yow the myghty prince the Duke of Excetter, Duke of Bokyngham, Duke of Northefolke, Erlys and barons of this londe: and then shall he be the Richest Kyng cristen.

Also desirith his trewe Comyns punysshement of the fals traitours, the which contreuyd and ymagyned the deeth of our excellent prince the Duke of Glowcetter, the whiche is to myche to reherse, the whiche Duke was opynly proclamyd at the Parlement of Bury a traytour, vpon the which quarell we purpose to lyue and dye that it is false.

Also the Duke of Exceter, and our holy fader the Cardenall of Wynchester, the nobill princes the Duke of Somersett,[11] the Duke of Warrewike, delyuered and distroyed by the same meanys.

Also the Realme of Fraunce, the Duchie of Normandy, Gasguyn, and Guyen, Angoy, and Mayn lost by the same traytours, and our trewe lordes and knygtes, Squyers and good yemen lost and sold or [*i.e. before*] they went ouer the See, which is gret pite and gret losse to our soueraigne lord and distruccion to his Realme.

Also desirith the Capteyn with the commons of Kente, that all the extorcions may be leid down, that is to sey, the grete extorcion of grene wex, that is falsly vsed to the perpetuall distruccion of the Kynges liege men and the Comons of Kente with out prouision. [Also the King's bench, the which is greefefull to the shire of Kent without prouision of][12] our Soueraigne lorde and his trewe Counsell.

Also in takyng whete and other Grayne, Beeff, Moton, and other vitaill, the whiche is vnportable to the said Commons, with oute breff provision of our soueraigne lorde and his trewe counseill, they may no longer bere hit: and also vnto the statute of laborers and grete extorcioners beyng in Kente, that they be punysshed, and that is to say, the traytours, Slegge,[13] Crowmere,[14] Ysele,[15] and Robert Est.[16]

---

[11] The duke of Somerset is not named in Stow's copy of this petition.

[12] There is an apparently accidental omission here of the first part of the sentence which, however, is found in full in Stow's version. *EHL*, 362 n. 2.

[13] Stephen Slegge, for whom see Ch. 2, sect. IV, above.

[14] William Crowmer, for whom see ibid.

[15] William Isle, for whom see ibid.   [16] For whom see ibid.

APPENDIX B
THE COMPOSITION OF THE PARDON ROLL OF JULY 1450[1]

IN Chapter 5 the matter is addressed as to who Cade's followers were. The roll which was drawn up in July 1450 of the names of those who received a pardon is rejected as straightforward evidence with which to answer the question. But if the pardon roll is no mere list of rebels, what is it? It is a list of those men—and a small number of women—who early in the July of 1450, for whatever reason, wished to have in their hands a free royal pardon. In his pardon the king promised every recipient that he or she was excused all transgressions they might have committed prior to 8 July 1450 and guaranteed that they would go unmolested by his justices, escheators, sheriffs, coroners, or bailiffs. The roll comprises a complex mixture of individuals who fall into three broad categories. There are those who clearly did not rise (these are in the minority); there are those who are there apparently as representatives of their communities and who may or may not personally have involved themselves in the rising but whose communities perhaps were implicated in it in some way, if only by living in the vicinity of the rebels' routes; then there are those who in all likelihood are actual rebels.

Such a mixture means, of course, that nothing hard and fast can be said about the geographical distribution of the rebels. One can speak only about the geographical distribution of those on the roll—but that in itself is worth noting. In broad terms, the bulk (65 per cent) of the 3,000 or so names appear to have come from almost the entire length and breadth of Kent; from eastern and mid-Sussex (14 per cent); from eastern Surrey, particularly from the north-eastern corner nearest to London (12 per cent); and from all along the Essex bank of the Thames estuary, and from a band of Essex running south–west to north–east across the county (8 per cent).[2] That is to say, these names come from along the main lines of communication between London and the coastal ports of the South-East. Joining dots on the sketch map down through Essex,

---

[1] Two articles on this subject appeared during the last century by the same author: W. D. Cooper, 'John Cade's Followers in Kent', *Arch. Cant.*, 7 (1868) and 'Participation of Sussex in Cade's Rising, 1450', *Sussex Archaeological Collections*, 18 (1866). Cooper's work has been more or less completely superseded by the section in R. A. Griffiths, *The Reign of King Henry VI: The Exercise of Royal Authority, 1422–1461* (London, 1981), 619–23, which provides the best account of the rebel host.
[2] I take these percentages from Griffiths, *Henry VI*, 622.

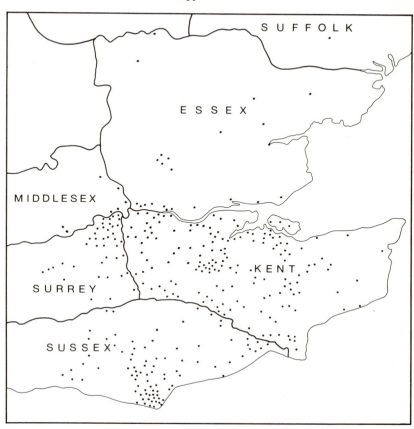

The Distribution of the Places Named on the Pardon Roll of 6 and 7 July 1450

beginning with Hadleigh in Suffolk, just to the west of Ipswich, and finishing in the eastern suburbs of London, produces the lines of the old Roman roads, Essex's main arteries of communication, converging upon Chelmsford from Braintree and from Colchester to travel down through Brentwood to London. In Kent the dots describe the main London to Dover road which passed through the northern and most populous section of the county, through Greenwich, Gravesend, Faversham, and Canterbury. The middle of the county was served by the Greenwich–Maidstone–Ashford route down to Folkestone in Kent and to Rye in Sussex. The villagers of the Weald of Kent were likely to have travelled to the capital on the main road which went out to the coast from London through Sevenoaks, Wadhurst, Battle, and Hastings.

The men of mid-Sussex and Surrey may well have moved along the main Greenwich to Lewes road.[3]

Only a score or so of names appear on the pardon list from areas beyond the South-East—a scattering of men from fifteen other counties. Richard Goldyng, a Shrewsbury yeoman, took out a pardon for himself and for all his fellow townsmen, and in their pardon the two Cornishmen included for good measure all the inhabitants of their home county, but the remainder of this scattering are named solely as individuals.[4] They are a miscellaneous group: their mix includes a Leicestershire knight; three gentleman from Hereford-shire, Cornwall, and Oxfordshire respectively; a York merchant; a Bristol chapman; a Hertfordshire miller; a Bedfordshire clerk; a Derbyshire mason; and a Cambridgeshire butcher. These were men who were perhaps in the vicinity of London during the weeks of the revolt and who willingly or unwillingly became caught up in its events. At least two of them were among the prisoners in the Marshalsea in Southwark which Cade had opened on the night of the battle on the bridge. These were the Cornishmen, a gentleman and a yeoman, whom the king's bench that year had ordered the sheriff of Cornwall to bring before it within fifteen days of Easter to answer for diverse transgressions.[5] Besides these, two others had earlier criminal records: Thomas Boll, the clerk from Temysford in Bedfordshire had raped a female servant at Hakeney in 1436 and stolen goods from her,[6] whilst Richard Goldyng of Shrewsbury had stolen from a religious house near Tonbridge in Kent in 1448 (although he is described as a yeoman in 1450 and as a soldier in 1448).[7] Not all of these geographical erratics need, however, have been press-ganged into the events of the rising. It is very suggestive that the yeoman and the butcher from Cambridgeshire both came from Babraham where Edmund

---

[3] On the subject of medieval roads, see B. P. Hindle, 'The Road Network of Medieval England and Wales', *Journal of Historical Geography*, 2 (1976), 207–21.

[4] Their names as printed, *CPR*, 1446–52, are as follows (in alphabetical order by county/country): Bedfordshire—Thomas Boll, clerk, of Tempsford (p. 366); Thomas Hamlyn, husbandman, of Pulloxhill (p. 353); Berkshire—Thomas Hakkere, yeoman, of Maidenhead (p. 355); Cambridgeshire—Henry Fraunces, yeoman, of Babraham (p. 351); John Glover, butcher, of Babraham (p. 351); Cornwall—John Bainton, gent., of Flexbury [manor] (p. 370); William Bainton, yeoman, of Burn alias of Flexbury, bailiff (p. 370); Derbyshire—William Crauford, mason, of Higham (p. 359); Devon—John Merymouth, fuller, of Honiton (p. 342); Hampshire—John Russell, mariner (p. 354); Herefordshire—John Holmiton, gent., of Holme Lacy (p. 351); Hertfordshire—John Mayster, miller, of Cheshunt (p. 370); Ireland—John Hereford of Kilkenny (p. 359); Leicestershire—William Trussell, kt., of Elmesthorpe (pp. 355, 356); Oxfordshire—Richard Bowle, yeoman, of Banbury (pp. 366, 367); Thomas Stone, gent., of Oxford (p. 345); Shropshire—Richard Goldyng, yeoman, of Shrewsbury (p. 361); Bristol—Peter Hereford of Bristol (p. 359); William Savage, chapman, of Bristol (p. 359); York—William Snawedon, merchant, of York (p. 354).

[5] KB27/755 *rex* side, m. 13ᵛ; *CPR*, 1446–52, 370.

[6] KB9/255/2, m. 44; *CPR*, 1446–52, 366.

[7] KB9/273, m. 8; *CPR*, 1446–52, 361.

Beaufort, duke of Somerset, a figure associated with losses in France, had been given the manor in 1444. They may well have been his tenants.[8]

To return to the names from the South-East, released prisoners may be found here too, but from the Fleet prison in London with its moated site in the ward of Farringdon Without. John Mars, a gentleman from Rickling in Essex had been in debt in 1448, had been outlawed in 1449, and had come to the king's bench on 30 June 1450 and been committed—with the city then under siege—to the Fleet.[9] Another inmate with John Mars would have been John Cutler, a husbandman from Detling in Kent. He had been committed to the Fleet prison in October 1449 in considerable debt to William Isle, the one-time sheriff of Kent. A Richard Cutler, husbandman, from Detling appears on the pardon roll and is likely to be the same man or a kinsman.[10]

It may (or it may not) say something for the workings of the common law in mid-fifteenth-century England that from this sample of many hundreds of individuals, which Professor Griffiths has described as 'a cross-section of society in the south-east of England',[11] only a few dozen individuals are to be found among the records of the king's bench being brought to book for engaging in criminal activities during the twelve years prior to 1450. This figure only just exceeds the number of people on the roll who were victims of major crimes during the period. To name some examples of crime in the South-East, Walter Brenchesle of Benenden had been part of a gang who in 1446 had allegedly killed a man in his home village; William Pilcher and John Pery, both of Chatham, had been fined for having together assaulted a man in Clerkenwell in 1443; Richard Nicoll, a tinker from Rochester, had attacked the city bailiff in court in 1445.[12] During the dozen years prior to 1450 some ten cases of theft, seven cases of assault, and three cases of murder are to be found amongst the king's bench indictments allegedly committed by men who are named on the pardon roll.[13] Other miscellaneous offences range from poaching to the selling of worthless charcoal.

Apart from the bulk of names, which as we have seen are designated as coming from the South-East and the score which did not, there are sixty-two names occurring throughout the roll which are given no place of origin. Just one or two of them are accompanied by their occupation, such as, for example, 'Robert Perry, trumpet', a man who perhaps had been of service to Cade

---

[8] *CPR*, 1446–52, 351. [9] C88/134/127; *CPR*, 1446–52, 340.
[10] C88/134/207; *CPR*, 1446–52, 355. [11] Griffiths, *Henry VI*, 621.
[12] KB9/254, m. 53; /250, m. 100; /251, m. 123.
[13] The ten cases of theft: KB9/234, m. 18; /242, m. 7; /248, m. 59; /233, m. 96; /997, m. 52; /256, m. 95; /245, m. 89; /253, m. 51 (*bis*); /255/2, m. 44. The seven cases of assault: KB9/250, m. 100; /253, m. 38; /240, m. 49; /251, m. 123; /1050, m. 130; /235, mm. 7, 9. The three cases of murder: KB9/229/1, m. 24; /229/3, m. 29; /254, m. 53. To give some idea of the incidence of recorded crime, during the ten years 1440–9 there was an annual average of 8 indictments from the county of Kent among the term indictments of the king's bench.

during the encampment on Blackheath.[14] To omit the place of origin from only sixty people from all the hundreds suing for pardons would seem to be a small percentage of error. No clue is given as to how exactly any of the names were given in, but, since a few names occur in triplicate with slight variations of spelling, perhaps some individuals obtained pardons not only for themselves but for friends at the same time and some persons had more than one friend doing this for them.

There is a more intriguing group of names of no given place of origin which totals three hundred and thirty-nine. These are not, as the last group of sixty-two was, a scattering of oversights, but are written out in a single list as coming from the same place. The very frequent occurrence of the same surnames (sometimes up to six of the same name) strengthens this impression. Of these three hundred and thirty-nine, a hundred and fourteen are, most unusually, women.[15] Since only ten names on the entire roll are designated as coming from London it might seem obvious to suggest that the three hundred and thirty-nine come from there. This is not necessarily the case: Londoners did not see themselves as conniving with the revolt. Indeed, when it was all over the Court of Aldermen held an inquiry and decided that Cade's army had been allowed into the city by an accident. No commission of oyer and terminer was sent into London after the events of the rising, unlike the experience of every other affected area.[16] It is more likely that this long list is of the inhabitants of Greenwich or Southwark who may have fed and accommodated the rebels. This would help account for the appearance here of women on the pardon roll.

As for the form in which the pardons were taken out, all but seven, that is to say, almost nine-tenths of all the numerous hundreds of Kent, are named through one means or another on the pardon roll. Several are cited because a single individual from there sought a pardon, such as the weaver from Brookland who is the only man named from Aloesbridge Hundred on Walland marsh. It is far more typical, however, that a hundred is represented by two constables who accept a pardon for themselves and all other men of their hundred, besides whom there may be named some half a dozen individuals from villages or towns of the hundred who accept a pardon for themselves and for all the other men of their respective parishes. Nearly a third of all the Kentish hundreds follow this pattern and twenty-two of the thirty-three Sussex hundreds named do so, although several of these have the hundred represented merely by the two constables alone without any further names. For some reason the men of the six Surrey and the twelve Essex hundreds on the roll are represented in a less systematic way: the lists of names for certain towns are, erratically, quite fulsome, as in the cases of Charlwood, Southwark,

---

[14] *CPR*, 1446–52, 361.   [15] Ibid. 357–8.
[16] C. M. Barron, 'The Government of London and its Relations with the Crown, 1400–1450', Ph.D. thesis (London, 1970), 538–9.

Croydon, Merton, and Streatham in Surrey, and of Great Waltham and Maldon in Essex—although here the hundred constables are often absent.

To return to the question of who these names on the roll are, Chapter 5 lists some of the most conspicuous examples of individuals who were patently not rebels. Indeed, they include some of the very men Cade's followers were out to condemn.[17] But, besides the infamous, their relatives, and associates, there are on the pardon roll examples of unlikely (although not impossible) rebels amongst the respectable and locally well esteemed. Sir John Cheyne, kt., of Eastchurch on the Isle of Sheppey was a royal serjeant-at-arms by 1445, MP for Kent in 1449, would be sheriff of Kent in 1454–5, and would serve as JP for Kent through from 1447 to 1460.[18] The mayor of Faversham, John Seyncler, is there too. He helped in the capture of Cade only a few days after the pardons were issued. So are former officials of the archbishop of Canterbury.[19] From Essex there is on the pardon roll Robert Darcy esq., whose father had been keeper of writs and rolls at the court of Common Pleas and one of the county's most prominent JPs.[20] Robert Darcy the younger himself followed such a public career and would be a member of the commission appointed in September 1450 to arrest and imprison all traitors and rebels in Essex. He went on to undertake frequent duties as a JP throughout the 1450s and was later to be knighted.[21] Another JP from Essex on the roll is William Tyrell the younger, esq., also destined to become a knight and often appointed on to the same commissions as Robert Darcy. He too would be on the commission to go into Essex in September 1450, and made an equally unlikely rebel, more especially since he and his brother, Sir Thomas, helped to capture rebels in Kent early in 1450 and after Cade's revolt did the same in Essex.[22] Matthew Hay, named alongside William Tyrell on the pardon roll, had served on commissions in Essex. In January 1450 he had been appointed as justice to deliver the gaol of Colchester castle, and in 1451 he would serve on the commission led by the duke of Norfolk to investigate Lollards and heretics in Essex. His active service on commissions of all kinds in Essex was to extend throughout the 1450s and 1460s.[23] Among the men from Sussex Bartholomew Bolney of West Firle and Bolney stands out as an implausible rebel; a yeoman-farmer of property, he had sat on a couple of commissions in Sussex during the 1440s, in May 1451 he would sit on a

---

[17] For further examples, see Griffiths, *Henry VI*, 619–23.
[18] *CPR*, 1446–52, 339; Griffiths, *Henry VI*, 620; Wedgwood, *Biographies*, 181.
[19] Griffiths, *Henry VI*, 620, 621.
[20] Ibid. 672, 703; *CPR*, 1436–41, 471, 532–3; *CPR*, 1446–52, 22.
[21] *CPR*, 1446–52, 348, 431, 477; *CPR*, 1452–61, 490, 558, 665; *CPR*, 1461–67, 564.
[22] *CPR*, 1441–46, 470; *CPR*, 1446–52, 338, 431, 440, 443; *CPR* 1452–61, 299, 665; *CPR*, 1467–77, 211; E403/784, m. 14; E404/67, m. 20. For the way in which William was accused as a follower of Cade, see Ch. 6, above.
[23] *CPR*, 1446–52, 136, 338, 433, 440; *CPR*, 1452–61, 220, 222, 299, 347, 406, 558, 665; *CPR*, 1461–67, 278, 564.

commission to investigate all treasons and offences in his native county since the time of Cade's revolt, and he would go on to serve on numerous commissions throughout the 1450s, acting regularly as Justice of the Peace. Moreover, he was employed as steward both by the abbot of Battle and the archbishop of Canterbury.[24]

Thomas Tebbe, a yeoman from Brenchley, Kent, and William Sandherst, a yeoman from Lamberhurst on the Sussex border, who in 1451 was to be one of the constables of the hundred of Brenchley, are two associates who appear on the pardon roll and who yet pursued active hostilities against the insurgents of their district of the Weald throughout the 1450s.[25] In April 1451 during troubles associated with the local Sussex leader Henry Hasilden, a gang of artisans from Brenchley, East Peckham, and Yalding lay in wait to attack them.[26] In 1456 followers of a Kentish captain rising up at Lamberhurst broke into William Sandherst's house and attacked him because he did not want to join their cause.[27] Then the tables turned and in 1458 Tebbe led a large gang attack upon a local rebel, Stephen Christmas (the gentleman from Staplehurst who had excited men in the Weald in January 1451 with rumours about the king's plan to invade Kent with Northern soldiery). In 1459 Sandherst alongside Tebbe was party to another such attack on Christmas. Two more gang ambushes set upon Christmas led by Tebbe's associates in 1460 and 1461.[28] There could scarcely be a clearer example of two men on the pardon roll who wanted nothing to do with the insurgents of their area and who were in turn victims and victimizers of such rebel elements.

It would appear that some men had their names enrolled among the pardon seekers not as rebels, but as representatives of their communities. There is evidence that some communities produced their natural representatives to add weight to their corporate pardon. In Chapter 5 Canterbury is cited as an example of a city which chose to take out a pardon for its population, the names from there having been included on the roll as representatives not as rebels. At the queen's manor of Great Waltham in Essex of the twenty-nine men who were named as chief pledges at the view of frankpledge which was held for the manor on 28 May 1450, fifteen subsequently appear on the pardon roll amongst the total of sixty-one from Great Waltham.[29]

Although it is quite possible to enumerate categories of individuals who appear on the roll but who are unlikely to have been followers of Cade, this exercise answers for only a handful of the total number. It looks likely that the bulk of names are those of the insurgents themselves. This likelihood is made all the stronger by the circumstance that several of the men on the roll were

---

[24] Griffiths, *Henry VI*, 622, 656; and, for example, *CPR*, 1441–46, 479; *CPR*, 1446–52, 88, 478, 540, 595; *CPR*, 1452–61, 679.   [25] *CPR*, 1446–52, 364, 373.
[26] Virgoe, 'Ancient Indictments', 250.
[27] KB9/289, m. 88; KB27/788 *rex* side, m. 19.   [28] KB9/298, m. 79.
[29] Essex Record Office, D/D Tu 243, m. 23; *CPR*, 1446–52, 370, 371.

involved in subsequent uprisings in the South-East. Henry Bedill, a husbandman from Thurnham went on to join a series of Kentish uprisings in April 1451;[30] in May 1452 John Newman of Halstow, husbandman, supported a newly arisen captain of Kent;[31] in August 1452 Henry Hamon, a sawyer from Headcorn, and William atte Chamber, a fuller from Harrietsham, complained with all the vigour of personal injury that the king and his bishops had rescinded on their promises to Cade's followers;[32] and in April 1456 John Badisden, tailor, and Henry Pelham, cooper, of Hawkhurst supported the rising of John Percy.[33] In Sussex, too, men on the pardon roll are to be found rising up in the September, October, and November of 1450.[34]

However, although it is noteworthy that men who took out a pardon in July 1450 would later be indicted for rising under subsequent captains, more striking is the absence of individuals from the pardon roll in the lists of later insurgents. They form only a very minor percentage of the total numbers indicted for the risings of 1450–6. Of the fewer than thirty men alleged to have been followers of Parmynter in Kent and Sussex (though this must represent a very small proportion of the total number) no more than one appears on the pardon roll; one among the sixty-one indicted for the risings associated with Hasilden; thirteen among the 137 indicted as supporters of Wilkyns; and a mere two among the 126 indicted for supporting Percy. This points to the very different nature of these subsequent uprisings which although they declared allegiance to Cade's aims stemmed as much from the economic and social difficulties of the industrial villages of the Weald and mid-Kent as from political indignation. So that in asserting that the bulk of names on the pardon roll are those of insurgents the evidence comes not from their later histories as rebels but from the plainly stated grievances of the bills of 1450. They are the grievances of these constables, parkers, tax collectors, farmers, and yeomen.

[30] *CPR*, 1446–52, 350, 374; Virgoe, 'Ancient Indictments', 244, 247, 249.
[31] *CPR*, 1446–52, 374; KB9/273, m. 11.
[32] *CPR*, 1446–52, 342, 372; KB9/955/2, m. 2.
[33] *CPR*, 1446–52, 353; KB9/49, mm. 5, 6, 10, 13, 14, 15; /284, m. 42; /288, mm. 58, 59. Henry Pelham is sometimes designated as a husbandman, but more often as a cooper.
[34] *CPR*, 1446–52, 356, 361; KB9/122, mm. 15, 21, 40.

SELECT BIBLIOGRAPHY

A. Original Authorities: Unpublished

Public Record Office, London

All documents referred to in footnotes, unless otherwise stated, are from the PRO, Chancery Lane, London.

C1 (Early chancery proceedings)
C66 (Patent rolls)
C67 (Pardon rolls)
C237 (Bails on special pardons)
C244 (*Corpus cum Causa*)
DL28 (Duchy of Lancaster—various accounts)
DL29 (Duchy of Lancaster—ministers' accounts)
DL30 (Duchy of Lancaster—court rolls)
E28 (Council and Privy Seal—ancient deeds)
E40 (Ancient deeds)
E101 (Accounts various)
E136 (KR Escheators' accounts)
E159 (KR Memoranda rolls)
E199 (Sheriffs' accounts)
E207 (King's Remembrancer *Bille*)
E357 (LTR Escheators' accounts)
E368 (LTR Memoranda rolls)
E372 (Pipe rolls)
E379 (Enrolled sheriffs' accounts)
E403 (Issue rolls)
E404 (Warrants for issues)
KB9 (Ancient indictments)
KB27 (Plea rolls)
KB29 (Controlment rolls)
SC6 (Original ministers' accounts)

British Library, London

Cotton Roll IV
Harleian MSS 530, 543, 545
Additional MS 14848
Additional Rolls

Canterbury Cathedral, MSS of the Dean and Chapter

Sacrist Rolls 37–8

East Sussex Record Office, Lewes

Ashburnham MSS 198–200A
Battle Abbey Estate MSS XA 3/2, 15 (Battle and Barnhorn court rolls)

Essex Record Office, Chelmsford

D/B 3/3/28–30 (Maldon borough records)
D/D Tu 243 (Great Waltham court rolls)
D/DBy M5 (Walden court rolls)
D/DM M33 (Writtle court rolls)
D/DP M255 (Moulsham court rolls)
D/DWg M18 (Navestock court rolls)
T/A 206/1 (Barking Abbey rental)

Essex Record Office, Colchester

D/B 4/38/8 (Harwich borough rolls)

Kent Record Office, Maidstone

PRC 17/5 and 32/2 (Archdeaconry and Consistory Registers)
Fa/Z3 (Pardon to inhabitants of Faversham)
Sa/AC1 (The Old Black Book of Sandwich)

Lambeth Palace Library, London

ED various (Estate documents)

Suffolk Record Office, Ipswich

C8/1/1–2 (Ipswich sessions rolls)
E3/15 (Ministers' accounts and court rolls)

Westminster Abbey, London, MSS of the Dean and Chapter

MS 12239

B. Original Authorities: Published

AMUNDESHAM, J., *Annales monasterii S. Albani*, ed. H. T. Riley (2 vols., RS, 1870–1).

BABINGTON, C. (ed.), *The Repressor of Over Much Blaming of the Clergy* (2 vols., RS, 1860).

BASIN, T., *Histoire des règnes de Charles VII et de Louis XI*, ed. J. E. J. Quicherat (4 vols., Paris, 1855–9).

—— *Histoire de Charles VII*, ed. C. Samaran (2 vols., Paris, 1933, 1944).

BLACMAN, J., *Henry the Sixth*, ed. M. R. James (Cambridge, 1919).

BLONDELL, R., *De reductione Normanniae*, in J. Stevenson (ed.), *Narratives of the Expulsion of the English from Normandy* (RS, 1863), 23–238.

BRIE, F. W. D. (ed.), *The Brut, or the Chronicles of England*, ii. (EETS, 136, 1908).

Calendar of the Charter Rolls, 1427–1516 (HMSO, 1927).

Calendar of the Close Rolls, Henry VI, i–vi and Edward IV (HMSO, 1933–54).

Calendar of the Fine Rolls, xiv–xxi (HMSO, 1934–61).

Calendar of the Patent Rolls, 1391–1485 (HMSO, 1897–1911).

Calendar of State Papers, Venice (HMSO, 1864).

Catalogue of Ancient Deeds, i–vi (HMSO, 1890–1915).

CHRIMES, S. B., and BROWN, A. L. (eds.), *Select Documents of English Constitutional History, 1307–1485* (London, 1961).

CLOUGH, M. (ed.), *The Book of Bartholomew Bolney* (Sussex Record Soc., 63, 1964).

COLLIER, J. P. (ed.), *Trevilian Papers*, pt. 1 (Camden Soc., OS 67, 1857).

DAVIES, J. S. (ed.), *An English Chronicle of the Reigns of Richard II, Henry IV, Henry V, and Henry VI* (Camden Soc., OS 64, 1856).

DAVIS, N. (ed.), *Paston Letters and Papers of the Fifteenth Century* (2 vols., Oxford, 1971–6).

ELLIS, H. (ed.), *Original Letters Illustrative of English History*, 1st ser. (3 vols., 1825); 2nd ser. (4 vols., 1827); 3rd ser. (4 vols., 1846).

D'ESCOUCHY, M., *Chronique*, ed. G. du Fresne de Beaucourt (3 vols., Paris, 1863–4).

FABYAN, R., *The New Chronicles of England and France*, ed. H. Ellis (1811).

FLEMING, J. H. (ed.), *England under the Lancastrians* (London, 1921).

FLENLEY, R. (ed.), *Six Town Chronicles* (Oxford, 1911).

FORTESCUE, J., *The Governance of England*, ed. C. Plummer (Oxford, 1885).

FURNIVALL, F. J. (ed.), *Political, Religious, and Love Poems* (EETS, OS 15, 1866).

GAIRDNER, J. (ed.), *The Historical Collections of a Citizen of London in the Fifteenth Century* (Camden Soc., NS 17, 1876).

—— (ed.), *Three Fifteenth-Century Chronicles* (Camden Soc., NS 28, 1880).

—— (ed.), *The Paston Letters* (6 vols., library edn., 1904).

GASCOIGNE, T., *Loci e libro veritatum*, ed. J. E. T. Rogers (Oxford, 1881).

GENET, J.-P. (ed.), *Four English Political Tracts of the Later Middle Ages* (Camden Soc., 4th ser., 18, 1977).

GILES, J. A. (ed.), *The Chronicles of the White Rose of York* (London, 1845; repr. Gloucester, 1974).

GILES, J. A. (ed.), *Incerti Scriptoris Chronicon Angliae de Regnis Trium Regum Lancastrensium Henrici IV, Henrici V, et Henrici VI* (London, 1848).

HALL E., *The Union of the Two Noble and Illustre Famelies of Lancastre and Yorke* (1550).

HALLIWELL, J. O. (ed.), *A Chronicle of the First Thirteen Years of the Reign of King Edward the Fourth by John Warkworth* (Camden Soc., OS 10, 1839).

HARDYNG, J., *Chronicle*, ed. H. Ellis (1812).

HARRISS, G. L., and HARRISS, M. A. (eds.), 'John Benet's Chronicle for the Years 1400 to 1462', *Camden Miscellany*, 24 (Camden Soc., 4th ser., 9, 1972), 151–252.

HARROD, H. D., 'A Defence of the Liberties of Chester, 1450', *Archaeologia*, 57 (1900), 71–86.

HINGESTON, F. C. (ed.), *John Capgrave, Liber de illustribus Henricis* (RS, 1858).

Historical Manuscripts Commission, iv. (1874); v. (1876); vi. (1877); viii. (1881); ix. (1883); ix. pt. 2 (1884); xiv. pt. 3 (1894).

HOLINSHED, R., *Chronicles of England, Scotland and Ireland*, ed. H. Ellis (6 vols., 1807–8).

KINGSFORD, C. L. (ed.), *The Chronicles of London* (Oxford, 1905).

—— (ed.), *Survey of London by John Stow* (2 vols., Oxford, 1908).

—— 'An Historical Collection of the Fifteenth Century', *EHR* 29 (1914), 505–15.

LE BOUVIER, G., 'Recouvrement de Normandie', in J. Stevenson (ed.), *Narratives of the Expulsion of the English from Normandy* (RS, 1863), 245–376.

MACCRACKEN, H. N. (ed.), *The Minor Poems of John Lydgate*, pt. 2 (EETS, 192, 1934).

MYERS, A. R., 'A Parliamentary Debate of the Mid-Fifteenth Century', *BJRL* 22 (1938), 388–404.

—— (ed.), *English Historical Documents*, iv. *1327–1485* (1969).

—— 'A Parliamentary Debate of 1449', *BIHR* 51 (1978), 78–83.

NICHOLS, J. G. (ed.), *The Chronicle of the Grey Friars of London* (Camden Soc., OS 53, 1852).

NICOLAS, N. H. (ed.), *Proceedings and Ordinances of the Privy Council of England* (7 vols., RC, 1834–7).

—— and TYRELL, E. (eds.), *A Chronicle of London, 1189–1483* (1827).

PUTNAM, B. H. (ed.), *Proceedings before the Justices of the Peace in the Fourteenth and Fifteenth Centuries: Edward III to Richard III* (London, 1938).

RILEY, H. T. (ed.), *Ingulph's Chronicle of the Abbey of Croyland* (1854).

—— (ed.), *Registrum abbatiae Johannis Whethamstede* (2 vols., RS, 1872–3).

ROBBINS, R. H. (ed.), *Historical Poems of the Fourteenth and Fifteenth Centuries* (New York, 1959).

Rotuli Parliamentorum (7 vols., 1832).

RYMER, T. (ed.), *Foedera, conventiones, literae . . .* (London, 1704–35).

SALTER, H. E. (ed.), *Registrum cancellarii Oxon.*, i. (Oxford, 1930).

SHARPE, R. R. (ed.), *Calendar of the Letter-Books preserved among the Archives of the Corporation of the City of London: Letter-Book K* (1911).

SHEPPARD, J. (ed.), *Literae Cantuarienses*, iii. (RS, 1889).

SHIRLEY, J. (ed.), *A Parisian Journal, 1405–1449* (Oxford, 1968).

STEVENSON, J. (ed.), *Narratives of the Expulsion of the English from Normandy, 1449–1450* (RS, 1863).

—— (ed.), *Letters and Papers Illustrative of the Wars of the English in France during the Reign of Henry the Sixth, etc.* (2 vols. in 3, RS, 1861–4).

STOW, J., *The Chronicles of England, from Brute unto this Present Yeare of Christ, 1580* (1580).

—— *Annales, or a Generall Chronicle of England*, ed. E. Howes (London, 1631).

THOMAS, A. H., and THORNLEY, I. D. (eds.), *The Great Chronicle of London* (London, 1938).

VIRGOE, R. (ed.), 'Some Ancient Indictments in the King's Bench referring to Kent, 1450–1452', in *Documents Illustrative of Medieval Kentish Society*, ed. F. R. H. Du Boulay (Kent Record Soc., 1964), 214–65.

WARNER, G. (ed.), *The Libelle of Englysche Polycye* (Oxford, 1926).

WAURIN, J. DE, *Recueil des croniques et anchiennes istories de la Grant Bretaigne*, ed. W. Hardy and E. L. C. P. Hardy (5 vols., RS, 1864–91).

WRIGHT, T. (ed.), *A Collection of Political Poems and Songs relating to English History, from the Accession of Edward III to the Reign of Henry VIII* (2 vols., RS, 1859–61).

C. Secondary Authorities

ALLMAND, C. T., 'The Anglo-French Negotiations, 1439', *BIHR* 40 (1967), 1–33.

—— 'The Lancastrian Land Settlement in Normandy, 1417–50', *Econ. HR*, 2nd ser., 21 (1968), 461–79.

—— *Lancastrian Normandy 1415–1450: The History of a Medieval Occupation* (Oxford, 1983).

—— *The Hundred Years War: England and France at war c.1300–c.1450* (Cambridge, 1988).

ARMSTRONG, C. A. J., *England, France and Burgundy in the Fifteenth Century* (London, 1983).

ASTON, Margaret E., *Lollards and Reformers: Images and Literacy in Late Medieval Religion* (London, 1984).

ASTON, T. H., and HILTON, R. H. (eds.), *The English Rising of 1381* (Cambridge, 1984).

BAGLEY, J. J., *Margaret of Anjou: Queen of England* (n.d. [1948])

BAKER, A. R. H., 'Open Fields and Partible Inheritance on a Kent Manor', *Econ. HR*, 2nd ser., 17 (1964), 1–23.

—— 'Some Fields and Farms in Medieval Kent', *Arch. Cant.*, 80 (1965), 152–74.

BARRON, C. M., 'London and the Crown 1451–61', in *The Crown and Local Communities in England and France in the Fifteenth Century*, ed. J. R. L. Highfield and R. Jeffs (Gloucester, 1981), 88–109.

BEAN, J. M. W., *The Estates of the Percy Family, 1416–1537* (Oxford, 1958).

BELLAMY, J. G., *The Law of Treason in England in the Later Middle Ages* (Cambridge, 1970).

—— *Crime and Public Order in England in the Later Middle Ages* (Cambridge, 1973).

BENNETT, H. S., *The Pastons and their England* (Cambridge, 1951).

—— *Six Medieval Men and Women* (Cambridge, 1955).

BLATCHER, M., *The Court of King's Bench, 1450–1550* (London, 1978).

BOLTON, J. L., *The Medieval English Economy 1150–1500* (London, 1980).

BOSSUAT, A., *Perrinet Gressart et François de Surienne, agents de l'Angleterre* (Paris, 1936).

BRANDON, P. F., 'Cereal Yields on the Sussex Estates of Battle Abbey during the Later Middle Ages', *Econ. HR*, 2nd ser., 25 (1972), 403–20.

BRITNELL, R. H., *Growth and Decline in Colchester, 1300–1525* (Cambridge, 1986).

BROWN, A., 'London and North-West Kent in the Later Middle Ages: The Development of a Land Market', *Arch. Cant.*, 92 (1976), 145–55.

BROWN, A. L., 'The King's Councillors in Fifteenth-Century England', *TRHS*, 5th ser., 19 (1969), 95–118.

—— *The Governance of Late Medieval England 1272–1461* (London, 1989).

BROWN, R. ALLEN, COLVIN, H. M., and TAYLOR, A. J. (eds.), *The History of the King's Works*, i. *The Middle Ages* (London, 1963).

BUTCHER, A. F., 'The Origins of Romney Freemen, 1433–1523', *Econ. HR*, 2nd ser., 27 (1974), 16–27.

CAMPBELL, B. M. S., 'The Diffusion of Vetches in Medieval England', *Econ. HR*, 2nd ser., 41 (1988), 193–208.

CARPENTER, C., 'The Beauchamp Affinity: A Study of Bastard Feudalism at Work', *EHR* 95 (1980), 515–32.

CARR, A. D., 'Welshmen and the Hundred Years War', *Welsh History Review*, 4 (1968), 21–46.

CARUS WILSON, E. M., *Medieval Merchant Venturers* (3rd edn., London, 1967).

—— and COLEMAN, O., *England's Export Trade, 1275–1547* (Oxford, 1963).

CHRIMES, S. B., *English Constitutional Ideas in the Fifteenth Century* (Cambridge, 1936).

—— *Henry VII* (London, 1972).

—— ROSS, C. D., and GRIFFITHS, R. A. (eds.), *Fifteenth-Century England, 1399–1509* (Manchester, 1972).

CLARK, P., *English Provincial Society from the Reformation to the Revolution: Religion, Politics and Society in Kent 1500–1640* (Hassocks, Sussex, 1977).

CLARKE, D., and STOYEL, A., *Otford in Kent: A History* (Otford and District Historical Society, Otford, 1975).

COMPTON-REEVES, A., 'William Booth, Bishop of Coventry and Lichfield (1447–52)', *Midland History*, 3 (1975), 11–29.

CONWAY, A. E., 'The Maidstone Sector of Buckingham's Rebellion, Oct. 18, 1483', *Arch. Cant.*, 37 (1925), 97–120.

COOPER, W. D., 'Participation of Sussex in Cade's Rising, 1450', *Sussex Archaeological Collections*, 18 (1866), 19–36.

—— 'John Cade's Followers in Kent', *Arch. Cant.*, 7 (1868), 233–71.

DARBY, H. C. (ed.), *A New Historical Geography of England before 1600* (Cambridge, 1976).

DAVIES, C. S. L., *Peace, Print and Protestantism 1450–1558* (London, 1976).

DAVIS, J. F., 'Lollard Survival and the Textile Industry in the South-East of England', *Studies in Church History*, 3 (1960), 191–201.

—— *Heresy and Reformation in the South East of England 1520–1559* (London, 1983).

DICKINSON, J. G., *The Congress of Arras, 1435* (Oxford, 1955).

DOBSON, R. B., *The Peasants' Revolt of 1381* (London, 1970).

—— (ed.), *The Church, Politics and Patronage in the Fifteenth Century* (Gloucester, 1984).

DU BOULAY, F. R. H., 'The Pagham Estates of the Archbishops of Canterbury during the Fifteenth Century', *History*, NS 38 (1953), 201–18.

—— 'A Rentier Economy in the Later Middle Ages: The Archbishopric of Canterbury', *Econ. HR*, 2nd ser., 16 (1964), 427–38.

—— 'Who were Farming the English Demesnes at the End of the Middle Ages?', *Econ. HR*, 2nd ser., 17 (1964), 443–55.

—— *The Lordship of Canterbury: An Essay on Medieval Society* (London, 1966).

—— *An Age of Ambition* (London, 1970).

DULLEY, A. J. F., 'Four Kent Towns at the end of the Middle Ages', *Arch. Cant.*, 81 (1966), 95–108.

DUNHAM, W. H., 'Notes from the Parliament at Winchester, 1449', *Speculum*, 17 (1942).

DUNKIN, J., *The History and Antiquities of Dartford* (London, 1844).

DYER, C. C., 'A Redistribution of Incomes in Fifteenth Century England?', *Past and Present*, 39 (1968), 11–33.

—— 'A Small Landowner in the Fifteenth Century', *Midland History*, 1 (1972), 1–14.

—— *Lords and Peasants in a Changing Society: The Estates of the Bishopric of Worcester, 680–1540* (Cambridge, 1980).

—— *Standards of Living in the Later Middle Ages: Social Change in England c.1200–1520* (Cambridge, 1989).

DYMOND, D., and VIRGOE, R., 'The Reduced Population and Wealth of Early Fifteenth-Century Suffolk', *Proceedings of the Suffolk Institute of Archaeology and History*, 36 (1986), 73–100.

EDWARDS, J. G., 'The Huntingdonshire Parliamentary Election of 1450', in T. A. Sandquist and M. R. Powicke (eds.), *Essays in Mediaeval History Presented to Bertie Wilkinson* (Toronto, 1969), 383–95.

—— *The Second Century of the English Parliament* (Oxford, 1979).

EVANS, J., *English Art 1307–1461* (Oxford, 1949; repr. New York, 1981).

EVERITT, A. M., *Landscape and Community in England* (London, 1985).

—— *Continuity and Colonization: The Evolution of Kentish Settlement* (Leicester, 1986).

FERGUSON, J., *English Diplomacy, 1422–1461* (Oxford, 1972).

FLEMING, P. W., 'Charity, Faith, and the Gentry of Kent 1422–1529', in A. Pollard (ed.), *Property and Politics: Essays in Later Medieval English History* (Gloucester, 1984), 23–54.

FLENLEY, R., 'London and Foreign Merchants in the Reign of Henry VI', *EHR* 25 (1910), 644–55.

FOURQUIN, G., *The Anatomy of Popular Rebellion in the Middle Ages* (Amsterdam, 1978).

FRYDE, E. B., *Studies in Medieval Trade and Finance* (London, 1983).

FURLEY, R., *A History of the Weald of Kent* (3 vols., London, 1871–4).

GAIRDNER, J., 'Jack Cade's Rebellion', *Fortnightly Review*, OS 14 (1870), 442–55.

GIRAUD, F. F., 'Faversham: Regulations for the Town Porters', *Arch. Cant.*, 20 (1893), 219–21.

GIUSEPPI, M. S., 'Alien Merchants in England in the Fifteenth Century', *TRHS*, NS 9 (1895), 75–98.

GRANSDEN, A., *Historical Writing in England II: c.1307 to the Early Sixteenth Century* (London, 1982).

GRAY, H. L., 'Incomes from Land in England in 1436', *EHR* 49 (1934), 607–39.

GREENSTREET, J., 'Jack Cade's Rebellion', *Antiquarian Magazine and Bibliographer*, 2 (1883), 165–71.

GRIFFITHS, R. A., 'Gruffydd ap Nicholas and the Fall of the House of Lancaster', *Welsh History Review*, 2 (1965), 213–31.

—— 'The Trial of Eleanor Cobham: An Episode in the Fall of Duke Humphrey of Gloucester', *BJRL* 51 (1968–9), 381–99.

—— 'Local Rivalries and National Politics: The Percies, the Nevilles, and the Duke of Exeter, 1452–55', *Speculum*, 43 (1968), 589–632.

—— 'Duke Richard of York's Intentions in 1450 and the Origins of the Wars of the Roses', *Journal of Medieval History*, 1 (1975), 187–209.

—— (ed.), *Patronage, the Crown and the Provinces in Later Medieval England* (Gloucester, 1981).

—— *The Reign of King Henry VI: The Exercise of Royal Authority, 1422–1461* (London, 1981).

—— 'The King's Council and the First Protectorate of the Duke of York, 1453–1454', *EHR* 99 (1984), 67–82.

—— and SHERBORNE, J. (eds.), *Kings and Nobles in the Later Middle Ages: A Tribute to Charles Ross* (Gloucester, 1986).

GUNN, S. J., 'Peers, Commons and Gentry in the Lincolnshire Revolt of 1536', *Past and Present*, 123 (1989), 52–79.

HARDING, A., *The Law Courts of Medieval England* (London, 1973).

HARRISS, G. L., 'The Struggle for Calais: An Aspect of the Rivalry between Lancaster and York', *EHR* 75 (1960), 30–53.

—— 'Cardinal Beaufort, Patriot or Usurer', *TRHS*, 5th ser., 20 (1970), 129–48.

—— 'Marmaduke Lumley and the Exchequer Crisis of 1446–9', in J. G. Rowe (ed.), *Aspects of Late Medieval Government and Society* (Toronto, 1986), 143–78.

—— *Cardinal Beaufort: A Study of Lancastrian Ascendancy and Decline* (Oxford, 1988).

HARVEY, B., 'The Leasing of the Abbot of Westminster's Demesnes in the Later Middle Ages', *Econ. HR*, 2nd ser., 22 (1969), 17–27.

—— *Westminster Abbey and its Estates in the Middle Ages* (Oxford, 1977).

HASTED, E., *The History and Topographical Survey of the County of Kent* (repr. of 2nd edn., 12 vols., Wakefield, 1972; orig. edn., 12 vols., Canterbury, 1797–1801).

HASTINGS, M., *The Court of Common Pleas in Fifteenth-Century England* (Ithaca, NY, 1947).

HATCHER, J., *Rural Economy and Society in the Duchy of Cornwall, 1300–1500* (Cambridge, 1970).

HAWARD, W. I., 'Economic Aspects of the Wars of the Roses in East Anglia', *EHR* 41 (1926), 170–89.

—— 'Gilbert Debenham: A Medieval Rascal in Real Life', *History*, 13 (1929), 300–14.

HICKS, M. A., 'The Yorkshire Rebellion of 1489 Reconsidered', *Northern History*, 22 (1986), 39–62.

HILTON, R. H., *The Decline of Serfdom in Medieval England* (London, 1969).

—— *Bond Men Made Free: Medieval Peasant Movements and the English Rising of 1381* (London, 1973).

—— *The English Peasantry in the Later Middle Ages* (Oxford, 1975).

—— *Class Conflict and the Crisis of Feudalism: Essays in Medieval Social History* (London, 1985).

HINDLE, B. P., 'The Road Network of Medieval England and Wales', *Journal of Historical Geography*, 2 (1976), 207–21.

JACOB, E. F., *The Fifteenth Century, 1399–1485* (Oxford, 1961).

—— *Essays in Later Medieval History* (Manchester, 1968).

JEFFS, R. M., 'The Poynings–Percy Dispute: An Example of the Interplay of Open Strife and Legal Action in the Fifteenth Century', *BIHR* 34 (1961), 148–64.

JOHNSON, P. A., *Duke Richard of York 1411–1460* (Oxford, 1988).

JOHNSTON, C. E., 'Sir William Oldhall', *EHR* 25 (1910), 715–22.

JONES, M. K., 'Somerset, York and the Wars of the Roses', *EHR* 104 (1989), 285–307.

JUDD, A., *The Life of Thomas Bekynton* (Chichester, 1961).

KEEN, M. H., *England in the Later Middle Ages* (London, 1973).

—— 'The End of the Hundred Years War: Lancastrian France and Lancastrian England', in *England and her Neighbours 1066–1453: Essays in Honour of Pierre Chaplais*, ed. M. Jones and M. Vale (London, 1989), 297–311.

—— and Daniel, M. J., 'English Diplomacy and the Sack of Fougères in 1449', *History*, 59 (1974), 375–91.

KEMPE, A. J., *Historical Notices of the Collegiate Church of St Martin-Le-Grand* (London, 1825).

KENNY, A. (ed.), *Wyclif in his Times* (Oxford, 1986).

KINGSFORD, C. L., *English Historical Literature in the Fifteenth Century* (Oxford, 1913).

—— *Prejudice and Promise in Fifteenth-Century England* (Oxford, 1925; repr. London, 1962).

KIRBY, J. L., 'The Issues of the Lancastrian Exchequer and Lord Cromwell's Estimates of 1433', *BIHR* 24 (1951), 121–51.

KNECHT, R. J., 'The Episcopate and the Wars of the Roses', *University of Birmingham Historical Journal*, 6 (1957–8), 108–31.

KNOOP, D., and JONES, G. P., 'The Building of Eton College, 1442–1460', *Transactions Quatuor Coronati Lodge*, 46 (1933), 70–114.

KRIEHN, G., *The English Rising in 1450* (Strasburg, 1892).

LANDER, J. R., 'Henry VI and the Duke of York's Second Protectorate, 1455 to 1456', *BJRL* 43 (1960), 46–69.

—— *The Wars of the Roses* (London, 1965).

—— *Conflict and Stability in Fifteenth-Century England* (London, 1st edn., 1969; 3rd edn., 1977).

—— *Crown and Nobility, 1450–1509* (London, 1976).

LEWIS, P. S., *Later Medieval France* (London, 1968).

List of Sheriffs for England and Wales (PRO, Lists and Indexes, 9, 1898).

LLOYD, T. H., *The English Wool Trade in the Middle Ages* (Cambridge, 1977).

LYLE, H. M., *The Rebellion of Jack Cade, 1450* (Historical Association, 1950).

MACCULLOCH, D., 'Kett's Rebellion in Context', *Past and Present*, 84 (1979), 36–59.

MCFARLANE, K. B., *John Wycliffe and the Beginnings of English Nonconformity* (London, 1952).

—— *Lancastrian Kings and Lollard Knights* (Oxford, 1972).

—— *The Nobility of Later Medieval England* (Oxford, 1973).

—— *England in the Fifteenth Century: Collected Essays*, ed. G. L. Harriss (London, 1981).

MCKENNA, J. W., 'Piety and Propaganda: The Cult of King Henry VI', in

B. Rowland (ed.), *Chaucer and Middle English Studies in Honour of R. H. Robbins* (London, 1974), 72–88.

MCRAE, S. G., and BURNHAM, C. P., *The Rural Landscape of Kent* (Wye, 1973).

MADDICOTT, J. R., 'Law and Lordship: Royal Justices as Retainers in Thirteenth and Fourteenth Century England', *Past and Present Supplement*, 4 (1978).

—— 'The County Community and the Making of Public Opinion in Fourteenth-Century England', *TRHS*, 5th ser., 28 (1978), 27–43.

MATE, M., 'Pastoral Farming in South-East England in the Fifteenth Century', *Econ. HR*, 2nd ser., 40 (1987), 523–36.

MEEKINGS, C. A. F., 'Thomas Kerver's Case, 1444', *EHR* 90 (1975), 331–46.

MOLLAT, M., and WOLFF, P., *The Popular Revolutions of the Late Middle Ages* (London, 1973).

MULLETT, M., *Popular Culture and Popular Protest in Late Medieval and Early Modern Europe* (London, 1987).

MUNRO, J. H. A., *Wool, Cloth and Gold* (Toronto, 1972).

MURRAY, K. M. E., *The Constitutional History of the Cinque Ports* (Manchester, 1935).

MYERS, A. R., *Crown, Household and Parliament in Fifteenth Century England* (London, 1985).

NICOLAS, H., *History of the Battle of Agincourt* (London, 1833).

OMAN, C., *The Great Revolt of 1381* (2nd edn., Oxford, 1969).

ORRIDGE, B. B., *Illustrations of Jack Cade's Rebellion* (1869).

OWST, G. R., *Preaching in Medieval England* (Cambridge, 1926).

PAYLING, S. J., 'The Widening Franchise—Parliamentary Elections in Lancastrian Nottinghamshire', in D. Williams (ed.), *England in the Fifteenth Century: Proceedings of the 1986 Harlaxton Symposium* (Woodbridge, 1987), 167–85.

PERROY, E., *The Hundred Years War* (London, 1951).

POLLARD, A. J., *John Talbot and the War in France, 1427–1453* (London, 1983).

—— *The Wars of the Roses* (London, 1988).

POSTAN, M. M., 'Some Social Consequences of the Hundred Years' War', *Econ. HR*, 12 (1942), 1–12.

—— 'The Costs of the Hundred Years' War', *Past and Present*, 27 (1964), 34–53.

—— *Medieval Trade and Finance* (Cambridge, 1973).

POWELL, J. E., and WALLIS, K., *The House of Lords in the Middle Ages* (London, 1968).

POWER, E., and POSTAN, M. M. (eds.), *Studies in English Trade in the Fifteenth Century* (London, 1933).

POWICKE, F. M., and FRYDE, E. B. (eds.), *The Handbook of British Chronology* (2nd edn., London, 1961).

POWICKE, M. R., 'Lancastrian Captains', in T. A. Sandquist and M. R. Powicke (eds.), *Essays in Medieval History Presented to Bertie Wilkinson* (Toronto, 1969), 371–82.

PUGH, T. B., 'Richard Plantagenet, Duke of York as the King's Lieutenant in France and Ireland', in J. G. Rowe (ed.), *Aspects of Late Medieval Government and Society* (Toronto, 1986), 107–42.

RAMSAY, J. H., *Lancaster and York: A Century of English History, 1399–1485* (2 vols., Oxford, 1892).

RAWCLIFFE, C., *The Staffords, Earls of Stafford and Dukes of Buckingham, 1394–1521* (Cambridge, 1978).

RICHMOND, C. F., 'The Keeping of the Seas during the Hundred Years' War, 1422–1440', *History*, 49 (1964), 283–98.

—— 'English Naval Power in the Fifteenth Century', *History*, 52 (1967), 1–15.

—— 'Fauconberg's Kentish Rising of May 1471', *EHR* 85 (1970), 673–92.

—— *John Hopton: A Fifteenth Century Suffolk Gentleman* (Cambridge, 1981).

ROSENTHAL, J. T., 'The Estates and Finances of Richard, Duke of York (1411–1460)', in W. M. Bowsky (ed.), *Studies in Medieval and Renaissance History*, 2 (Lincoln, Nebr., 1965), 115–204.

ROSKELL, J. S., *The Commons and their Speakers in Medieval English Parliaments* (Manchester, 1965).

—— *Parliament and Politics in Late Medieval England* (3 vols., London, 1981–3).

ROSS, C. D., *Edward IV* (London, 1974).

—— (ed.), *Patronage, Pedigree and Power in Later Medieval England* (Gloucester, 1979).

—— 'Rumour, Propaganda and Popular Opinion during the Wars of the Roses', in R. A. Griffiths (ed.), *Patronage, the Crown and the Provinces in Later Medieval England* (Gloucester, 1981).

—— *Richard III* (London, 1981).

ROSS, C. D., and PUGH, T. B., 'The English Baronage and the Income Tax of 1436', *BIHR* 26 (1953), 1–28.

RUDDOCK, A. A., *Italian Merchants and Shipping in Southampton, 1270–1600* (Southampton, 1951).

SCATTERGOOD, V. J., *Politics and Poetry in the Fifteenth Century* (London, 1971).

SCOFIELD, C. L., *The Life and Reign of Edward the Fourth* (2 vols., London, 1923).

SEARLE, E., *Lordship and Community: Battle Abbey and its Banlieu, 1066–1538* (Toronto, 1974).

STOREY, R. L., *The End of the House of Lancaster* (London, 1966).

SWANSON, R. N., *Church and Society in Late Medieval England* (Oxford, 1989).

THIELEMANS, M.-R., *Bourgogne et Angleterre: relations politiques et économiques entre les Pays-Bas Bourguignons et l'Angleterre, 1435–1467* (Brussels, 1966).

THOMSON, J. A. F., 'A Lollard Rising in Kent: 1431 or 1438?', *BIHR* 37 (1964), 100–2.

—— *The Later Lollards, 1414–1520* (Oxford, 1965).

—— 'Orthodox Religion and the Origins of Lollardy', *History*, 74 (1989), 39–55.

THRUPP, S. L., *The Merchant Class of Medieval London* (Chicago, 1948; repr. Ann Arbor, Mich., 1962).

TUCK, A., *Crown and Nobility 1272–1461* (Totowa, 1985).

VALE, M. G. A., *English Gascony, 1399–1453: A Study of War, Government, and Politics during the later Stages of the Hundred Years War* (Oxford, 1970).

—— *Charles VII* (London, 1974).

VALLANCE, A., 'A Curious Case at Cranbrook in 1437', *Arch. Cant.*, 43 (1931), 173–86.

VAUGHAN, R., *Philip the Good: The Apogee of Burgundy* (London, 1970).

VICKERS, K. H., *Humphrey, Duke of Gloucester* (London, 1907).

VIRGOE, R., 'The Death of William de la Pole, Duke of Suffolk', *BJRL* 47 (1964–5), 489–502.

—— 'Three Suffolk Parliamentary Elections in the Mid-Fifteenth Century', *BIHR* 39 (1966), 185–96.

—— 'The Composition of the King's Council, 1437–61', *BIHR* 43 (1970), 134–60.

—— 'William Tailboys and Lord Cromwell: Crime and Politics in Lancastrian England', *BJRL* 55 (1973), 459–82.

—— 'The Cambridgeshire Election of 1439', *BIHR* 46 (1973), 95–101.

—— 'The Murder of James Andrew: Suffolk Faction in the 1430s', *Proceedings of the Suffolk Institute of Archaeology and History*, 34 (1980), 263–8.

—— 'The Crown, Magnates and Local Government in Fifteenth-Century East Anglia', in J. R. L. Highfield and R. Jeffs (eds.), *The Crown and Local Communities in England and France in the Fifteenth Century* (Gloucester, 1981), 72–87.

—— 'The Parliamentary Subsidy of 1450', *BIHR* 55 (1982), 125–38.

—— 'Aspects of the County Community in the Fifteenth Century', in M. Hicks (ed.), *Profit, Piety and the Professions in Later Medieval England* (Gloucester, 1990), 1–13.

WALLENBERG, J. K., *The Place-Names of Kent* (Uppsala, 1934).

WEDGWOOD, J. C. (ed.), *History of Parliament: Biographies of the Members of the Commons House, 1439–1509* (HMSO, 1936).

—— (ed.), *History of Parliament: Register of the Ministers and of the Members of both Houses, 1439–1509* (HMSO, 1938).

WELCH, E., 'Some Suffolk Lollards', *Proceedings of the Suffolk Institute of Archaeology and History*, 29 (1963), 154–65.

WILKINSON, B., *Constitutional History of England in the Fifteenth Century, 1399–1485* (London, 1964).

WILKINSON, B., 'Fact and Fancy in Fifteenth-Century English History', *Speculum*, 42 (1967), 673–92.

WOLFFE, B. P., 'Acts of Resumption in the Lancastrian Parliaments, 1399–1456', *EHR* 73 (1958), 583–613.

—— *Henry VI* (London, 1981).

D. Theses

ARTHURSON, I., '1497 and the Western Rising', Ph.D. thesis (Keele, 1981).

BARRON, C. M., 'The Government of London and its Relations with the Crown, 1400–1450', Ph.D. thesis (London, 1970).

BLATCHER, M., 'The Working of the Court of King's Bench in the Fifteenth Century', Ph.D. thesis (London, 1936).

BROWN, A. F., 'The Lands and Tenants of the Bishopric and Cathedral Priory of St Andrew, Rochester, 600–1540', Ph.D. thesis (London, 1974).

CARLIN, M. N., 'Christ Church, Canterbury, and its Lands, from the Beginning of the Priorate of Thomas Chillenden to the Dissolution 1391–1540', B.Litt. thesis (Oxford, 1970).

FLEMING, P. W., 'The Character and Private Concerns of the Gentry of Kent 1422–1509', Ph.D. thesis (Swansea, 1985).

HARE, J. N., 'Lords and Tenants in Wiltshire *c*.1380–*c*.1520 with Special Reference to Regional and Seigneurial Variations', Ph.D. thesis (London, 1976).

JAMES, L. E., 'The Career and Political Influence of William de la Pole, First Duke of Suffolk 1437–1450', B.Litt. thesis (Oxford, 1979).

JOHNSON, P. A. 'The Political Career of Richard, Duke of York, to 1456', D.Phil. thesis (Oxford, 1981).

MADDERN, P. C., 'Violence, Crime and Public Disorder in East Anglia, 1422–1442', D.Phil. thesis (Oxford, 1984).

RICHMOND, C. F., 'Royal Administration and the Keeping of the Seas, 1422–1485', D.Phil. thesis (Oxford, 1962).

SMITH, A. R., 'Aspects of the Career of Sir John Fastolf (1380–1459)', D.Phil. thesis (Oxford, 1982).

VIRGOE, R., 'The Parliament of 1449–50', Ph.D. thesis (London, 1964).

INDEX

Index